About this Book

This landmark volume on the history, application and teaching of anthropology in post-colonial Africa is timely and entirely welcome. At a time when appeals to cultural difference are becoming increasingly central to various political and economic interventions in Africa and beyond, anthropological knowledge would seem to be indispensable, both as a critique of emerging trends and as a domain that can facilitate their very emergence. In addition to highlighting the relevance of anthropology in the twenty-first century, this book successfully debunks various myths. Most significantly, it analyses how African anthropologists are redefining the historical legacy of European and American disciplinary hegemony and developing distinctively African contributions to anthropological theory and practice.

While illustrating the diverse national traditions of anthropological practice that have developed in sub-Saharan Africa since decolonisation, the contributors exemplify the diversity of professional work carried out by the discipline's practitioners, united by use of anthropological perspectives and commitment to fieldwork to realise change. This book has the additional value of going beyond a critical reappraisal of the trajectory of anthropology to examine the very conditions of knowledge production in Africa.

About this Series

The books in this new series are a new initiative by CODESRIA, the Council for the Development of Social Science Research in Africa, to encourage African scholarship relevant to the multiple intellectual, policy and practical problems and opportunities confronting the African Continent in the 21st century.

Publishers

CODESRIA in association with Zed Books

Titles in the Series

African Intellectuals: Rethinking Politics, Language, Gender and Development
EDITED BY Thandika Mkandawire (2005)

Africa and Development Challenges in the New Millennium: The NEPAD Debate
EDITED BY J. O. Adésínà, A. Olukoshi and Yao Graham (2005)

Urban Africa: Changing Contours of Survival in the City
EDITED BY A. M. Simone and A. Abouhani (2005)

Liberal Democracy and Its Critics in Africa:
Political Dysfunction and the Struggle for Social Progress
EDITED BY Tukumbi Lumumba-Kasongo (2005)

Negotiating Modernity: Africa's Ambivalent Experience
EDITED BY Elísio Salvado Macamo (2005)

Insiders and Outsiders: Citizenship and Xenophobia in
Contemporary Southern Africa
Francis B. Nyamnjoh (2006)

African Anthropologies: History, Critique and Practice
EDITED BY Mwenda Ntarangwi, David Mills and Mustafa Babiker (2006)

Intellectuals, Youths and African Development: Pretension and Resistance in African Politics
EDITED BY Bjorn Beckman and Gbemisola Remi Adeoti (2006)

About the Publishers – CODESRIA

The Council for the Development of Social Science Research in Africa (CODESRIA) is an independent organisation whose principal objectives are facilitating research, promoting research-based publishing and creating multiple forums geared towards the exchange of views and information among African researchers. It challenges the fragmentation of research through the creation of thematic research networks that cut across linguistic and regional boundaries.

CODESRIA publishes a quarterly journal, *Africa Development*, the longest standing Africa-based social science journal; *Afrika Zamani*, a journal of history; *African Sociological Review*; *African Journal of International Affairs* (AJIA); *Africa Review of Books* and *Identity, Culture and Politics: An Afro-Asian Dialogue*. It co-publishes the *Journal of Higher Education in Africa* and *Africa Media Review*. Research results and other activities of the institution are disseminated through 'Working Papers', 'Monograph Series', 'CODESRIA Book Series', and the *CODESRIA* Bulletin.

African Anthropologies
History, Critique and Practice

Edited by
Mwenda Ntarangwi, David Mills and Mustafa Babiker

CODESRIA
DAKAR

in association with

Zed Books
LONDON & NEW YORK

African Anthropologies: History, Critique and Practice was first published by Zed Books Ltd., 7 Cynthia Street, London N1 9JF, UK and Room 400, 175 Fifth Avenue, New York, NY 10010, USA in 2006.
www.zedbooks.co.uk

in association with

CODESRIA,
Avenue Cheikh Anta Diop,
X Canal IV, BP3304 Dakar, 18524 Senegal.
www.CODESRIA.org

Distributed exclusively in the United States by Palgrave Macmillan, a division of St. Martin's Press, LLC, 175 Fifth Avenue, New York 10010, USA.

Designed and set by Long House , Cumbria
Cover design by Andrew Corbett
Printed in Malta by Gutenberg Ltd

CODESRIA would like to express its gratitude to the Swedish International Development Cooperation Agency (SIDA/SAREC), the International Development Research Centre (IDRC), Ford Foundation, MacArthur Foundation, Carnegie Corporation, the Norwegian Ministry of Foreign Affairs, the Danish Agency for International Development (DANIDA), the French Ministry of Cooperation, the United Nations Development Programme (UNDP), the Netherlands Ministry of Foreign Affairs, Rockefeller Foundation, FINIDA, NORAD, CIDA, IIEP/ADEA, OECD, IFS, OXFAM America, UN/UNICEF and the Government of Senegal for supporting its research, training and publication programmes.

A catalogue record for this book is available from the British Library.
Library of Congress Cataloging-in-Publication Data is available.

ISBN: CODESRIA: · 2 86978 168 7
ISBN: Zed Books edition: 1 84277 762 9 (cased)
                              1 84277 763 7 (limp)
                          978 1 84277 762 6 (cased)
                          978 1 84277 763 3 (limp)

Contents

We dedicate this book to the next generation of African anthropologists who will take the discipline to greater heights in service to Africa and its friends

Contributors

Séverin Cécile Abega teaches social and cultural anthropology at the Catholic University of Central Africa, Yaoundé. He also leads the research group IRSA (Institut de recherches socio-anthropologiques). His main fields of interest are youth sexuality in relation to the prevention of AIDS, social change, cultural ecology and gender issues. Besides works in the oral literature genre he is author of (among other books) *Les Choses de la forêt. Les masques des Princes Tikar de Nditam* (Yaoundé: Presses de l'UCAC) and *Contes du Sud du Cameroun. Beme et le fétiche de son père* (Paris: Karthala). scabega@yahoo.fr

Mary Amuyunzu-Nyamongo is an applied anthropologist working in the area of reproductive health. She worked for the African Medical and Research Foundation (AMREF), the Population Council and the African Population and Health Research Centre (APHRC) in Nairobi before joining the Africa Institute of Health and Development. mnyamongo@aihd.org

Mustafa Babiker teaches anthropology at the University of Khartoum, Sudan, where he is also Director of the Development Studies Research Centre. His research, publications and consultancy work address issues of development and social change amongst pastoral communities in Sudan. mababiker@hotmail.com

P.-J. Ezeh, who teaches in the Department of Sociology and Anthropology at the University of Nigeria, Nsukka, has published on the practice of anthropology in Africa, on African art and expression, and on linguistic anthropology. A firm advocate of participant observation, he used this method in his study of the Orring of south-eastern Nigeria for Master's and doctoral degrees. His latest book is *Signs and Society*. pitjazi@yahoo.com

Johannes Fabian is chair of the Cultural Anthropology Department at the University of Amsterdam and the author of numerous books, including *Time and the Other: How Anthropology Makes Its Object*; *Moments of Freedom: Anthropology and Popular Culture*; *Remembering the Present: Painting and Popular History in Zaïre* and *Out of Our Minds: Reason and Madness in the Exploration of Central Africa*. fabian@pscw.uva.nl

Robert Launay is Professor of Anthropology at Northwestern University. His ethnographic research, based on fieldwork in northern Côte d'Ivoire, focuses specifically on the anthropology of Islam, the subject of his most recent book, *Beyond the Stream: Islam and Society in a West African Town*. He is also the author of *Traders without Trade: Responses to Change in Two Dyula Communities*. Currently he is conducting research on the history of anthropology, dealing, among other things, with the Enlightenment quarrel of the ancients and the moderns at the beginning of the eighteenth century as it relates to the discipline. rgl201@northwestern.edu

David Mills lectures at the University of Birmingham and is the Anthropology Coordinator within Sociology, Anthropology, Politics (C-SAP), a part of the Higher Education Academy. He has published on the post-war history of British social sciences, the history of African universities, and the ethnographic study of educational institutions. Co-editor of *Teaching Rites and Wrongs* and *The Qualities of Time*, he is currently completing a book on the political history of British social anthropology. d.mills@bham.ac.uk

Victor Ngonidzashe Muzvidziwa is currently an Associate Professor in the Department of Sociology at the University of Swaziland (UNISWA), on leave of absence from the University of Zimbabwe. He is also Dean of the Faculty of Social Sciences, UNISWA. He holds an MSc. in Sociology and Social Anthropology from the University of Zimbabwe, and a doctorate in Anthropology from Waikato University, New Zealand. His areas of research are in culture, urban studies, tourism and gender studies. His forthcoming volume, *Women Without Borders*, is a study of Zimbabwean cross-border women traders. vnmuzvidziwa@yahoo. co.uk

Mwenda Ntarangwi teaches anthropology in the Department of Sociology, Anthropology and Social Welfare at Augustana College. Previously he directed the St Lawrence University's semester abroad in Kenya. He is the author of *Gender, Identity and Performance* and his current research looks at education and cross-cultural encounters. sontarangwi@augustana.edu

Christine Obbo is a Ugandan cultural anthropologist who has taught at a number of American Universities. She has written extensively on work, urbanisation and gender in Africa. Obbo is the author of *African Women* and has in the last two decades been working on HIV/AIDS and gender issues in Africa, including the co-edited book *Experiencing and Understanding AIDS in Africa* . She is currently writing on the politics of the epidemic, from the domestic to the global, and how it has led to 'jammed' North/South dialogues. She also works for intervention programmes that promote an AIDS-free generation. obbo@mageos.com

Washington Onyango-Ouma is a Research Fellow at the Institute of African Studies, University of Nairobi. Awarded his doctoral degree in medical anthropology by the University of Copenhagen, he continues to research health and illness. His current interests and publications relate to sexual and reproductive health, children and childhood, health communication, health systems and ethics in research. onyango.ouma@uonbi.ac.ke

Alula Pankhurst is Associate Professor in the Department of Sociology and Anthropology, Addis Ababa University. His research interests include the history of anthropology in Ethiopia, migration and re-settlement, natural resource management and responses to HIV/AIDS. He is the author of *Resettlement and Famine in Ethiopia* and co-editor of *Peripheral People* and *Living on the Edge*. His current research into well-being looks at the links between poverty, inequality and quality of life in developing countries. alulapankhurst@telecom.net.et

Abbreviations

AMREF African Medical and Research Foundation
AUF Agence Universitaire de la Francophonie
CARE Cooperation for Assistance and Relief Everywhere
CDAW Colonial Development and Welfare Act
CICIBA Le Centre International des Civilisations Bantu
CODESRIA Council for the Development of Social Science Research in Africa
CRO Commonwealth Relations Office
CSSRC Colonial Social Science Research Council
EAISR East African Institute of Social Research
FHI Family Health International
HSIU Haile Selassie I University
IAI International African Institute
ICAES International Congress of Anthropological and Ethnological Sciences
IDRC International Development Research Centre
IFAN Institut Français d'Afrique Noire
IMF International Monetary Fund
IRD Institut de Recherche pour le Développement
IUCN International Union for Conservation of Nature and Natural Resources
KEMRI Kenya Medical Research Institute

NORAD Norwegian Agency for Development Cooperation
ORSTOM Organisation Recherche Scientifique et Technique Outre Mer
OSSREA Organisation for Social Science Research in Eastern and Southern Africa
PAAA Pan African Anthropology Association
PAR participatory action research
PLA participatory learning and action
PPA participatory poverty assessment
PRA participatory rural appraisal
PRSP poverty reduction strategy paper
RAI Royal Anthropological Institute
RLI Rhodes Livingstone Institute
RRA rapid rural appraisal
SIDA Swedish International Development Agency
UNAIDS Joint United Nations Programme on HIV/AIDS
USAID United States Agency for International Development
UZ University of Zimbabwe
WAISR West African Institute for Social Research
WHO World Health Organisation
WWF World Wildlife Fund
ZIDS Zimbabwe Institute of Development Studies
ZIMWESI Zimbabwe Programme on Women's Studies, Extension, Sociology and Irrigation

Preface

The idea for this edited volume germinated at the meeting of the Association of Social Anthropologists of the United Kingdom and Commonwealth (ASA) held in April 2002 in Arusha, Tanzania. The event occasioned a number of stimulating presentations on the role of anthropology and anthropologists in twenty-first-century Africa. David Mills co-convened the Arusha meeting with Wendy James, and the debate helped inspire Mwenda Ntarangwi and Mustafa Babiker with their own visions for this book. Several of the chapters collected here were originally presented at this meeting, but all have since been extensively revised. Both Obbo and Fabian made their presentations as conference keynote addresses. Chapters by Ntarangwi, Mustafa Babiker and Pankhurst were contributions to a conference panel entitled 'Practising Anthropology and Archaeology – Past, Present and Future'. Onyango-Ouma's chapter was originally presented at the Pan-African Anthropological Association meetings in Nairobi in August 2002. We are indebted to the organisers of these meetings. In seeking to ensure a balanced, continent-wide perspective, we have also sought out further contributions on West Africa by Launay, Ezeh and Abega.

The book is divided into three broad sections, mirroring the volume's three-pronged emphasis – history, critique and practice. The first prong takes a historical and comparative perspective – illustrating and reflecting on a number of the national anthropological traditions that have developed within sub-Saharan African universities during and since the colonial period. Contributors draw on both historical sources and their own career narratives to retell and reflect upon these traditions of teaching, training and research.

Several of the chapters highlight and detail policy issues facing the teaching of anthropology in Africa today, including the effects of economic liberalisation on higher education and the implications of growing student numbers and limited access to teaching materials. They also document innovative ways in which people are surmounting and dealing with these changes, demonstrate the importance of a reflexive approach to teaching and working with students, and add to the growing body of scholarship on the teaching of anthropology. In this regard, the book serves partly to enlarge on the debates addressed in the 1989 volume *Teaching and Research in Anthropology and Sociology in Eastern African Universities* (edited by Seyoum Selassie and El-W. Kameir) that documented the history and practice of the two disciplines across East Africa.

Alula Pankhurst provides a comprehensive political sociology of research traditions within and about Ethiopia, focusing particularly on the – often overlooked – contribution of Ethiopian scholars and students of anthropology at Addis Ababa University College over the last 50 years. In his chapter, David Mills documents the founding of the East African Institute for Social Research in 1950, using it to untangle the complicated history of colonial anthropology and to explore the relationship of mutual suspicion that existed between anthropologists and administrators at the time. Victor Muzvidziwa documents the development of academic anthropology within Zimbabwe over the past forty years, relating the intellectual debates to the growth of university institutions within the turbulent political context of that country. Robert Launay's chapter looks at the long and close relationship between anthropology and Islam, especially in West Africa where a heavy presence of Islam shapes the everyday reality of many residents. Despite Islam having been appropriated by many Africans into their indigenous socio-cultural practices, many anthropologists avoided it altogether because of its possible role in tampering with the 'authentic' African small-scale communities that they sought to study and understand. Abega uses Cameroon as a case to illuminate the practice of anthropology in many Francophone African countries, where anthropological training is closely tied to initial training in philosophy and in France.

The volume's second prong demonstrates the growing importance of anthropological engagement. In a philosophical opening contribution, Johannes Fabian discusses the history of forgetting Africa amongst Western scholars. As well as pointing to the unequal politics of knowledge production about Africa, he uses examples of popular Swahili idioms for memory in the Shaba region of Congo to make the point that there is an important tradition of popular African historiography and memory work that should never be neglected or 'forgotten' by anthropologists. Many African anthropologists now work, at least partly, outside the academic sector, and in particular within NGOs and applied research centres. Christine Obbo's chapter weaves her personal biography of anthropological engagement into a history of disciplinary teaching and practice in post-colonial Africa, insisting on the continued relevance of African anthropology today. Mustafa Babiker provides an autobiographical account of his anthropological work on the study of pastoralism, showing how the persistence of 'crisis scenarios' and the simplistic use of the 'herder/farmer' dichotomy within the social sciences has sometimes limited the debate. He calls for a more historically-aware analysis of agricultural and social change.

The volume's third prong demonstrates the important contributions to knowledge that African anthropologists have made through practising and applying their disciplinary skills, whether in the fields of social development or public health. Contributors to this section highlight the importance of maintaining a dialogue between university-based academics and those anthropologists employed by NGOs or working as research consultants. P.-J. Ezeh's piece shows the complementary roles of individual intervention and institutional innovativeness in promoting anthropology as a discipline in higher education. Mwenda Ntarangwi's chapter reflects on the potentials and dilemmas of teaching anthropology to American exchange students in Kenya, and his attempts to help them deal with their often simplistic understandings of Kenyan politics and culture while developing anthropological skills through their 'study abroad' experience. Mary Amuyunzu Nyamongo describes the varied responsibilities and roles she has had working in multidisciplinary teams, whilst Onyango-Ouma discusses the particular ethical and professional challenges faced by anthropologists working in their 'home' communities, with such ramifications as involvement in consultancy and biomedical research. As all our contributors show, it is an exciting and intellectually invigorating time to be practising anthropology in Africa today, despite the many challenges it faces. We are greatly indebted to many who have read various drafts of this manuscript for their very helpful comments.

Mwenda Ntarangwi, David Mills and Mustafa Babiker

1

Introduction
Histories of Training,
Ethnographies of Practice

Mwenda Ntarangwi, Mustafa Babiker and David Mills

What unites a Ugandan social scientist working for the Population Council in Nairobi, an academic from Lesotho teaching at the University of Zimbabwe and a Khartoum-based academic doing a short-term consultancy for Oxfam in Southern Sudan? All share an anthropological identity and a commitment to shaping an African discipline that critically contributes to both social knowledge and social reform. Whilst aware of colonialism's influence on the development of African anthropology, its practitioners are forging new intellectual agendas, working practices and international collaborations. The expansion of anthropology worldwide and its willingness to tackle a broadening set of intellectual challenges presented by globalisation – religious revival, ethnic conflict and genocide, street children, child soldiers, human trafficking, grinding rural and urban poverty, pandemic diseases, good governance, brain drain, to name but a few – are revitalising anthropological practice. In Africa, the new face of the discipline is developing through ever-closer association between academic anthropologists and those working in multidisciplinary research teams, between consultants and teachers.

This volume engages African anthropologists as well as Africanist anthropologists in a rare combination to draw together writings on the history, application and teaching of anthropology (predominantly social and cultural) in post-colonial Africa. It heeds Southall's call – following Owusu's (1978) critique of Western anthropology – for a willingness and capacity by Western anthropologists to achieve that degree of rapport and mutual respect for human equality with African intellectuals which they always claim to have achieved in the African bush (1983: 74). We do so by looking at the history of the discipline (selectively, to match our current aim) to re-examine the principal critiques, particularly of anthropology's links with colonialism and how the discipline produces its object (to borrow Fabian's 1983 phrase), and some of the ways it is practised in Africa today. There exist several accounts that tell the story of the development of African anthropology. Among the most informative and especially relevant to the focus of this volume are Keith Hart's review of the social anthropology of West Africa (1985); Aidan Southall's essay on the contribution of anthropology to African studies (1983); and the essays on ethnographic traditions of sub-Saharan Africa by Wendy James (Sudan and Ethiopia), Elizabeth Tompkin (West Africa), Richard P. Werbner (South Central Africa) and David Parkin (Eastern Africa) in the volume edited by Richard Fardon (1990).

What our volume does is to consider some neglected or under-emphasised aspects of the history of African anthropology, with comments on the probable future of an evolving discipline. In so doing we show how African anthropologists are redefining the historical legacy of European and American disciplinary hegemony and developing distinctively African contributions to anthropological theory and practice. By reflecting on disciplinary pasts we demonstrate paths to the future. To illustrate the diverse national traditions of anthropological practice that have developed in sub-Saharan Africa since decolonisation, and particularly during the last 25 years, the contributors to this volume exemplify the diversity of professional work carried out by the discipline's practitioners, united by their use of anthropological perspectives to make a difference. Their commitment to this disciplinary identity demonstrates the place that exists for a critical anthropology that is reflective about both its potentials and its limitations.

A key tenet of this book is that the pure/applied dichotomy – consistently mobilised by some in Western anthropology, and especially British social anthropologists who conceptualised applied anthropology as inferior to the standard type anthropology[1] – is an unhelpful way of categorising the discipline, particularly in the African context. All too often this rhetorical divide is used to reinforce the originative and core status of 'pure' theoretical anthropological work, from which applied research is seen to derive, and on which it is said to depend. It is not enough to insist on the indivisibility of pure and applied research, or on the close links between theory and practice. The pure/applied distinction is itself a construction and may only make sense in the particular context in which a discipline's practitioners view their institutional location as key to their intellectual self-definition. This is because, as Schapera (1949) showed many decades ago, social anthropology is best seen as a three-tiered discipline that combines the descriptive (ethnography), the explanatory (theoretical) and the practical (applied). We suggest, therefore, that this pure/applied dichotomy, developed within a European and American historical context, does not travel easily to an African setting, neither does it represent the spirit of the discipline's historical identity. Many African anthropologists are increasingly finding themselves straddling two worlds – that of consultancy for purposes of accessing research funds while offering much-needed anthropological knowledge, and that of the academy for purposes of producing anthropological knowledge and training students. This situation is not unlike that faced by many anthropologists in the West as Grillo (1985: 3) shows when he states that 'the ASA meeting of 1980 had a section devoted to discussing the prospects of anthropologists working in development, industry, commerce, and public services as the resources that had earlier supported traditional research dwindled'.

Contributions to this book shift the focus away from conventional scholarly wisdom that often locates anthropology in the academy, and reveal a diverse, energised and engaged African discipline that struggles to survive through a combination of various strands of practice. They also show how, forsaking the colonial anthropological project that sought to study small, isolated (primitive) societies, many African anthropologists are moving from the marginal/local studies that were (are) traditionally favoured by many anthropologists (mostly Western anthropologists or those trained in the Western tradition) to adopt perspectives that address broader national issues. They do this, however, by locating themselves within the local, where fieldwork occurs, and then relating their results and experiences to the national and regional contexts.

Lila Abu-Lughod has recently and rightly called for 'ethnography in/of nations' noting somewhat misleadingly that 'only in the last couple of decades have anthropologists gotten serious about nations' (2004: 1). As Julia Paley correctly points out, the late 1950s and 1960s saw US anthropologists grouped into 'The Committee for the Comparative Study of New Nations' at the University of Chicago set out to study Asian and African countries that had gained independence from colonial rule in the post-Second World War period. Their goal was to understand the problem of democracy in the new states, the forces that erode it and the factors that might establish or strengthen it. Participants, who included Johannes Fabian and Maxwell Owusu as graduate students, were concerned especially with how to integrate local identities – or 'primordial sentiments' in the words of Clifford Geertz – into a unified civil order and modern political systems associated with democracy. The important thing to note here, as Paley emphasises, is that the New Nations Committee's interests were not merely academic, because participants sought to educate advisers to the newly independent states and also to intervene in policy matters. Full-length ethnographies written shortly thereafter assessed the success or failure of democracy in the social and institutional context of various national societies and within local frameworks, and one of the most outstanding and groundbreaking publications of this genre is Owusu's (1970). In addition Paley observes that in these early studies anthropologists sought to make their work relevant to political change. A second wave of anthropological interest in democracy would not emerge until the 1990s and the fall of the Berlin Wall (Paley 2002: 472).

This shift in focus and practice has been observed by Clifford Geertz, who has written about what he calls the 'permanent crisis of Western socio-cultural anthropology' (1991: 48) by addressing the implications of specific important changes in the field that have affected how Western anthropologists do their work. Among some of the changes he observes are, first, the rise of indigenous anthropology, namely 'the practice of anthropology in one's own country, society, and/or ethnic group in the Third World but also increasingly in the West'; second, the transformation and/or the disappearance of the subject matter of socio-cultural anthropology, namely 'primitive' and 'tribal' societies, and perhaps most importantly the loss of research isolation, which has resulted in the invasion of Third World societies (the research field once considered the preserve of socio-cultural anthropology) by an army of researchers from a wide variety of allied disciplines such as economics, history and political science; third, the popularity of the hermeneutic-semiotic perspectives in opposition to scientific positivist perspectives in the study of culture and society (quoted in Owusu 1986: 47–8). The changes identified by Geertz have reordered the significance of the pure and applied dichotomy and also the scientific nature of the discipline.

Ironically, all the factors cited above by Geertz as contributing to the 'permanent identity crisis' of Western anthropology are precisely those that are shaping the emerging academic identity of anthropology in post-colonial Africa. Indeed, Malinowski's (1938: xii) claim that 'anthropology begins at home', made over half a century ago, has been prophetic given what is going on in African anthropology today, as shown by contributions to this volume. Multidisciplinarity, research at home, and applied research are all very critical aspects of African anthropology that will continue to shape its future. It is in this context that we can locate an African anthropology, one that cherishes the proven tools of fieldwork and mobilises them to address larger social problems and challenges of development and underdevelopment. This is where ethnographic, archival or survey research done through consultancies comes into play, addressing national issues while remaining true to the anthropological process of localised fieldwork. This volume also draws on Grinker and Steiner's valuable discussion (1997: xix) of the relationship between perspective as technique, objective and metaphor, and Africa as a concept that has been constructed, invented and interpreted in much of anthropological writing.

In this introduction, therefore, we provide a scholarly background to our venture in three different ways. We begin by retelling the history of African intellectual engagement with anthropology during the colonial and early post-colonial period, as well as discussing the changing role of African higher education as it bears on anthropology over this period. The history of the expansion of African anthropology in the late colonial period allows one to explore the relationship between anthropology and social administration more broadly. We go on to document the contemporary state of the discipline and its teaching in Francophone and Anglophone Africa. Finally we discuss the role of regional research organisations like the Organisation for Social Science Research in Eastern and Southern Africa (OSSREA) and the Council for the Development of Social Science Research in Africa (CODESRIA), through whose funds African anthropological research has been revitalised to give some shape to African anthropology. Interspersed in this discussion is an exploration of what constitutes African anthropology, showing the many facets it exhibits as well as its contemporary challenges. A recurring theme in this volume, therefore, is the way anthropology reflects and is linked to broader narratives of national public policy within post-colonial Africa. Some of the issues addressed by anthropologists include the rise of ethnic nationalism, crises of health and education, and the role of academic activism. Rather than seeking academic isolation from pressing political questions, our contributors show how disciplinary theory, method and debate are intertwined with the life of national political communities.

Histories of practice have important implications for the present, and the question of engagement is alive, contentious and ongoing. Whilst seeking to avoid 'Afro-pessimism', our contributors do not shy away from the dilemmas and challenges faced by the discipline on the continent today, whether describing the political economy of knowledge production, or the time demands imposed by applied and consultancy research. Each recounts challenges faced, some not always overcome. Each seeks to communicate something of the intellectual vibrancy, political reflexivity and social engagement demonstrated by contemporary African anthropologists. Each chapter is intended to inspire new generations of scholars in Africa to study and train to be anthropologists, aware of the histories of practice to which they contribute and motivated, too, by a commitment to progressive social change that leads to the reduction of human suffering and poverty, improves the general quality of life, and advances freedom and justice, democracy and human rights for all.

Histories of academic anthropology and application in Africa

Members of academic disciplines, like all communities, craft identities for themselves through the histories they tell and the memories they nurture. All too often these histories are written for a purpose, that of explaining and legitimating the present, rather than in order to understand the events and disjunctures of the past. We want to ask which histories of African anthropology get told, when, and by whom? Which pasts get revisited, and which lie undisturbed? And how should we go about creating new accounts, particularly of the discipline's involvement with colonialism, undoubtedly a formative moment for the social sciences in Africa?

The histories one tells depend partly on how one draws boundaries around the discipline. One way of doing so is to draw it very tightly, defining the discipline primarily as an ongoing intellectual dialogue, and thus focusing primarily on the internal history of ideas and theoretical debates. Such accounts can be revealing (Kuper 1996, for example), but they also risk being internally self-contained, straying little from the academic seminar and the senior common room. Goody's history of British anthropology in Africa from 1918 to 1970, entitled *The Expansive Moment*, is a case in point (Goody 1995). This is an account of British social anthropology's theoretical developments, in which Africa's role as a research laboratory for the metropolitan academy is all too clear. Whilst the description of the rivalries and intrigues amongst British anthropologists is titillating, the discipline's relationship with colonial administrations and anti-colonial politics is played down. So too are all the other hidden histories of anthropological practice, such as the work of scholar travellers, missionary ethnographers, African intellectuals or colonial adminis- trators themselves. Geertz is 'exceedingly unfond' of what he calls 'practitioner histories' because they start with an 'almost Cartesian, clear and self-evident perception of what anthropology is ... and work back from that to find rudimentary, prefigurative examples of it *avant la lettre*' (Geertz 1999: 306). They risk simplifying the past in order to explain the present, rather than seeking to relate the past to the present. Ignoring the institutional and political contexts in which ideas unfold and blossom, such histories also overlook key aspects of their own disciplinary reproduction, and in particular practical aspects of teaching and training

There is another, diametrically opposed, approach to the past. This is to define anthropology by the colonial contexts in which it was practised, exploring its links, patronage and funding by colonial administrations. This external definition has been most powerfully adopted by the discipline's critics, and was particularly dominant amongst African and leftist academics in the 1960s and 1970s. Some focused on how anthropology had emerged from the colonial context (Asad 1973: 8–19), others on the limits of its functionalist methods (Goddard 1972) or empirical methods (Banaji 1970; Magubane 1973) whilst others still emphasised the continuing and influential legacy of colonial ideologies (Magubane 1971; Owusu 1975). Some, such as Banaji and Goddard, came out of a Marxist tradition of social theorising; others were concerned to demonstrate the developing contradictions between the administrators' philosophy of just rule and the growing nationalist movements, with anthropologists caught in the middle. There were those questioning the ethnographic project itself and its ability to produce valid and authentic knowledge of Africa given the (Western) anthropologist's questionable competence in local vernacular (Owusu 1978), as well as the over-reliance on native interpretations that often tended to reproduce colonial discourse about the native culture (Jones 1974).

Over time the diverse aspects and nuances of this critique have begun to merge, and the general question asked of the past has become more focused on anthropology's 'complicity' with colonial rule – caricatured as the 'anthropology as the handmaiden of colonialism' debate – as well as its distinctiveness from other social sciences engaged in fieldwork. A number of authors have continued to develop this strong critique (Mafeje 1996; Rigby 1996; Magubane 2000) from the groundwork laid by others in the 1970s such as Chilungu (1976), Nzimiro (1979), Onoge (1979), Amadiume (1987) and Owusu (1978, 1979). The ideological shadow of Western influence, such writers insist, continues to delegitimise anthropology. For them, the future of the African social sciences lay in escaping from its colonial past: anthropology is past rather than future. One of the problems in this position is its implied assumption of a radical disjuncture between the colonial past and the post-colonial future, and that it depicts anthropology's past in a singular and un-nuanced way. The colonial and post-colonial are so intricately tied together that even attempts to reclaim a pre-colonial African cultural past (often favoured by those persuaded by radical Afrocentricism) can become 'the indigenisation of colonial culture itself' (A. Apter 1999: 591) or the fossilising of cultural practices otherwise characterised by innovativeness and flexibility (Owusu 1972: 27). It is thus more productive to note that the problematic embodied in the colonial and post-colonial relations is not dichotomous but rather symbiotic and almost mutually reinforcing.

Could we then assume that anthropology, as some have contended, was simply colonialism's 'child', 'tool' or 'handmaiden'? Stocking reminds us that 'casual metaphorical characterisation' (1995: 368) is of little help in understanding the issues at stake. The accusation gains what moral insight it has from its very lack of specificity. Can one talk about colonialism in general, or should one focus on particular colonial administrations and polities at specific moments in time? Were French and British colonial anthropological projects similar? Are particular professional and institutional linkages that developed between scholars and administrators at issue, or is the broader issue of anthropology's 'ideological entanglement' (Wolfe 1999) ultimately what matters? The issue of scale is important to an analysis of this sort. At the most general level, most anthropologists were members of European societies that participated enthusiastically in the imperial project and so share some responsibility for the patronising moral attitudes and exploitative social relations it espoused. At a more individual level, there were many who sought to develop a critique of these relations, not to mention the African scholars and activists who, as we will argue, sometimes used anthropology's tools in new and oppositional ways. In view of this complex set of identities and activities associated with anthropology, we may well be best served by looking at some of the roles anthropology played over time.

The faces of anthropology during colonialism

Writing about the emergence of social anthropology, Evans-Pritchard (1962) shows that it is hard to state when anthropology started, given the fact that whenever humans started thinking deeply about culture and society could have indicated a rudimentary stage in anthropological thinking. However, he makes it clear that no discipline could claim any autonomy before it was taught at the university. We follow this thinking by Evans-Pritchard to show that anthropology does have a long presence in Africa, starting in the pre-colonial and early colonial period with the pre-professional anthropologists, who included European missionaries, Arab and European travellers, and administrators on the one hand and local educated Africans, chiefs and church leaders on the other. The former established the vision of Africa for the world, creating biblical, racist colonialist and bio-technological frameworks that have continued to shape the way the West perceives and deals with Africa (Vansina 1986).

Between the First and Second World Wars the International African Institute (IAI) was created with two specific aims: first, to provide an international centre that would promote research and dissemination of information and knowledge on African cultures; and, second, to increase and strengthen the links between scientific knowledge and practical activities and needs for administrators, educators and missionaries (Schapera 1949). The IAI went on to publish the journal *Africa* and became instrumental in anthropological work in Africa, especially in Britain. Out of this mandate established by the IAI came the work of anthropologists who were commissioned by the colonial government, such as Isaac Schapera, who was asked to look at the way the government could benefit from anthropology, especially in the colonies. This commissioning led to his monograph on problems of anthropological research in Kenya (1949). There were others like Philip Gulliver, who was hired by the colonial government to work as an administrator and use his anthropological training to understand local administrative structures and problems for better colonial governance within the framework of indirect rule. His work in East Africa, especially in the then Tanganyika, was instrumental in shaping colonial administrative work there but also in continuing applied anthropological work (Gulliver 1985). Later on came the anthropologist who was invited to give his/her expertise in conducting research on a specific social problem and whose report was used to shape public policy and thinking. This has morphed into what we see as consultancy work and applied anthropology in Africa (see Mary Amuyunzu-Nyamongo, this volume). Grillo (1985: 13–14) gives a fitting example of this kind of anthropology.

One example was the East African Institute of Social Research's survey of migrant labour in Uganda, which Stanner and Schapera had recommended should be initiated by the protectorate government. Preliminary work was done by two colonial Social Research Fellows (the Sofers) and a lecturer at Makerere University College (Powesland), but later research was organised by the Institute through a steering committee comprising representatives of government departments; several Institute Fellows (Fallers, Middleton and Southall), carrying out their own independent fieldwork in Uganda, were also drawn into the survey.

These anthropologists (Fallers, Middleton and Southall) later became teachers who then trained many African and Africanist anthropologists, including Maxwell Owusu and Johannes Fabian, who worked with Fallers at the University of Chicago. Thus this anthropological research that had been initiated by the government not only engaged government researchers, a lecturer and independent researchers, but also paved the way for the future of this kind of anthropology in relation to Africa. This face of anthropology has continued in Africa to date.

As the opaque moral clouds of colonialism have dispersed, a more nuanced and historically subtle position has developed. Yes, as Stocking notes, British colonialism did represent a potential market for a new kind of anthropology, one which Malinowski was the first to recognise with his bids for Rockefeller funding. Yes, it did help in the process of facilitating the institutionalisation of academic social anthropology in Britain in the inter-war and immediate post-war years (Stocking 1995: 368). And, as we have showed above in reference to IAI, anthropology did benefit from significant Colonial Office funding and was mobilised to give specific service to colonial administration structures of the time. But there is evidence of the systematic use of extant anthropological ideas (even when aligned to the then-prevailing nineteenth-century philosophies of social evolutionism) to produce very useful descriptions of cultural practices of various African societies through what were called 'ethnographic surveys'. The relationship between the Colonial Office and anthropology was thus both fraught with misunderstanding and fruitful. At times anthropologists were in direct confrontation with colonial administrators (David Mills, this volume) while at other times there was no clear divide between anthropological work and colonial administrative work. If this debate on the relationship between anthropology and colonialism continues, this is partly because Africa's relationship to British and French colonialism and now the neo-colonial relations shaped by international aid and its conditions continues to change and develop over time. Rather than fading away, the issues are re-framed. The discipline has changed greatly, but mistrust of it within Africa remains: throughout this volume we explore the reasons for this suspicion and its consequences.

An alternative way of telling this history is to closely attend to historical events whilst seeking to understand their implications for the present. By opening a dialogue with the past one can work towards a history of anthropological practice that neither denies colonialism nor lets it overdetermine intellectual debate. We do this by foregrounding the work of African scholars and political activists, showing how they worked within, challenged and reworked the colonial context they found. Where does one start such a history? There are plenty of potential precedents. Pels and Salemink (1998) focus on the pre-professional anthropology as practised by missionaries, travellers and colonial administrators. We would add the educated Africans and informants who worked with them. An example here would be Apollo Kaggwa, the Regent of Buganda, who liaised closely with the missionary John Roscoe in interviewing Baganda chiefs, as part of Roscoe's ethnography of the Buganda

(Roscoe 1911). It is notable that, like a number of other Baganda analysts, Kaggwa saw the power of the written word, publishing his own influential accounts of Kiganda customs and clans (Kaggwa 1907). Yet we cannot ignore the harsh reality of privileging the written word over oral histories that often led to the reproduction and recuperation of colonial culture in indigenised forms (see Jones 1974 and Obbo, this volume). All these three (missionaries, colonial administrators and indigenous African intellectuals) constitute the amateur phase of anthropological work that produced some interesting cultural accounts of native peoples.

We then trace the beginning of African anthropology to those Africans who became attracted to anthropology as students (such as Kenyatta and Nkrumah), those who carried out graduate-level research themselves (such as Kofi Busia and Nnamdi Azikiwe), and those who constitute part of the next phase we may refer to as that of anthropologists working outside of the academy. Let us start with the work of writer and social activist turned politician, Jomo Kenyatta. This choice is not an arbitrary one. Whilst his subsequent political career left behind this early model of the engaged academic, his patriotic ethnography *Facing Mount Kenya* (1938) was an attempt to bring together a record of the Kikuyu past with a vision of a post-colonial Kenyan future as he struggled with what Owusu (1997: 21) terms 'the problem of mistranslation of African cultures by Europeans and Africans trained by Europeans in European institutions'. His work serves as a model of how one activist put anthropology to use, turning it against itself. Malinowski was aware of this subversive potential of the discipline, commenting once that 'anthropology might one day be turned against us' (cited in Onoge 1979: 48).

Kenyatta first came to Britain in 1929 as a representative of the Kikuyu Central Association, and, two years later, as a delegate to Colonial Office talks on the future of Kenya. He remained abroad for 16 years (Kenyatta 1961: 16), his belief in self-government vastly out of step with other leading Kenyan politicians who found it hard to look beyond British colonial rule. In his time in London he tried on very different personae. The first was as an aspirant communist revolutionary, spending time with Trinidadian anti-colonial activist and writer George Padmore, with whom he went to Moscow.

They gradually began to realise that African socialism had to be African as well as socialist, and, falling out with Stalin, were expelled in 1933 from the Communist Party. On return to Britain, they set up their own organisational machine, the International African Service Bureau, and continued a hectic round of campaigning against the injustices of British Imperialism in Africa. Mixing in a cosmopolitan circle, Kenyatta soon met Bronislaw Malinowski, leader of the now famous social anthropology seminars on culture change at the London School of Economics (LSE), and ended up receiving a diploma in anthropology under Malinowski (Kenyatta 1968). Both showmen, they apparently got on famously, seemingly sharing a prejudice in their dislike of Indians. Prince Peter of Greece recalls how Malinowski had once opened a seminar saying 'My lectures are not for Indians', with Kenyatta following up by describing how Indians had exploited Africans in Kenya (quoted in Murray-Brown 1972: 177). Their disdain for Indians, however, has to be understood in context. Both were not necessarily intolerant of Indians *per se* but were opposed to the colonial system that produced a hierarchy in which Indians, Arabs and Europeans not only had representation in the Legislative Council that excluded Africans but also exploited Africans. Malinowski's five-month sojourn in Africa (East, Central and South) showed him the unjust system put together by colonialism, in which Europeans collaborated with other racial groups such as the Indians and the Arabs to exterminate, enslave and/or exploit native peoples (Malinowski 1961). This system privileged Europeans, Indians and Arabs in Africa, creating a racial divide and hatred that led to great atrocities, as seen in what happened in Uganda under Idi Amin. Kenyatta, however, was more open to reconciliatory gestures, extended to both Europeans and Indians after independence.

In November 1935, it was Kenyatta's turn to give a paper at the seminar, and he chose the topic of female circumcision. Prince Peter took notes on Kenyatta's talk, recording: 'Europeans and missionaries consider this rite disgusting and barbarous, the Kikuyu consider it very important for the solidity of the social structure' (ibid.: 190). Interestingly, missionaries among the Kikuyu adopted the notion of initiation rites of passage for young girls by presenting the Virgin Mary as a circumcised girl who was unmarried in order to win over Kikuyu converts (Greenfield 1978). Thus Kenyatta's spirited attacks on missionaries did elicit a response. In capitalising on anthropology's 'going concerns', Kenyatta thus developed the core of an argument for imagining the Kikuyu nation. He used a form of cultural relativism to challenge the administrative philosophy of 'enlightened' progressive colonialism. Indeed, while in London between 1930 and 1939 he gave lectures on anthropology and colonial development sponsored by Southampton University and taught Kiswahili through the University of London's School of Oriental and African Studies (Kenyatta 1968). With funding from the International African Institute, Kenyatta's ideas about culture and colonialism developed into the book, Facing Mount Kenya, which Malinowski provided with a fulsome introduction, praising the combination of 'his full competence of a trained Western scholar', and the 'illuminating sidelights inspired by the inside knowledge of an African' (Malinowski 1938: viii). Despite a few cavils about 'European bias' and Kenyatta's unproblematic description of the Kikuyu magician's 'telepathy', Malinowski declares that the book is one of the 'first really competent and instructive contributions to African ethnography by a scholar of pure African patronage' (ibid.: xiii). The book itself is a persuasive mix of detailed empirical description and the occasional more campaigning appeal to the dignity and cohesion of Kikuyu culture. The material is organised into the usual chapters on land tenure, kinship, economics, religion and marriage, as befitting the Malinowskian ethnographic genre, but each has a twist in the tail. The conclusion is unashamedly political, berating the way that when a European 'robs the people of their land, he is taking away not only their livelihood but the material symbol that holds family and tribe together. In doing this, he gives one blow which cuts away the foundations from the whole of Kikuyu life, social, moral and economic' (Kenyatta 1938: 317). Similar critiques of European missionaries and teachers are made at the end of chapters on education and initiation rites. These critiques, rather than maintaining the scholarly façade of an untouched 'ethnographic present', remind the reader that Kenya is being changed by settlers, missionaries, administrators and even scholars. There is also a swipe at the 'professional friends of Africa' in his introduction – a veiled reference to anthropologists. Thus, like his friend and teacher Malinowski, Kenyatta mobilises anthropological knowledge to argue for an unpolluted Kikuyu polity, one that was best left alone if its cultural autonomy was to be preserved.

It is too easy to judge a book by its author. Kenyatta's subsequent career, his rewriting of his role within the anti-colonial struggle, the divisions caused by Kikuyu nationalism and his own sometimes autocratic presidential rule, make it easy to overlook the book's scholarly contributions. It openly uses anthropology to challenge colonial rule. It could fairly be labelled as the first ethnography in the colonial period written by an African. Not simply one step on an academic career ladder, the brand of anthropology presented in *Facing Mount Kenya* contributed to, and built upon, a renewed interest in traditional African cultures. Mirroring debates within the Negritude movement, this was a strategic reclamation and celebration of Africanity in ways that would challenge Western and colonial perceptions and constructions of Africa.

Kenyatta increasingly prioritised his political campaigning for African rights, and his work with Padmore eventually led to the Fifth Pan African Congress in Manchester in 1945. Amongst other Diaspora African activists, in attendance was W. E. B. DuBois, the history professor whose 1903 work *The Souls of Black Folk* was a seminal text for those writing about racial discrimination and pan-Africanism. The event was formative for many of the African delegates who attended, including Kwame Nkrumah. Kenyatta's African roots gave him an authority that the Caribbean intellectuals envied, but also helped him see the Kenyan situation in its global racial context. This important intellectual and political connection between Africans, West Indians and African-Americans has continued to flourish. Indeed, among notable African-American anthropologists who have studied and written about Africa are Sinclair Drake (Ghana), Elliot Skinner (Burkina Faso), James Gibbs (Liberia), Sheila Walker (Ivory Coast), Leith Mullings (Ghana), William Shack (Ethiopia), Carolyn Martin-Shaw (Kenya and Zimbabwe), Niara Sudakarsa (Nigeria and Ghana), Walton Johnson (South Africa), George Bond (Zambia) and Gwen Mikell (Ghana).

Whilst Kenyatta chose to pursue a political career, he had recognised the progressive potential offered by anthropology. He wasn't the only one to do so. Nkrumah also took courses in the discipline at University College London, and as Ghanaian Prime Minister encouraged the Africanisation of the university curriculum, in which anthropology and African studies played a prominent role. He established the Institute of African Studies at the University of Ghana, Legon, and called for a pan-African study of African cultural practice. Speaking in 1964, he attacked anthropology, arguing that scholars of African studies had 'begun to give accounts of African society which were used to justify colonialism as a duty of civilisation ... this explains, I believe, the popularity and success of anthropology' (Nkrumah, quoted in Brokensha 1966). This critique, we would argue, was not about the efficacy of anthropology as a discipline capable of understanding African social realities and contributing to the solutions of practical problems in Africa, but about the abuse of that anthropological knowledge, what Sichone (2001) calls 'pure anthropology'. Indeed, Nkrumah's critique of anthropology was rooted in what he saw as anthropologists' role in providing colonial administrators with information about local practices that would enhance the divide-and-rule strategy preferred by the colonial government: the anthropologists were helping to identify indigenous forms of governance (chieftaincy), enhancing the role of chiefs in colonial administration while sidelining Western-educated Africans like Nkrumah. He scoffed at the notion of encouraging 'Africans' to remain 'African' which was being mobilised through applied anthropology (Nkrumah 1962).

Both Nkrumah and Kenyatta knew the value of anthropology in defining and reclaiming an African cultural identity, yet both took different paths with it. It is prudent to speculate on the cause of this departure from anthropology by these African leaders. Within the colonial education system that saw the rise of higher education institutions in Kenya and Ghana, there was no room for the discipline of anthropology. This was partly because the discipline was embroiled in its own crisis of identity and because within the University of London social science curriculum that had been exported to the colonies, social anthropology was understood as the sociology of primitive people. The University of London's sociology programme was the primary location for social anthropology and students who specialised in anthropology ended up getting a degree in sociology. Sociology students would often choose one of two options of study – the first option would allow them to focus on industrial or Western societies, and the second option would allow them to focus on non-Western societies studied by anthropologists.[2] This approach to studying world cultures and peoples is what sociologist Immanuel Wallerstein calls the Western division of intellectual labour, carved out in the late nineteenth century when modern European and European-settler states were studied by economists, historians, political scientists and sociologists; non-Western areas with a long-standing written culture were studied by 'Orientalists'; and backward peoples were studied by anthropologists (1983: 155). It is no wonder, therefore, that anthropology was not to take root as a discipline in higher education in Africa until the second decade after political independence (except for South Africa, where it started in 1920 but had its own internal divisions instigated by apartheid). The dominant discipline was thus sociology, which continues to be home to many African anthropologists to date.

Kofi Busia, leader of the Ghanaian opposition and Nkrumah's eventual successor after the military coup of 1966, was initially recruited to help Fortes in a social survey of Asanteland in the 1940s. This led him to do a PhD at Oxford with Fortes, published in 1951 as *The Position of the Chief in the Modern Political System of Ashanti* (Busia 1951). Building on Rattray's work, Busia's study differs from his peers in that it was carefully situated within, and critical of, British colonial rule. He starts from the premise that 'the British occupation of 1900 disintegrated the Ashanti union' (*ibid.*: 101). He goes on to describe local uprisings, destoolments and challenges to Chiefly authority, explaining them as a result of true power having been vested in the colonial government and its agents, 'which the people associate with limitless power, endless wealth and a high prestige' (*ibid.*: 117). He saw the direct relevance of anthropological debates to contests of colonial authority. Alex Kyerematen, another Ghanaian, was also a student of anthropology with Busia at Oxford during this period, writing a thesis on Ashanti royal regalia. One other noted Ghanaian intellectual is J. B. Danquah (John Stewart Mill scholar in the philosophy of mind and logic at the University of London) who was highly praised by Meyer Fortes and went on to write a critical work on Akan laws and customs that aimed at providing an indigenous perspective of cultural practices. Danquah 'was seriously worried about the possible distortions of African cultures in European accounts ... and thus wrote his work from a purely African perspective' (Owusu 1997: 23).

It is thus evident that notable indigenous anthropological activity continued in Ghana through the colonial period (D. Apter 1970). Busia, for instance, continued to write about the implications of colonialism for African culture, and became the first Ghanaian to hold a Professorship and chair in sociology at the University of Ghana, Legon (Goody 1995) although he was a trained anthropologist. He was not afraid to be critical of the more romantic elements of the Negritude movement that had developed in Paris in the 1930s. First propounded by Césaire and Leopold Senghor, the Negritude movement can again be too easily criticised for its essentialist depictions of African culture. It has to be understood, like Kenyatta's work, as an intellectual resource for consciousness-raising developed during a period when direct anti-colonial activism was repressed by the French authorities. As Young notes, if 'the Anglophone activists tended to be political philosophers, the leaders of the anti-colonial revolution in the French Caribbean and Africa, Césaire and Leopold Senghor, were both poets' (2002: 265).

Unsurprisingly, Anglophone African social scientists like Busia were less convinced by such poetry. In The Challenge of Africa Busia reflects on the notion of the 'African personality' being propounded within the Negritude movement. Drawing on his anthropological training, he develops an early critique of Negritude, asking 'what is the shared social tradition with reference to which the abstraction of an African personality is conceived? Where does it prevail? In the whole continent? In parts of the continent? Which parts?' (1962: 43) He goes on to criticise the concept of African personality as a political myth, which given its 'profound social consequences' can be 'extravagantly' abused. Yet he too recognises it as a quest for the 'vindication of the dignity of persons of African descent', given that 'colonialism rests on force and violence', and that 'its persistence constitutes the most burning challenge in Africa today' (ibid.: 63). Notions of African personality and Negritude differed greatly in principle. The former was rooted in a Marxist-socialist identity that sought to restore African dignity through anti-colonial campaigns. Nkrumah's pan-Africanist agenda was based on this idea and has been analysed extensively by Drake (1964), who went on to become Professor of Anthropology in the Sociology Department at the University of Ghana, Legon. Negritude sought to encourage Africans in the diaspora to be proud of their African heritage as well as encouraging the study of African culture and life. The pan-African movement saw Negritude as too mellow and only interested in literary aspects of culture that were not revolutionary; hence the critique levelled against it by Nkrumah and Busia.

There is one final figure to add to this coterie of anti-colonial activists who engaged with anthropology – Dr Nnamdi Azikiwe, later the first president of Nigeria, and also a founder of a Nigerian university. He went to the US to study, doing a degree in political science at Lincoln University and an MSc in anthropology at Pennsylvania, writing his thesis on 'Mythology in Onitsha Society'. Malinowski attended a seminar he gave on 'The Origins of the State' at Pennsylvania and invited him to join the Royal Anthropological

Institute (RAI). He also sought to recruit him to his seminar, but in 1934 Azikiwe returned to West Africa to a career first in newspaper publishing and then politics, becoming an icon of the nationalist movement. He, too, saw the potential anthropology offered to the debate over national cultures. And he, too, met George Padmore whilst in the US; in his autobiography Azikiwe recalls how Padmore led a student protest against British colonial policy during the visit of the British Ambassador to Howard University.

A key aspect of this history of anti-colonial intellectual debate is the space that the metropolitan universities offered to these young scholars. Nationalists like Azikiwe, Kenyatta and Nkrumah used the opportunity of studying abroad both to develop their ideas and their political networks. Nkrumah and Azikiwe specifically chose to study in the US because of the ease with which they could get into the American system of higher education compared to the British one; another inducement was the fact that their mentor Dr J. K. Aggrey (reputed to be the first African student to study in the US at the close of the nineteenth century, he was a coastal Fanti from Anomabo, Ghana) encouraged them to study in America. Anthropology was to become part of their education, even though they were very critical of various aspects of its practice.

Whilst one may wish to dismiss anthropology as an intimate part of a colonial knowledge structure, one also has to acknowledge the interstitial space that the discipline offered to those of a critical bent, both in nurturing an anti-colonial consciousness and in inviting the first steps in Africanising the discipline. It was, indeed, anthropology's role as the 'sociology of primitive people' that allowed social scientists to engage with people that were often overlooked or neglected by other social sciences (sociologists, economists and political scientists, just to name a few), and which in turn equipped these African leaders with the social and cultural data necessary to demand informed politico-economic changes for their citizenry. One of the lasting colonial contributions to anthropology is the ethnographic surveys commissioned by IAI that produced very detailed accounts of African cultures. As Sichone (2001: 371) reflects, anthropology challenged him to let workers, peasants and other strata define themselves rather than imposing concepts like class on their complex lives. In their written work both Kenyatta and Busia were percipient about the potential for a post-colonial anthropology. That none of them pursued their scholarly work is a reflection of their political careers, the way that the discipline's reputation became increasingly tarnished by the funding and support it received from the British Colonial Office, and the nature of academic structures imported into their countries from the University of London. This apparent slight of the discipline must also be understood in perspective. Anthropology like all other social sciences was/is Eurocentric in its origin and orientation and the opposition and critique it has aroused, especially in Africa, is not of the discipline as such but of the agenda that made it lose its 'democratic and progressive side to the irritating language of primitive studies' (ibid.). Thus the critiques are mostly of the discipline's subject matter (it stands accused of focusing on tribal/'primitive' peoples), its methodology (of participant observation – even when local language competencies may be in question as both Owusu (1978) and Sichone (2001) have noted), its concepts and theories (of social evolution, with Africans located on the lowest rungs of the social ladder), and its objectives (mostly seen as serving the European colonial agenda or the Western academic enterprise). Other disciplines that have similar methodological and theoretical orientations have often escaped similar critiques because of their agendas and seemingly practical value.

The history of academic disciplines is a story of both ideas and institutions. How did anti-colonial politics gradually intersect with the establishment of universities in Africa? Before the Second World War, there were already a number of higher-education colleges scattered across British-controlled Africa, such as Fourah Bay College in Sierra Leone, first established in 1826 and later linked to the academic standards of Durham University in England. Makerere in Uganda, and Achimota in the Gold Coast both offered post-secondary vocational education by 1935. But most African higher education institutions were developed after the Second World War, with colleges being formed in Ibadan and Legon in 1949, and Makerere being upgraded to university status in 1963. Ashby (1964) describes how the Asquith commission of 1951 became 'Britain's blueprint for the export of universities to her people overseas'. Acknowledging this as one of the few 'lasting legacies' of British colonialism, with much time, effort and funding going into these new universities, he also points out that the policy was 'a vivid expression of British cultural parochialism', for its basic assumption was that a university system 'appropriate for Europeans brought up in London and Manchester and Hull was also appropriate for Africans brought up in Lagos and Kumasi and

Kampala' (ibid.: 19). As with new provincial universities in the UK, they initially had to teach to London University curricula and maintain the same entrance standards. This meant that quite often places went unfilled – there were 100 vacancies in University College Ghana in 1955. The principle of academic autonomy may be a good one, but in practice in Africa in the 1950s this meant a senate composed primarily of expatriate scholars defining university policy. As Tadesse (1999) notes, these universities were lavishly funded, often located on campuses away from urban centres. Several of the universities were started as regional institutions serving various countries and later became national universities. All of this contributed to a growing public backlash against such racialised 'ivory towers', and there was strong pressure on universities to become more publicly accountable. The initial focus on standards was gradually replaced by a call for relevance and usefulness.

The situation in Francophone Africa was rather different. The French did not support the early creation of African universities, and the only university founded prior to independence was in Dakar. Young African scholars all graduated from French universities, and Coquery-Vidrovitch suggests that this led them to oppose vigorously the 'brutal' assimilation of the Francophone model, and to 'construct a national history separate from their French heritage' (Mudimbe 1991). Both Mamadou Diouf and Achille Mbembe, founders of the Senegal school of cultural philosophy, and leaders of a movement to develop an autochthonous African scholarly project, were trained in France (Diouf and Mamdani 1994). The picture is complex and country-specific. Nkwi (2000) describes the teaching of ethnology within sociology at the University of Yaoundé in Cameroon, firstly led by a French anthropologist in the 1960s, and gradually evolving until anthropology became, in 1993, a recognised degree in its own right.

Anthropological work in Anglophone Africa was both aided and abetted by British support for social research, through the funding provided by the Colonial Social Science Research Council (Mills, this volume). In Francophone Africa, such work was aided by the creation of the Institute of Ethnology at the University of Paris in 1925 and later by the founding of the Société des Africanistes (Society of Africanists) to mirror the British-dominated International African Institute (Coquery-Vidrovitch 1999). Couched in a paternalist rhetoric of colonial development and welfare, different social research projects were established across British Africa in the 1950s, many of which were anthropologically informed. The funding also led to the creation of regional research institutes including the Rhodes Livingstone Institute (RLI) in Northern Rhodesia (Zambia), the East African Institute of Social Research (EAISR) at Makerere College in Uganda, and the West African Institute for Social Research (WAISR) in Nigeria. Yet the very prestige and visibility of such projects led, in the minds of many African observers, to the discipline being closely associated with colonial administrations. This had not been the intention, and back in 1944 Max Gluckman had stated his hope that Africans would use the 'sociologist's knowledge' to challenge the colonial administration (Schumaker 2001).

The original purpose of the centres had been to build research capacity and train local researchers; this did not always materialise. Schumaker describes how many of the research assistants employed at the RLI were never offered permanent appointments within the institute, despite developing a strong commitment to the discipline, and went on to develop non-academic careers. Like Kenyatta, however, they made anthropology their own, making use of their nationalist political credentials to gain access to sensitive urban contexts, and also using their research appointments to further their own political careers. In Makerere, Ugandan research assistants left for careers in journalism and politics.

With independence, the research concerns of both the RLI and the EAISR shifted away from anthropological to economic topics; and the debates begun in the early years of the RLI had more influence on scholarly work in Manchester than in Lusaka. The RLI was shifted first to Lusaka and then to Salisbury (Harare) during the years of the federation. The first, and last, Zambian director of the institute, Philip Nsugbe, presided over its renaming as an Institute for African Studies. His memories of that period are revealing: 'In Zambian eyes, the Rhodes Livingstone Institute was viewed as an embarrassing colonial relic, indeed as an open window through which the same old Colonial eyes pried … it still bore to the oversensitive Zambian nostrils the unpleasant skin odour of its Colonial ancestry' (Nsugbe 1977: 335). He recalls the battle for its future amongst expatriate researchers, some of whom had an inevitably 'strong emotional attachment' to the RLI. These research institutes were plagued by their history and their semi-autonomous status in relation to the new universities, few of which established departments of anthropology.

Not one of the universities in English-speaking Africa, save for South Africa, created a single-discipline anthropology department, though a number of joint departments of anthropology and sociology were created, including in Nigeria, Sudan, Zimbabwe and Ethiopia.

Nigeria was one exception to this general relegation of anthropology in the post-colonial period. A strong tradition of anthropological research was begun when Nathaniel Fadipe became the first Nigerian to receive a PhD in social anthropology in 1939. There followed a succession of scholars who, whilst calling themselves sociologists, trained in social anthropology in Europe and America, some of them in departments of sociology. These included Philip Nsugbe, G. K. Nukunya, Onige Otite, Victor Uchendu, M. Onwuejeogwu, Azuka Dike and F. Ekijuba, several of whom wrote classic anthropological monographs on their peoples (Otite 1999).

From the mid-1960s onwards, flourishing universities like Makerere came under increasing state control, and growing social pressure to Africanise their faculty. This was also a time during which dynamic new schools of thought emerged within the radical social sciences, such as the Dar es Salaam school of political economy (Rodney 1972; Shivji 1976) and new schools of thinking within history. Professional associations and regional research centres like CODESRIA began to emerge. Tadesse characterises this period as 'a euphoric one, seemingly full of intellectual promise', yet he notes that a 'tradition of research and publishing was not institutionalised' (1999: 148).

Viewed historically, the omens for anthropology in late-colonial Africa were never auspicious, born as it was amidst a rising tide of anti-colonial sentiment and the increasingly scholarly and metropolitan concerns of academic social anthropology. The inevitable consequence of being associated with colonialism was that anthropology in Anglophone Africa became the scapegoat. With the exception of South Africa, most African anthropologists taught in cognate disciplines because no stand-alone departments of anthropology existed in their institutions. Thus many who were trained as anthropologists taught in sociology departments. With neither a presence in the new universities nor support from African intelligentsia, the loss of independent identity of the discipline in the 1960s and 1970s was almost complete, although there were ongoing discussions about the relationship between anthropology and sociology in countries such as Nigeria (Otite 1972) and about the

Africanisation of the university curriculum in Kenya (Ogot 1999). Brokensha felt that 'most African intellectuals are at best indifferent to, or mildly tolerant of, social anthropology, and frequently they have a strong feeling of hostility to the subject and its practitioners' (Brokensha 1966: 16). With anthropology suddenly out of fashion, its approaches and research practices were adopted to great effect within African history – as in the sudden scholarly emphasis on the importance of the collection of oral history using fieldwork methods and participant observation – as well as in other social science disciplines that, it seemed, had suddenly seen the value of ethnography and multidisciplinarity. We will discuss later how this appropriation of anthropological tools continues today as the project of economic development demands more situated accounts of cultural processes in local communities and processes of change and adaptation.

New academic fashions developed, including the Dar es Salaam school of scholars such as Walter Rodney (1972), Mafeje (1971), Shivji (1976) and Mamdani (1976) and African revolutionary leaders such as Cabral (1969), all building a growing activist community of African social scientists. Structural Marxism, revisionist histories and dependency theory analyses threw light on the history of colonialism and the structurally peripheral economic and political relationships enmeshing Africa. However, Marxism's explanatory ambitions took it away from the more modest tasks of making empirical sense of changing African social forms. This was a period of grand narratives about African history, politics and economics, but rather less attention was paid to social relations or cultural forms, 'society' being the tarnished analytical tool of the anthropologists. If, as Mamdani (1999: 192) argues, 'ethnicity (tribalism) was simultaneously the form of colonial control over "natives" and the form of revolt against it', then ethnicity was unlikely to be the analytical frame of choice. As Brokensha noted in 1966, 'any appearance of anthropologists fostering interest in this potentially divisive and disruptive force would be regarded with deep suspicion' (Brokensha 1966: 15). At the first International Congress of Africanists in 1964, anthropology was attacked for its portrayal of African societies in a way that justified colonial rule (Bown and Crowder 1964). Paul Nkwi notes that this critique was repeated at the 1971 Algiers Congress of African Intellectuals (Nkwi 1998a).

The growing influence of Marxist theory was mirrored by the growth of institutes of development studies and of 'developmentalist' ideology within African universities and civil society. As Obbo shows in her contribution to this volume, scholars were primarily interested in 'modern' Africa, and had little interest in documenting rural African life. The focus was on nation building as a means to development. The paradox was that neither the modernisation paradigm nor its critique engaged with the everyday reality of life in impoverished villages and urban slums on the continent. Applied anthropology continued during the 1960s as Brokensha indicates (1966, 1969), but was primarily carried out by Western expatriate scholars who had their own agendas that never quite resonated with those of the target communities (Onoge 1979). Furthermore, many élite Africans during the anti-colonial movement saw anthropology as a threat because of its interest in Africans and their cultures – an implicit celebration of cultural diversity at a time of 'forced' ideas of culturally integrated nationhood necessary for independence (Southall 1983).

Debate over the epistemological and racial politics inherent in the Western academic study of Africa continues to this day, particularly in the US. A heated conflict over the racial composition of faculty in African studies departments in the US (Curtin 1995; Atkins et al. 1995) brought to the surface strong divisions over the 'conceptions, institutions and communities dedicated to the study of Africa' (Martin and West 1999: 1). Those who provided a critique of the 'Africanist' establishment decry its narrow and compartmentalised construction of Africa, and 'gatekeeping practices' within area studies. This compartmentalisation has led established white scholars to ignore the work of African-Americans and other New World Africans in the diaspora whose research and writing they consider less scholarly and more ideological and politically motivated. The problem-focused approach in anthropology (favoured by those opposed to the Africanist paradigm) seems to be the direction being taken by African anthropology, especially given the nature of research supported by such external donors as USAID, Family Health International (FHI), Global Fund, the Population Council or the Swedish International Development Agency (SIDA), as well as a desire by practitioners for social change. We may make a distinction here between African and Africanist anthropology. The former refers to Africans, primarily based in the continent, who are engaged in anthropological work that ranges beyond knowledge production to include an understanding that allows for empathy with the people and societies they study because they as researchers are also part of these same societies. They are using their social science skills to study Africa primarily for the benefit of Africans' understanding of themselves, as is the practice of all other social scientists across the globe – where social science research is used to generate knowledge about self and society. It is unlikely that these African anthropologists can abandon the study of their own societies, no matter how deplorable the socio-economic or political conditions may be. They cannot give up on Africa as Gavin Kitching (2000) did by abandoning African studies, which he found depressing. The future of African scholars is intimately tied to the study of their societies, and the future of African anthropology and social science is dependent on such scholars (Owusu 1978, 1997; Sichone 2001). Africanist anthropology, comprising mostly Western scholars, whose research priorities and interests may differ drastically from those of their African colleagues, may not have a personal commitment to African development or tolerate the physical hardships and inconveniences that extended residence among their study population entails. This may explain why a number of them 'abandon' such communities as soon as their funding dries up. Others may lack the necessary grounding in local cultural practices and yet write about African cultures with authority even after a 'brief encounter with an arbitrary array of informants' (Sichone 2001: 377).

Such a division between African (local and indigenous) and Africanist (Western and foreign) in the academy need not exist, yet it is discernible in much of the history of African studies in the West (primarily in North America). Martin and West suggest that an 'examination of the origin of the study of Africa outside the Africanist establishment indicates both a different history of the field and the foundations of an alternative, non-Africanist future for African studies' (1999: 14). They point to the continuing importance of what they call 'transcontinental' scholarship, a tradition begun by W. E. B. DuBois, that explores Africa in relation to its diasporic communities. DuBois not only theorised about this relationship but also went on to relocate in Ghana, taking up Ghanaian citizenship and upon his death being buried there. If such a connectivity were to be revived in the anthropology of Africa, the discipline would survive beyond its current challenges. Such collaboration would make African anthropology much more inclusive and hence avoid the marginalisation of African anthropologists by their Western counterparts, who write reviews of the anthropology of Africa without a single mention of anthropological work by African scholars based in the continent, even when the reviewers themselves have done fieldwork in Africa and interacted with locally based anthropologists (Owusu 1997).

Creative marginality? The teaching and practice of anthropology in Africa today

Does the absence of the acknowledgement of African anthropologists in Western writing mean that African anthropology was non-existent? After a half-century of being out of favour, how and where is anthropology being taught in Africa today? How are anthropologists being employed? There is a growing literature and debate about the history of the discipline and its teaching in Africa (for example, Gordon 1993; Nkwi 2001; Mamdani 1998), and it is now possible to piece together a continent-wide picture of disciplinary practice.

Within Anglophone Africa there are very few academic institutions with autonomous anthropology departments. Exceptions include a number of joint sociology and anthropology departments in Nigeria, Moi University in Kenya, the University of Khartoum and a number of anthropology departments in South Africa. The record for the longest tradition of teaching within a department of anthropology is held by Sudan, where it has been taught since 1955 (Kameir and Elbakri 1989). In Nigeria there has also been a long tradition of anthropology teaching, within either sociology departments or joint departments of sociology and anthropology, with the particular emphasis of each dependent on the scholars founding the department (Otite 1999). The University of Nigeria, Nsukka, founded by Nnamdi Azikwe, was one of the first to teach anthropology (see Ezeh, this volume). As Pankhurst (this volume) demonstrates, anthropology has also had a relatively unbroken record in Ethiopia, where it has been taught at the University of Addis Ababa since the late 1960s. Each country and institution has a different and very specific history and relationship with the discipline. As Joshua Akong'a, once a Dean of the Faculty of Cultural and Development Studies at Moi University (where anthropology has been taught since 1994), puts it in relation to the situation in Kenya: 'We have broken away from European anthropology, we're not about writing ethnographies, but rather we're seeking to solve societies' problems' (Akong'a, personal communication).

South Africa has a rather different history (Gordon 1993; Hammond-Tooke 1997), both because of the early development of anthropology departments in South Africa – Radcliffe-Brown taught at the University of Cape Town (UCT) in the 1930s – and because of its years of isolation under apartheid which led to *volkekunde* in Afrikaans-language universities. Yet, even in other parts of Southern Africa, one often finds a contradictory situation. Anthropologists are usually 'hidden' within sociology departments, and yet most of the empirical research done for masters and doctorates in countries such as Namibia, Botswana, Lesotho, Swaziland and Zimbabwe is carried out by anthropologists. As LeBeau and Gordon (2002) note, this has been carried out primarily by Western expatriates rather than local scholars. Mamdani (1998) has been a vocal critic of the shape of the social sciences in Southern Africa, pointing out that if students wished to study the 'native' rather than White experience at the University of Cape Town, they were expected to go to the Centre for African Studies rather than to the disciplinary departments (see also Hall's response, 1998). He calls for the 'deracialisation of intellectual production' through state action to change the institutional context of knowledge production (Mamdani 1999:134), citing similar govern-ment interventions in the 1960s as a key catalyst to intellectual debate across sub-Saharan Africa. If there are relatively few universities teaching anthropology in Anglophone Africa, there are even fewer in Francophone Africa. Instead, as Abega shows in this volume, anthro-pologists were usually trained first in philosophy, often within the seminary.

One way of understanding the ongoing epistemological legacy of the discipline's relationship within the colonial metropole is to explore the degree to which, 40 years after independence, university lecturers are still being appointed after having completed research degrees outside Africa. An informal sample of the situation in Anglo-phone Africa can be taken from those listed as teaching in sociology or anthropology departments in the 2002 Commonwealth University Yearbook. Of the 170 or so academics listed, roughly two-thirds had a Masters or PhD degree from a non-African university. The sample is a casual one, potentially skewed by a selective listing of only the senior faculty within departments, but it is nonetheless revealing. It raises the issue of the extent to which 'endogenisation' is occurring in African universities. Crossman uses the term to evaluate the extent to which African universities are developing 'new and original approaches to the practices of their own disciplines – in short, their own schools of thought' (1999: 27).

African anthropology continues to be characterised by an imbalance in its disciplinary networks. The international networks that are a legacy of colonial rule outweigh the regional and national networks that one might have predicted. This has both positive and negative consequences. African anthropology has thrived on its contacts and exchanges with British, French, American and other European anthropologies via scholarships and sabbaticals, workshops and conferences, exchange of teachers and students, research funding, and participation in joint research projects. Although this has protected African anthropology from provincialism, it has been at the expense of forging similar contacts and exchanges among African anthropologists, even amongst those within a single country. It is instructive that anthropologists in Africa communicate less across national boundaries within Africa than they do with colleagues in Europe and North America or Australia. The separation seems even greater between Anglophone and Francophone African anthropologists, where language is a major hindrance. An exception is Cameroon, where both English and French have often been used simultaneously as media of instruction in the education system.

One example of this is the relative paucity of linkages between South African anthropologists and those from the rest of the continent. De Jongh sees this as partly the result of South Africa's years of isolation during apartheid, which led to a 'relative ignorance of the discipline and its practitioners in the rest of Africa' (1997: 443). Two distinct traditions of anthropology also developed in South Africa, one catering to the intellectual interests and linguistic needs of Afrikaans intellectuals, and the other to the more liberal English-speaking anthropological community. Neither addressed the interests or training needs of black academics.

The issue today for African anthropology is not simply one of redressing the geopolitical balance in favour of African scholarship but also one of sustaining its global networks, which have been seriously undermined by the more inward-looking economic and educational policies of the Western countries. It is also one of constantly re-evaluating the habit of Western anthropology that ignores the input of African scholars to the project of anthropology. As Owusu (1997: 20) has observed, the challenge of making African anthropology (anthropologies) truly African will entail a shift in focus away from the Western epistemological assumptions that have dominated African intellectual life for generations. It will be an anthropology ready to question basic empirical assumptions and realities, and to interrogate how African ideas about various cultural practices have been related at different times and places in order to provide explanatory or interpretive meanings that may not be captured through dominant Western perspectives and conceptual frameworks. African anthropology thus enters the twenty-first century not only fragmented and isolated from the international anthropological community, but with the burden of defending the dignity of Africa and its people, who too often have been used as laboratories for social sciences that seek to build theoretical paradigms of the West with no tangible benefits to Africa. This is a big challenge because the shortage of resources for research and teaching (such as up-to-date literature)[3] and low salaries have combined to cause a 'brain drain' and a disincentive to serious anthropological work of Africa by Africans. With resources of universities along with their prestige declining, intellectual outlooks are becoming narrow and provincial, and the best of faculty and graduates are emigrating to greener pastures overseas. These material constraints and inequities have been extensively explored in the existing literature (see Selassie and Kameir 1989; Ajayi 1995; Mamdani 1993, among others).

Those who stay behind are drifting into consultancy work with international organisations. Consultancies are not in themselves problematic, but they can result in the confining of intellectual production and debate to routine reports, sacrificing scholarly creativity to survival necessities. A particular problem for many African researchers has been the way they have ended up serving as local sources of basic information (raw data) for their more fortunate colleagues abroad, who add 'more value' to such information in the form of analytical, interpretive or expansive theoretical contributions to the literature for African consumption.

Within Africa a more positive aspect of the interaction between anthropology and its cognate disciplines has been the growing integration of qualitative and quantitative approaches within anthropological work. Partly driven by the conventions of biomedical research, African anthropologists have increasingly found ways of using quantitative tools to analyse qualitative research (as demon-strated in Mary Amuyunzu-Nyamongo's contribution to this book). This is not necessarily a new departure for anthropology, for Max Gluckman's students at the RLI constantly returned to the importance of bringing together qualitative and quantitative data, as was also noted by Schapera in reviewing anthropological work in Kenya (Schapera 1949).

A legacy of the ideological heritage of colonial anthropology is found in the continued divide between 'Africanists' and African scholars working in Africa. Whilst there has never been more potential for creative and collaborative linkages, between individuals, disciplines and countries, they are rarely in evidence. African scholars are well positioned to carry out empirical social research, partly because of their familiarity with local political contexts, competence in local languages, and understanding of local cultural nuances, but are often less exposed to relevant theoretical debates current in Northern institutions which may benefit African scholarship. Examples of such collaborative research projects between institutions are increasing, but the relationship is not always an equal one; this volume is a small step towards that much-needed scholarly collaboration. There are also a growing number of undergraduate study-abroad programmes being organised by US universities across Africa that call upon African anthropologists as key players (currently 33 US universities offer such programmes in Ghana). Mwenda Ntarangwi (this volume) explores the complex relationship between anthropology and study abroad, often evocative of polarised relations between modernised élites and the masses, who are thought of as stuck in 'tradition'.

A related question is the role of theory in African anthropology. Zeleza (1997: iv) expresses his frustration at the existing gap between disciplinary theory and practice: 'African scholars cannot afford the disengaged academic recreations of faddish theorising others seem to be able to indulge in. Their countries and communities cry out for clear and committed analyses, not the superficial travelogues they often get from foreign fly-by-night academic tourists.' Sichone, in an important critique of contemporary American anthropological trends, suggests that 'anthropological research is still a Western enterprise in a way that political science, development studies or any of the other social sciences are not' (2001: 371). He is particularly concerned about what he calls 'pure anthropology', which, in its 'insistence on creating meaning even when lacking information', ends up becoming even more imperial than colonial anthropology. For him, current trends in American anthropology are leading to anthropology 'that has no practical value' (ibid.). He ends by suggesting that it should be a requirement of the profession that 'all anthropologists do some research at home' (*ibid.*: 379). This further confirms Malinowski's sentiments about anthropology, mentioned above. It is our argument that the African anthropologies currently being carried out 'at home' and across the continent have a very real value, and represent an important disciplinary future. Yet given the international exchanges that do occur, African anthropology is inevitably torn between forging its own identity and building on the traditions of scholarship in the institutions where its practitioners are trained. For instance, anthropologists trained in the US and the UK under traditions such as the 'four field' approach (combining cultural anthropology, linguistic anthropology, physical/biological anthropology, and archaeology as it is in many institutions in the US) or the focus on social anthropology as separate from archaeology (common in many UK institutions where archaeology is linked more to history than social anthropology), could enrich or create problems for African anthropology. Those trained in the US bring a more broad-based approach that can be an advantage when it comes to course offerings and student advising; their UK counterparts, by contrast, are hardly required to take doctoral courses beyond research methods. At Moi University in Kenya, for instance, archaeology is listed in two departments – the departments of history and anthropology – but is only taught in the history department, and there is no evidence that anthropology students interested in archaeology have taken archaeology in the history department as part of their requirements for graduation. African scholars employed in the same national university who have trained in both the US and the UK thus bring very different experiences and perceptions of anthropology to their teaching.

Critiques of anthropology in Africa, including those by Zeleza and Sichone, do not merely question the discipline's epistemological ability to offer understandings of Africa and its complexities. They also point to how the social identities and institutional locations of academics shape the questions they ask and the conclusions they draw. The favoured disciplines of political science and development studies, seen as suitable for Africa in ways that 'pure anthropology' is not, are equally determined by the same Western epistemological assumptions. It is not only theories of post-modernism that have given rise to the 'superficial travelogues' that Zeleza criticises. Indeed, post-modern critiques have galvanised the discipline of anthropology, allowing for the legitimacy of other worldviews besides those of Western anthropologists.

In its practice African anthropology can decentre Western episte-mological traditions by unpacking African ways of knowing, creating its own traditions of reflexive anthropology and cultural critique (Marcus and Fischer 1986). This is not to say that every African anthropologist should conduct research 'at home'. Even they are studying not 'ourselves' but 'others' albeit in their 'own' geographi-cal locality, as Onyango-Ouma points out (this volume). We can neither ignore the critiques levelled against anthropology nor its utility. We instead suggest a more discriminating engagement with the discipline that is not predetermined by its colonial history or the dominance of the West. A precedent for such an engagement is offered in the discussion of the role of 'anthropologies of the South' in linking scholarship with politics (Quinlan 2000; Krotze 1997) and the role of a 'world anthropology network' in supporting and promoting the diversity of anthropological practice (Ribeiro and Escobar 2005). The discipline has a lot to offer African social scientists especially as they grapple with the enormous socio-economic and political challenges brought about by HIV/AIDS, which can best be compre-hended through the array of tools provided by anthropology, including multidisciplinary theory, observation and participatory methodology, intensity and holistic approaches, and fieldwork. Indeed, the failure of the 'development' project in much of Africa (especially the brand that is mostly conceived of by economists and political scientists, who tend to ignore the role of local culture, local meaning and local history) has clearly opened up opportunities for a complex and multilayered approach that is offered by anthropology. This point is skilfully made in Polly Hill's (1979) critique of development economists, in which she advocates an anthropological approach to development in order to inform the planning and implementation of development projects with local sensibilities.

The founding of the Pan African Anthropology Association (PAAA) in 1989 was an attempt to demonstrate anthropology's potential contribution to the understanding of Africa's social, cultural and political terrain. It marked the culmination of continued discussion about anthropology and a pan-African agenda located in the continent (Otite 1972). The PAAA was the brainchild of 14 African anthropologists who met in Zagreb at the Twelfth International Congress of Anthropological and Ethnological Sciences (ICAES). During the Congress, these anthropologists assembled a steering committee, chaired by Paul Nchoji Nkwi (Cameroon), and included

Adama Diop (Senegal), George Hagan (Ghana) and Ocholla Ayayo (Kenya). They acknowledged the 'serious problems facing African anthropologists', evidenced in the way that 'African ethnology and anthropology did not feature as prominently as it should have' at the Congress, and determined to launch an association of African anthropologists to 'come together and identify these problems more clearly' (Nkwi 1998a). Similar sentiments were expressed at an earlier meeting of Nigerian social scientists with the aim of forming such an association to promote anthropological research and teaching, produce a journal, and cooperate with national associations of anthropologists and sociologists with a view to promoting the formation of a pan-African association (Otite 1972 cited in Owusu 1979: 157).

The PAAA was launched in 1990 in Cameroon, with financial support from the Wenner-Gren Foundation, which has been supplemented by funds from the Carnegie Foundation, the UNFPA (UN Family Planning Association) and other UN funding bodies. Its journal, The African Anthropologist, has been published since 1995 with support from Wenner-Gren until 2005, when its support was taken up by CODESRIA. The association has attended closely to the issue of disciplinary reproduction, and, in collaboration with Wenner-Gren, has organised a number of training and mentoring initiatives (Nkwi 1998a, 1998b, 2000). Through its annual meetings held in different countries in Africa (mostly East, West and Southern) each year, the PAAA has created a forum for the exchange of scholarly ideas and experiences by African and Africanist anthropologists. This forum allows for interaction not only across national and disciplinary boundaries but also across generational levels as senior anthropologists meet and exchange ideas with younger colleagues.

Consultancies and African anthropology

At the 2002 PAAA conference, the outgoing executive secretary, Paul Nkwi, suggested that one of the biggest problems facing African anthropology was publication and the need for young scholars to develop writing skills, particularly in the generation of detailed 'thick' ethnographies. This raised the question of whether anthropology's identity is defined by its commitment to the production of 'ethnographic' texts. The link between the two now seems incontrovertible, but this has not always been the case, and post-war British anthropologists used to jest about 'mere' ethnographers – insisting that the real purpose of ethnographic research was to 'build' theory. This raises the question whether prioritising ethnographic monographs, and the time needed to write them, is always appropriate in an environment dominated by diminished resources, the short-term demands of applied social research and the use of consultancies to augment meagre professional salaries. But are consultancies an antithesis to ethnography and/or fieldwork? One could argue that in a well-funded, well-paid research university one could undertake consultancy as a complement to one's normal work and in underfunded institutions one could engage in consultancy as a way of survival. Be that as it may, consultancies may provide opportunities for new research projects and stimulate new thinking about an existing problem requiring in-depth examination and extended fieldwork. Such consultancy work could be rewritten into the sort of 'thick ethnographic descriptions' favoured by the scholarly community. Repeated consultancies in the same community or with the same group of people could result in an accumulated set of data that, over time, amounts to a critical ethnography. The relationship is not always one-way. Accepted techniques of academic research, such as those of participatory appraisal, first developed out of the world of consultancy.[4]

We may also point out that the time needed to finish a traditional ethnography that produces a thick description is quite different from that required in a topic- or problem-based research. If one is conducting research on a specific research project for testing for malaria in blood samples obtained from the placentas of women who delivered at home (Onyango-Ouma, this volume), one may successfully complete the project in a short time once a relevant sample size has been obtained.

At times the issue is not simply one of funding, but also of epistemology. There is an increasing reliance by both national and international funders and donors on a standardisation of research procedures, particularly within short-term consultancies. One consequence of this is a simplistic breakdown of the research and writing process into methodology, data collection, results and conclusions (see Amuyunzu-Nyamongo, this volume). We call this the 'bureaucratisation of anthropology'. Such chunky categories do not necessarily do justice to the nuances of anthropological knowledge, or the iterative process of carrying out anthropological research, during which 'results' gained can lead to both a change in methods used or even the research questions themselves. The genre of the consultancy report or project assessment equally serves to shape writing styles, privileging crisp analyses and succinct summaries rather than more subtle explorations of anthropological themes. The irony is that research projects often turn to anthropology because of its seeming promise to garner 'local knowledge', and overcome past failures of quantitative sociology to deliver tangible results (see Onyango-Ouma, this volume). Yet there is a tension between the expectations laid on the discipline by both national and international funding agencies and a lack of understanding of the timeframes and research conventions within which anthropological research operates. This could, however, be seen as a blessing in disguise as anthropologists continue to provide a necessary critique of the disengaged development work of which practitioners in other disciplines are so fond. There is often a tendency to confuse the roles played by consultancy and applied work in anthropology. While the difference between the two is often slight, depending on one's perspective, it is notable that an anthropologist could do consultancy work without engaging in applied anthropology. One could be consulting on a project because of one's experience and training without offering advice on the kind of policy or social change that characterises applied anthropological work (Stewart and Strathern 2005).

Unlike many of their counterparts in the North, African anthropologists working in the academy do not have access to research funds and are thus almost always compelled to seek these alternative methods of sustaining an active scholarship. As Michael Crowder observes, African lecturers 'are overburdened with teaching, do not have access to the latest books and journals, cannot obtain funds to travel to conferences outside their countries, and are unable to find funds even for local research' (1987: 110). Since most of these African scholars work for public universities that are highly dependent on government subsidies, or for private universities that are tuition-dependent, research funds is the last item on the priority list of these institutions, even as student enrolments continue to grow. One way of getting out of this academic quagmire it to seek out any consultancies available, especially those looking for the 'culture experts' to help make their projects become responsive to a new way of thinking about social phenomena. Some of these 'culture projects' do not end up in the hands of anthropologists as scholars from other disciplines claim to be doing anthropological work when their focus is on culture and local customs. It is not unusual for one, for instance, to sit in a PAAA annual conference and hear colleagues from other disciplines discussing culture in ways that do not acknowledge existing anthropological literature at all, even when such discussion hinges on socio-cultural change that has been well documented by anthropologists. This 'hijacking' of the discipline is not limited to African anthropology at all. In their edited volume *Culture Matters*, Harrison and Huntingtcn, together with a group of Harvard economists, political scientists and a few anthropologists, debate what seems to them the radical proposition that culture makes a difference in economic development. Yet they do so by falling into the trap long ago discerned by anthropologists (at least since the times of Oscar Lewis) of blaming all poverty on the malformed and defective cultures of underdeveloped countries (Wilk 2002). One may thus observe that anthropological practice is under siege, and when we combine this with the fact that anthropologists have to use consultancies to survive, we know that the discipline faces an overwhelming task of staying active and productive. With almost all research being driven by local or international donors, anthro-pological work in Africa is unable to produce the contributions to ethnography, comparative theory and applied work necessary to sustain local scholarship and teaching; instead, the main value of the work produced is to the specific funding agencies supporting it. Many anthropologists in the African academy have to moonlight to make ends meet and few students are enrolling for anthropology courses to be trained as anthropologists because many come to the discipline seeking specific skills that will make them employable (see Ezeh, this volume). Anthropology and consultancy in Africa therefore seem to have towed the line pursued by other applied anthropologists, the only difference being that – unlike in the colonial era, when applied work was mostly commissioned by the government for adminis-trative ends (Grillo 1985; Gulliver 1985) – current work is mostly commissioned by non-governmental organisations that seem to have absorbed the role of the many failed or unstable African governments. Sometimes this consultancy work ends up as reports to be used and stored by the respective donor agencies (both national or inter-national), with no involvement of the respective government. Rarely, for instance, do lecturers at Kenyan public universities get access to consultancy reports funded by international donors such as FHI, USAID, the Global Fund, or Care International. These reports may be known only to those in the institutions that funded the project and the consultants hired to undertake the project.

Training for the future: the role of regional research institutes

A key concern for the discipline in Africa is the continued low status of anthropology among the social sciences. On the one hand, anthropology continues to occupy a marginal position within university departments, and is accorded little attention by planners and funders in comparison to the other social sciences. On the other hand, independent regional organisations such as CODESRIA and OSSREA have received funding and supported anthropological work to varying degrees. Tadesse (1999) points to the growth in these organisations and their role in forging a cumulative knowledge base and a culture of critical inquiry. But how autonomous are such organisations? The social sciences, like all other disciplines, have always depended on government patronage and support, but in Africa anthropology is now mostly reliant on funding from Western development agencies and international donors such as the Ford Foundation, FHI, USAID, the Rockefeller Foundation, the Global Fund, the Norwegian Agency for Development Cooperation (NORAD), SIDA, the World Bank, the International Monetary Fund (IMF) and many others. Their influence on the contemporary discipline is conditioning the very shape of anthropological writing, even within universities.

In line with this trend, some of the independent Africa-based social science research institutes have been encouraged by funders such as the Rockefeller Foundation, SIDA and the Ford Foundation to conform to the expectations of a generic, evidence-based social science. Whilst they have prioritised support for students, the fellowships offered by both OSSREA and CODESRIA are for a year (or less) to do research and write up their findings, often leading to inadequate and poorly written dissertations. When available, such funding does not cover a time period sufficient for students to be guided through the complex and often lonely process of carrying out fieldwork and writing an anthropological PhD. They, like their Western counterparts, cannot come close to fulfilling the term of fieldwork experience (five to seven years) recommended by Schapera (1949:18). Anthropological research is thus undercut by the demands of funding agencies that, because of their own pressures and deadlines, have little respect for a disciplinary identity based on extended fieldwork. Yet it should be noted that if fieldwork is done repeatedly in the same community for short periods, it yields telling ethnographic data (see Babiker, this volume).

One possible change to this short-term research would be for research organisations to abandon their obsession with 'quantity' in favour of a quest for 'quality' by limiting the numbers of their annual research grants. In this way they could provide the young researchers with enough funds, and an ample and flexible timeframe, whilst also subjecting them to a rigorous process of monitoring and evaluation of research output. Such organisations inevitably have to operate under the constant risk of donors withdrawing funds. However, we do not think it is impossible to strike a balance between the bureaucratic requirements of donors and the effective use of funds to ensure the quality of the final output. If, as it stands, few of the research reports produced from these grants qualify for publication, the onus is on the organisations to clarify their aims in supporting junior research projects.

Limited resources mean that funds available for research may only be enough for individual rather than team research and thus compel young researchers to carry out every aspect of the research themselves, inadvertently discouraging the development of research teams and the use of research assistants. Yet anthropologists have long relied on the help provided by committed and systematic informants (school teachers, administrators, veterinarians, extension agents, rural nurses) who in fact become unpaid research assistants. In most cases these are not merely mechanistic data gatherers, but informed observers who offer insights and intelligent criticism. In the field, to use Thomas's phrase, 'one works not with informants, but with co-interpreters' (1999: 343). Therefore, research organisations could make provisions in the research design and financial support of young researchers for the employment of research assistant(s), whilst not divorcing young researchers from direct handling of the data. An education in research management is essential for the future development of the discipline as well as for the professional careers of the younger anthropologists.

Conclusion

So what is African anthropology and where is it headed? First, we have to acknowledge the dire straits the discipline is in across much of sub-Saharan Africa. Resources to support research have dramatically dwindled in the last 40 years yet the demands on anthropologists in African universities continue to grow. Unless the situation is dramatically improved, very few African anthropologists will be making much of an impact on the academic world in the coming years. Unlike in the 1960s and 1970s, when African scholarship stood shoulder to shoulder with that of any other continent, the 1980s and 1990s have been marked by structural adjustment programmes that have reduced African economies, and by extension African academic institutions, into sorry caricatures of the past. With the right kind of financial support, African anthropology will take up its rightful place as the 'mother' of African studies in leading other social science disciplines in shaping the future of Africa. It will do so by blending the descriptive (thick description), the analytical (theoretical) and the applied (consultancy) in confronting such issues as poverty, reproductive health and governance. It will be an anthropology that builds on the work of the Kenyattas, Busias, Amadiumes, Obbos, Azikiwes, Onoges, Ottites, Uchendus and Kyerematengs who primarily studied either their own cultures or national societies and made original contributions to African anthropology that should stimulate further comparative studies of African studies and cultures elsewhere (Owusu 1997).

The report of the recent Commission for Africa, *Our Common Interests: Commission for Africa* 2005, was launched on 11 March 2005 in London, Addis Ababa and Washington by its chair, UK prime minister Tony Blair. The seventeen-member commission, of whom nine were Africans, was set up to investigate the root causes of Africa's persistent poverty and to suggest solutions and remedies. Despite the inclusion of African members, there is no mistaking the influence exerted by Western interests on the final report. It is ironic that the British and other Western powers, who did little for African secondary and higher education in the colonial era, should promote the expansion of education in Africa nearly half a century after political independence. Perhaps it's better late than never. As the report states, 'expanding higher education is important not only for providing vital skills to governments and other professions, including the vital supply of teachers and administrators, crucial for delivering education at all levels, but also for accountability throughout society'. Predictably, the 450-page document does not give specific commitments on how to finance its recommendations. Nonetheless, anthropology's open and inclusive ways of working, and its demonstrated ability to combine theoretical debates with practical applications, leave it well placed to benefit from this suggested expansion of higher education in Africa. Provided anthropology communicates its relevance to new generations of academically and vocationally minded students, employers and policy makers, and demonstrates its theoretical and policy contributions, its future is assured.

The future of anthropology in Africa can be likened to what Hamilton (2003: 160) says of the discipline in Australia:

> I do not believe anthropology can conceivably exist, at least in the sense of being reproduced, outside the university. It certainly can be practised outside the university, and in some countries, notably the US, it is practised very widely. However only in the university environment is it possible for students to learn the discipline and progress in it, for the necessary research base to be maintained, for the conditions to exist so that a continuing freshness and vitality can be assured. It is true that in the nineteenth century groups of interested gentlemen could join together in the premises of the Royal Society, and read learned papers which interested them on a wide variety of topics. In these times of intense competition for dwindling resources in universities, the domination of 'market forces' and neo-liberalism, the spread of late global capitalism, and the instability of the emerging world system, it is clear that certain choices will determine which knowledge bases or systems will survive and thrive. There is no guarantee that an area of study and knowledge which was considered significant and influential at one time will automatically be so considered later.

Despite its original contributions in the colonial period anthropology in post-colonial African universities cannot claim to have been at the cutting edge of socio-cultural studies in the past and thus faces tough challenges in the future. It is important that scholarship in Africa become a major priority of both national and international development agendas. Governments and international donors have to invigorate research at the university through setting aside adequate research funds and supporting local publishing houses that will in return support local scholarship. In this way anthropology will take its rightful place as a discipline that understands and reflects African needs and aspirations.

Notes

1 Lucy Mair states in her book, *Anthropology and Social Change*, that Malinowski sent her to study social change because he felt that she did not know enough anthropology for fieldwork of the standard type (1969: 8). In his paper on applied anthropology in Britain, R. H. Landman interviewed about sixty British applied anthropologists and found overwhelming evidence of their sense of inferiority compared to the rest of the profession (Landman 1978).

2 We would like to thank Maxwell Owusu for his insights on sociology programmes at the University of London.

3 Recently one of the editors – Mustafa Babiker – was involved in a study of the social and economic impact of a sugar production project in the White Nile province of Sudan. He adds: 'Since this was in an area in which I had not done research before, I decided to acquaint myself with it by reading the available literature. My intensive search in the libraries of the University of Khartoum boiled down to a single article written by a colonial administrator and published in the 1930 volume of *Sudan Notes and Records*. Yet I knew that anthropological research had recently been done in the area by an Italian anthropologist, some of which was published in the journal *Nomadic People* in 1995. Unfortunately, that journal was not available in the library and I had to email a friend of mine, an anthropologist currently reading for his PhD degree in Bergen, Norway, in order to get hold of the material. As we go to press, it has been mailed, but God only knows how long will it take to travel the distance of 300 metres between the Post Office of Khartoum University and my Department, if it arrives at all.'

4 We acknowledge Stephen Maack's useful insights on applied anthropology.

References

Abu Lughod, L., 2004, 'Ethnography In/Of Nations', *General Anthropology Division Newsletter*, 10, 2 (Spring): 1–4.

Ajayi, J. F. and L. H. Goma, 1996, *The African Experience with Higher Education*, Oxford: James Currey.

Amadiume, I., 1987, *Male Daughters, Female Husbands: Gender and Sex in an African Society*, London: Zed Books.

Apter, A., 1999, 'Africa, Empire, and Anthropology: a Philological Exploration of Anthropology's Heart of Darkness', *Annual Review of Anthropology*, 28: 577–98.

Apter, D., 1970, 'Foreword' to M. Owusu, *Uses and Abuses of Political Power*, Chicago: University of Chicago Press, xii–xx.

Asad, T. (ed.), 1973, *Anthropology and the Colonial Encounter*, London: Ithaca Press.

Ashby, E., 1964, *African Universities and Western Tradition*, Oxford: Oxford University Press.

Atkins, K. and J. Higginson, 1995, 'Letter to the Editor', *Chronicle of Higher Education*, 7 April: B3–B4.

Azikiwe, N., 1970, *My Odyssey: an Autobiography*, London: Hurst and Company.

Banaji, M., 1970, 'The Crisis of British Anthropology', *New Left Review*, 64: 71–85.

Bown, L. and M. Crowder, 1964, *Proceedings of the First International Congress of Africanists*, London: International Congress of Africanists.

Brokensha, D., 1966, *Applied Anthropology in English-Speaking Africa*, Lexington, Kentucky: Society for Applied Anthropology.

Busia, K. A., 1951, *The Position of the Chief in the Modern Political System of Ashanti: a Study of the Influence of Contemporary Social Changes on Ashanti Political Institutions*, Oxford: Oxford University Press.

—— 1962, *The Challenge of Africa*, London: Pall Mall Press.

Cabral, A., 1969, *Revolutions in Guinea*, New York: Monthly Review Press.

Chilungu, S., 1976, 'Issues in the Ethics of Research Method: an Interpretation of Anglo-American Perspective', *Current Anthropology*, 17, 3: 457–81.

Commission for Africa, 2005, 'Final Report Issued 11 March 2005', available for download at www.commissionforafrica.org.

Coquery-Vidrovitch, C., 1999, 'The Rise of Francophone African Social Science: from Colonial Knowledge to Knowledge of Africa', in W. G. Martin and M. O. West (eds.), *Out of One Many Africas: Reconstructing the Study and Meaning of Africa*, Urbana: University of Illinois Press, pp. 39–53.

Crossman, P., 1999, *Endogenisation and African Universities: Initiatives and Issues in the Quest for Plurality in the Human Sciences*, Leuven: Africa Research Centre.

Crowder, M., 1987, '"Us" and "Them": the International African Institute and the Current Crisis of Identity in African Studies', *Africa* 57, 1: 109–22.

Curtin, P., 1995, 'Ghettoising African History', *Chronicle of Higher Education*, 3 (March): A44.

de Jongh, M., 1997, 'Africa Colonises Anthropology', *Current Anthropology*, 38, 3: 451–53.

Diouf, M. and M. Mamdani (eds.), 1994, *Academic Freedom in Africa*, Dakar: Council for the Development of Social Science Research in Africa (CODESRIA).

Drake, S., 1964, 'Pan Africanism, Negritude and the African Personality', in W. John Hanna (ed.), *Independent Black Africa: the Politics of Freedom*, Chicago: Rand McNully and Co., pp. 530–41.

DuBois, W. E. B. 1996 [1903], *The Souls of Black Folk*, Penguin Books: New York.

Evans-Pritchard, E., 1962, *Essays in Social Anthropology*, New York: Free Press.

Fabian, J., 1983, *Time and the Other: How Anthropology Makes Its Object*, New York: Columbia University Press.

Fardon, R. (ed.), 1990, *Localising Strategies: Regional Traditions of Ethnographic Writing*,

Edinburgh: Scottish Academic Press.

Geertz, C., 1999, 'The Introduction into Anthropology of a Genuinely Historical Eye', *Journal of Victorian Culture*, 4, 2: 305–9.

Goddard, D., 1972, 'Anthropology: the Limits of Functionalism', *Ideology in the Social Sciences*, New York: Vintage Books.

Goody, J., 1995, *The Expansive Moment: Anthropology in Britain and Africa 1918–1970*, Cambridge: Cambridge University Press.

Greenfield, R., 1978, 'The Passing of Burning Spear', *West Africa London*, 28 August, pp. 1677.

Grillo, R., 1985, 'Applied Anthropology in the 1980s: Retrospect and Prospect', in R. Grillo and A. Rew (eds.), *Social Anthropology and Development Policy*, London: Tavistock Publications, pp. 1–36.

Grinker, R. R. and C. B. Steiner (eds.), 1997, *Perspectives on Africa: a Reader in Culture, History and Representation*, Oxford: Blackwell Publishers Ltd.

Gulliver, P. H., 1985, 'An Applied Anthropologist in East Africa during the Colonial Era', in R. Grillo and A. Rew (eds.), *Social Anthropology and Development Policy*, London: Tavistock, pp. 37–57.

Hall, M., 1998, ' "Bantu Education?" A Reply to Mahmood Mamdani', *CODESRIA Bulletin*, 3–4: 33–6.

Hamilton, A., 2003, 'Beyond Anthropology, Towards Actuality-1', *Australian Journal of Anthropology*, 14, 2: 160–70.

Hill, P., 1986, *Development Economics on Trial: The Anthropological Case for a Prosecution*, Cambridge: Cambridge University Press.

Jones, G. I., 1974, 'Social Anthropology in Nigeria during the Colonial Period', *Africa*, 44, 3: 280–9.

Kaggwa, A., 1907, *Empisa za Baganda*, Kampala: Uganda Bookshop.

Kenyatta, J., 1938, *Facing Mount Kenya*, London: Martin Secker and Warburg.

——— 1968, *Suffering Without Bitterness: the Founding of the Kenyan Nation*, Nairobi: East African Publishing House.

Kitching, G., 2000, 'Why I left African Studies', *African Studies Review and Newsletter*, 22, 1: 21–6.

Krotze, E., 1997, 'Anthropologies of the South: Their Rise, Their Silencing and Their Characteristics', *Critique of Anthropology*, 17: 237–51.

Kuper, A., 1988, 'Anthropology and Apartheid', in J. Lonsdale (ed.), *South Africa in Question*, Oxford: James Currey, pp. 32–45.

——— 1996, *Anthropology and Anthropologists: the Modern British School*, London: Routledge.

LeBeau, D. and R. Gordon, 2002, 'The Renaissance of Anthropology in Southern Africa', in D. LeBeau and R. Gordon (eds.), *Challenges for Anthropology in the African Renaissance*, Windhoek: University of Namibia Press, pp. 56–69.

Mafeje, A., 1994, 'Beyond Academic Freedom: the Struggle for Authenticity in African Social Science Discourse', in M. Diouf and M. Mamdani (eds.), *Academic Freedom in Africa*, Dakar: Council for the Development of Social

Science Research in Africa (CODESRIA), pp. 17–28.

—— 1996, 'A Commentary on Anthropology and Africa', CODESRIA Bulletin, 2: 12–34.

—— 1997, 'Who Are the Makers and Objects of Anthropology? A Critical Comment on Sally Falk Moore's Anthropology and Africa', African Sociological Review, 1, 1: 1–15.

—— 1998, 'Anthropology and Independent Africans: Suicide or End of an Era?' African Sociological Review, 2, 1: 1–43.

—— 2000, 'Africanity: a Combative Ontology', CODESRIA Bulletin, 1: 66–71.

Magubane, B., 1971, 'A Critical look at Indices Used in the Study of Social Change in Colonial Africa', Current Anthropology, 12, 4–5: 419–45.

—— 1973, 'The Xhosa in Town, Revised Urban Social Anthropology: a Failure of Method', American Anthropologist, 75, 5: 1701–15.

—— 2000, African Sociology: Towards a Critical Perspective, Asmara: Africa World Press.

Mair, L., 1969, Anthropology and Social Change, London: LSE Monographs on Social Anthropology 38, Anthrolone Press.

Malinowski, B., 1938, 'Introduction', in J. Kenyatta, Facing Mount Kenya, London: Martin Secker and Warburg.

—— 1962, The Dynamics of Culture Change: an Inquiry in Race Relations in Africa, New Haven: Yale University Press.

Mamdani, M., 1993, 'University Crisis and Reform: a Reflection on the African Experience', ROAPE, 58: 7–19.

—— 1998, 'Is African Studies to Be Turned into a New Home for Bantu Education at UCT?', CODESRIA Bulletin, 2: 12–25.

—— 1999, 'No African Renaissance without an Africa-Focused Intelligentsia', in M. Makgoba (ed.), African Renaissance: the New Struggle, Cape Town: Mafube Publishing, pp. 34–49.

Marcus, G. and M. Fischer, 1986, Anthropology as Cultural Critique: an Experimental Moment in the Human Sciences, Chicago: University of Chicago Press.

Martin, W. and M. West, 1999, Out of One, Many Africas: Reconstructing the Study and Meaning of Africa, Urbana, Chicago: University of Illinois Press.

Mazrui, A., 1978, Political Values and the Educated Class in Africa, London: Heinemann.

Mkandawire, T., 1997, 'The Social Sciences in Africa: Breaking Local Barriers and Negotiating International Presence', African Studies Review, 40, 2: 15–36.

Mudimbe, V. Y. (ed.), 1991, The Surreptitious Speech: Presence Africaine and the Politics of Otherness 1947–1987, Chicago: University of Chicago Press.

Murray-Brown, J., 1972, Kenyatta, London: Allen and Unwin.

Nkrumah, K., 1962, Towards Colonial Freedom: Africa in the Struggle against Imperialism, London: Heinemann.

Nkwi, P., 1998a, 'An African Anthropology? Historical Landmarks and Trends', African Anthropology, 5, 2: 192–216.

—— 1998b, The Pan African Anthropological Association: Striving for Excellence, Yaoundé:

ICCASRT.

—— (ed.), 2000, The Anthropology of Africa: Challenges for the Twenty-First Century: Proceedings of the Ninth Annual Conference of the PAAA, Yaoundé: Pan African Anthropological Association.

Nsugbe, P. O., 1977, 'Brief but Black Authority 1968–1970', African Social Research, 24: 335–40.

Nzimiro, I., 1979, 'Anthropologists and Their Terminologies: a Critical Review', in H. Gerrit and B. Mannheim (eds.), The Politics of Anthropology: from Colonialism and Sexism toward a View from Below, The Hague: Mouton Publishers, pp. 67–83.

Ogot, B. E., 1999, Building on the Indigenous: Selected Essays 1981–1998, Kisumu: Anyange Press.

Onoge, O., 1977, 'Revolutionary Imperatives in African Sociology', in P. Gutkind and P. Waterman (eds.), African Social Studies: a Radical Reader, New York: Monthly Press, pp. 34–40.

—— 1979, 'The Counterrevolutionary Tradition in African Studies: the Case of Applied Anthropology,' in H. Gerrit and B. Mannheim (eds.), The Politics of Anthropology: from Colonialism and Sexism toward a View from Below, The Hague: Mouton Publishers, pp. 45–66.

Otite, O., 1972, 'An End to the Nigerian Sociology Debate', West Africa, 549.

—— 1999, 'Anthropology in Nigeria: a Bibliographic Survey', Annals of the Social Science Academy of Nigeria, 11: 105–20.

Owusu, M., 1970, Uses and Abuses of Political Power: a Case Study of Continuity and Change in the Politics of Ghana, Chicago: University of Chicago Press.

—— 1975, Colonialism and Change: Essays Presented to Lucy Mair, New York: Walter de Gruyter Publishers.

—— 1978, 'Ethnography of Africa: the Usefulness of the Useless', American Anthropologist, 80: 310–34.

—— 1979, 'Colonial and Postcolonial Anthropology in Africa: Scholarship or Sentiment?' in H. Gerrit and B. Mannheim (eds.), The Politics of Anthropology: From Colonialism and Sexism toward a View from Below, The Hague: Mouton Publishers, pp. 145–60.

—— 1986, 'An Ethnography of Ethnographers and Ethnography: Theory and Practice in Socio-cultural Anthropology, a Reconsideration', in M. D. Zamora and B. Erring (eds.), Human Intervention: Fieldwork in Cultural Anthropology, Trondheim, Norway: The Association of Third World Anthropologists and the Department of Social Anthropology, University of Trondheim, pp. 47–85.

—— 1997, 'Has African Anthropology a Future? An African View from Afar', keynote address presented at the Annual PAAA conference, University of Ghana, Legon, 8–12 September.

Paley, J., 2002, 'Toward an Anthropology of Democracy', Annual Review of Anthropology, 31: 459–96.

Pels, P. and O. Salemink, 1999, 'Introduction: Locating the Colonial Subjects of Anthropology', in P. Pels and O. Salemink (eds.), *Colonial Subjects: Essays on the Practical History of Anthropology*, Ann Arbor: University of Michigan Press, pp. 1–52.

Quinlan, T., 2000, 'Anthropologies of the South: the Practice of Anthropology', *Critique of Anthropology*, 20, 20: 125–36.

Ribeiro, L. and A. Escobar (eds.), 2005, *World Anthropologies: Disciplinary Transformations in System of Power*, Oxford: Berg Publishers.

Rigby, P., 1996, *African Images, Racism and the End of Anthropology*, Oxford: Berg Publishers.

Rodney, W., 1972, *How Europe Underdeveloped Africa*, Dar es Salaam: Tanzania Publishing House.

Roscoe, J., 1911, *The Baganda: an Account of Their Native Customs and Beliefs*, London: Macmillan.

Schapera, I., 1949, *Some Problems of Anthropological Research in Kenya Colony*, London: Oxford University Press.

Schumacker, L., 2001, *Africanising Anthropology: Fieldwork, Networks, and the Making of Cultural Knowledge in Central Africa*, Durham, NC: Duke University Press.

Selassie, S. G. and E. Kameir (eds.), 1989, *Teaching and Research in Anthropology and Sociology in Eastern African Universities*, New Delhi: Organisation of Social Science Research in Eastern Africa.

Shivji, I., 1976, *Class Struggles in Tanzania*, London: Heinemann.

Sichone, O., 2001, 'Pure Anthropology in a Highly Indebted Poor Country', *Journal of Southern African Studies*, 27, 2: 34–50.

—— 2002, 'The Social Sciences and Africa', in T. Porter and D. Ross (eds.), *The Cambridge History of Science Volume 7: Modern Social and Behavioural Sciences*, Cambridge: Cambridge University Press.

Southall, A., 1983, 'The Contribution of Anthropology to African Studies', *African Studies Review*, 26, 3–4: 63–76.

Stewart, P. and A. Strathern (eds.), 2005, *Anthropology and Consultancy: Issues and Debates*, New York: Berghahn Books.

Stocking, G., 1995, *After Tylor: British Social Anthropology, 1888–1951*, Madison: University of Wisconsin Press.

Strathern, M. (ed.), 2000, *Audit Cultures: Anthropological Studies in Accountability, Ethics and the Academy*, London: Routledge.

Tadesse, Z., 1999, 'African Academic Institutions', in W. G. Martin and M. O. West (eds.), *Out of One, Many Africas: Reconstructing the Study and Meaning of Africa*, Urbana: University of Illinois Press, pp. 145–54.

Thomas, N., 1999, 'Anthropological Epistemologies', *International Social Science Journal*, 153: 333–56.

Vansina, J., 1986, 'Knowledge and Perceptions of the African Past', in B. Jewsiewicki and D. Newbury (eds.), *African Historiographies: What History for Which Africa?*, Beverly Hills Sage.

Wallerstein, I., 1983, 'The Evolving Role of the African Scholar in African Studies', *African Studies Review*, 26, 3–4: 155–61.

Wilk, R., 2002, 'Why Haven't They Ever Heard of Economic Anthropology?' *Society of Economic Anthropology Newsletter*, Winter 2002.

Wolfe, P., 1999, *Settler Colonialism and the Transformation of Anthropology: the Politics and Poetics of an Ethnographic Event*, London: Cassell.

Young, R., 2002, *Postcolonialism: an Historical Introduction*, Oxford: Blackwell.

Zeleza, T., 1997, *Manufacturing African Studies and Crises*, Dakar: Council for the Development of Social Science Research in Africa (CODESRIA).

PART I

Regional Histories
of Anthropological Practice

2

Research and Teaching in Ethiopian Anthropology
An Overview of Traditions, Trends and Recent Developments

Alula Pankhurst

Ethiopia is unique in Africa in having largely escaped the effects of colonisation. But has this had an impact on the intellectual field of Ethiopian studies and on research training within Ethiopia? In this contribution[1] I provide a political sociology of Ethiopian studies, relating international research and teaching traditions to their historical and geopolitical contexts, as well as to the influence of leading scholars. I outline previous dominant scholarly images of Ethiopia, and propose three new images, those relating to the socialist experiment, the image of disasters, and ethnic federalism.

I consider the contributions of Ethiopian students and scholars in shaping the views of foreign scholars about Ethiopian societies and cultures. In so doing, I argue that student bulletins and theses in socio-logy and anthropology have been neglected as a scholarly resource. I go on to analyse trends in the training of Ethiopian anthropologists abroad, and assess their contributions to the *Journal of Ethiopian Studies* and to the series of international conferences of Ethiopian studies.

In the last part I describe changing trends in anthropology, sociology and social work training within Ethiopia over the last half-century, comparing the late imperial, revolutionary and recent periods, and assess the future prospects for anthropological teaching and research in the country.

Paucity, poverty and politics of social and cultural research traditions

Anthropology has long been seen as having aided and abetted the colonisation of Africa (Asad 1973; de Jongh 1997). Ethiopia, as an exception that largely escaped the effects of colonisation, offers an important case to explore the hypothesis that anthropology benefited from colonial rule. Indeed, a number of scholars have suggested that the dearth and poverty of research and teaching traditions in anthropology and sociology in Ethiopia can be attributed to the lack of a colonial tradition.

Shack (1984) suggested that due to the lack of a colonial context Ethiopian institutions did not consider social science research as an important adjunct to teaching, and argued that no dominant figures in the West directed or coordinated research carried out by younger scholars in Ethiopia. James (1990) contrasted ethnography in Sudan and Ethiopia, characterising the former tradition as 'investigative', grounded in field observation, promoted by the 'colonial encounter' and resulting in an 'engaged' and ultimately more acceptable style. In contrast, she labels the Ethiopian tradition as 'representative', based on Orientalist and fictional images deriving from a 'culture-history' school of German ethnology and a 'folkloristic' Italian school. Abbink (1992) contrasts the situation in Ethiopia and Eritrea, where the Italian colonial administration stimulated considerable research. He also notes the domination of an 'imperial tradition' in Ethiopia with attention to highland culture, which he attributes partly to visitors being confined to the central domains of the state. He also points out that Ethiopia avoided the impact of a Western style of colonial administration, a 'hegemonic' written discourse on its native peoples and the creation of 'tribes' as occurred in neighbouring Sudan and Kenya.

These three scholars stress *external* factors. They take a comparative African perspective, focus on the contribution of the colonial legacy, and characterise Ethiopia in negative terms, and in respect of the lack of a scholarly tradition. In contrast, Ethiopian scholars have focused on *internal* factors. In an analysis of the situation at the end of the 1980s, Seyoum and Admassie (1989) described the constraints faced by staff at Addis Ababa University, notably shortage of time since faculty are overloaded with teaching and committee work, limited resources, especially books and reference materials, few publishing opportunities, and the need for staff to engage in consultancy work, seldom leading to publications. Looking further back, Fecadu (1991) discussed the delay in institutionalising teaching and the carrying out of anthropological research within the Ethiopian state, which he attributes to several factors. These include a Semitic bias and consequent focus on history and language; a self-image of Ethiopia as a nation-state undergoing a process in which 'non-integrated groups' were becoming 'assimilated'; a 'civilisation syndrome', which under-valued indigenous cultures; a 'transformational model', which posited change as desirable and inevitable; and the inevitable stereotype of anthropology as concerned with 'primitive cultures'.

The argument that the lack of a colonial context hindered the development of research and teaching traditions has validity. It is noteworthy that Italian scholars contributed significantly to the existing scholarship.[2] However, the lack of colonial domination by one power probably also stimulated German and French anthro-pologists to take an early interest in Ethiopia.[3] Moreover, missionaries and travellers produced a large body of writings on Ethiopia, which, biased as they may be, provide important records for reconstructing ethno-histories, understanding cultural values and interpreting social change. Although it was easier for travellers to move within the central areas, already in the nineteenth century explorers were attracted to some of the less-known areas. The view that there was a Semitic bias is accurate in terms of the work of linguists and early anthropologists, though students and scholars during the twentieth century increasingly took an interest in non-Semitic cultures.[4] A southern perspective soon became dominant when field-based anthropologists began to come to Ethiopia in the 1960s. The lack of research institutions and journals also began to be rectified after 1950.[5] The points raised by Fecadu about the damaging effects of state bias, development ideologies and anthropology's own political image, however, were real and lasting constraints on the development of Ethiopian studies.[6]

The Ethiopian case suggests that the lack of a colonial heritage hampered the development of a research tradition. Yet the consensual wisdom that Ethiopian anthropology is comparatively weak, under-developed and dominated by linguistic and historical biases stereo-types early work and neglects contributions within the context of Italian colonialism and in spite of it. Moreover, anthropology has become increasingly important in Ethiopian studies in recent decades and Ethiopian student writings have made a significant contribution over the past fifty years, which has remained largely unknown abroad. Whereas colonial research traditions led to the international-isation of local knowledge outwards from the colonies, the lack of this heritage in Ethiopia has meant that local traditions have tended to be cut off from international exposure. This in turn suggests that there is a need for research and writing to relate international and local research cultures and traditions in a more systematic manner, with a view to producing global as well as local knowledge.

Political sociology of research traditions: characteristics, comparisons and contrasts

Research traditions and intellectual schools do not emerge in a vacuum, and the various national schools of Ethiopian studies that have emerged need to be situated in their international political and economic contexts. To take some early examples, sixteenth-century relations with Portugal, the Napier expedition in the nineteenth century, or the development of the Ethio-Djibouti Railway led first Portuguese, then British and French scholars to carry out research on Ethiopia. More recently, the Italian colonial interests in the late nineteenth century and then in the 1930s, and the changing post-Second World War alliances of Ethiopia with the US and then the USSR led scholars from Italy, the US and USSR respectively to take an interest in Ethiopian cultures and societies.

Religious influences also played a role. Links between the Ethiopian Orthodox Church and the Coptic Church in Egypt, as well as with Greek, Armenian and Russian Orthodox traditions, on the one hand, and on the other the expansion of Islam, notably with Ahmed Ibn Ibrahim's invasion of the highlands, became areas of historical interest in culture. The influence of Catholicism in the sixteenth century and later from the nineteenth century, and of Protestantism from the late nineteenth century and especially from the mid-twentieth century stimulated research, the latter associated particularly with a Scandinavian tradition (Arén 1978). The Bétä Esra'él (or Falasha), particularly with their organised exodus, and recently the Rastafarian immigrants have also attracted attention from scholars.

In what follows I outline, compare and contrast six major foreign research traditions – Italian, German, French, British, American and Japanese – in terms of their history and politics; their geographical and disciplinary interests; their period of involvement; and the group expeditions, institutional centres and influential scholars associated with the research traditions and current status of each country's interest in Ethiopia.[7]

In terms of historical interest and echoes from the past the early Italian and German traditions were initially influenced by Ethiopian monks in Europe. Later missionaries and explorers became important influences on these traditions, as well as on the French and British ones. Italian research was stimulated by that country's political interests in Eritrea and Somalia, the conflict with Emperor Menelik at the end of the nineteenth century, the Italian occupation in the 1930s, and the consequent requirements of administration. The German tradition can be related to the First World War and the backing of Lij Iyasu, rising German nationalism, the presence in Ethiopia of several scholars serving as officers, and initial support for Haile Selassie. The French tradition can be associated with the Djibouti connection, and the wish to forge links between their colonial interests in East and West Africa. British interests related to their colonial presence in neighbouring Sudan, Somalia and Kenya, Haile Selassie's period of exile in Britain and British involvement in his return, and continued post-war involvement in Eritrea and Somalia. American interests can be related to superpower rivalry in the Horn, their military mission, the role of the Peace Corps and the rise of black and ethnic consciousness. Finally, Japanese interests can be related to comparisons with Ethiopia in resisting colonisation led by an Emperor, the rising economic preponderance of Japan and a growing interest in North-East Africa. In terms of economic interests the Italians were concerned not to miss out in the colonial race and to find 'a place in the sun' for potential settlement, Germany was interested in trading with a non-colonised country, France had invested in the railway and traded in arms, Britain was concerned with the Nile valley, the US with trade links, notably in cotton, and Japan with trade and development.

In considering the anthropological research interests of these six traditions regarding time, space and ethnicity, some geographical expeditions took place in the late nineteenth century, but more detailed investigations were initiated prior to the Second World War from the 1920s by Italian anthropologists, and in the 1930s, by German and French anthropologists. It was only from the late 1950s, however, that more specifically and exclusively anthropological expeditions were carried out, notably by the Frobenius Institute. Longer individual field-based studies began in the late 1950s and became more common in the 1960s. These were carried out largely by American, British, French and German social anthropologists. Group expeditions became less common, except in the Japanese and American traditions.[8]

In terms of geographical area the Italians and Germans focused on the south and west, whereas the French were interested in the east and in the south-west. British anthropologists studied mainly the south and western borderlands, whereas American anthropologists concentrated on northern groups, with a particular American Jewish interest in the Bétä Esra'él, although there were also a number of Americans who studied southern peoples.[9] In terms of ethno-linguistic groups, the Italian, German and French scholars moved from an interest in Semitic studies to studying Cushitic and also Omotic groups. British scholars were concerned largely with Cushitic, Omotic and Nilotic groups, whereas American scholars focused largely on Semitic groups, although some studied Cushitic and Omotic groups. The Japanese tradition was distinctive in its focus on Nilotic and Omotic groups.

As for leading scholars, despite Shack's suggestion that European or American anthropologists interested in Ethiopia did not have a following, in the earlier period one can note the influence of Eike Haberland in Germany, Marcel Cohen in France, Enrico Cerulli in Italy, Edward Evans-Pritchard in Britain,[10] Donald Levine in the United States and Katsiyoshi Fukui in Japan. In the former two cases they organised expeditions involving colleagues, and in the case of the latter two they influenced other colleagues and students to continue with Ethiopian studies.

A crude characterisation of the past decade would be that Italian and British scholarship in Ethiopian anthropology is in relative decline;[11] American scholarship has been dominant numerically with a multitude of centres and scholars, a revival in the post-Derg period, and group research on specific issues. French, Japanese and especially German scholarship has been in the ascendancy. The French interest has been stimulated by the setting up of the Maison and later Centre Française des Études Éthiopiennes in Addis Ababa and the relaunching of the journal Annales d'Ethiopie. Japanese interest was stimulated by group research based on comparative studies of agro-pastoral societies, subsistence economy, ethnic conflict, and indigenous knowledge systems involving sixteen researchers (Fukui 1997). It was also given a boost by the creation of a newsletter Nilo Ethiopian Studies Newsletter and the journal Nilo Ethiopian Studies in 1993 and the holding of the Thirteenth International Conference of Ethiopian Studies in Kyoto in 1997. German interest has been stimulated by the fact that there are numerous centres where Ethiopian studies are taught, and leading scholars have influenced junior researchers.[12] The launching of the journal *Aethiopica* and the *Encyclopaedia Aethiopica*, and the holding of the International Conference of Ethiopian Studies in Hamburg in mid-2003 have had a significant effect in consolidating a German 'ascendancy' in Ethiopian studies.

In conclusion, comparing the six traditions one can notice similarities between the Italian and German traditions in terms of an early involvement, a move from linguistic to anthropological concerns, from north to south, and from Semitic to Cushitic and Omotic groups. The German tradition involved and continues to involve group research, and is the most vigorous tradition, whereas the Italian tradition is in greatest decline. The French tradition shares some similarities with the Italian and German ones in terms of an early interest, and changes in geographical and ethnic focus. However, despite a shift to the south (especially in the Gamo area), an interest in northern Ethiopia has continued, notably in terms of religion, and in eastern Ethiopia, notably in Afar studies, owing to the Djibouti connection. The most distinctive aspect of the French tradition, however, is its strong institutional interest within Ethiopia, its close cooperation with the Ministry of Culture and the setting up of the Centre des Études Éthiopiennes. There are also parallels and contrasts to be drawn between the British and American traditions. Levine (1974) treated them more or less as one, as sharing a concern with empirical field-based research. Here, however, we may suggest a dichotomy: whereas the British tradition was concerned mainly with 'primitive' simple societies – often attributed to the colonial 'civilising mission' and resulting in a focus on southern Ethiopia – American anthropology was more interested in complex societies and in the integration of different groups – reflecting the US role as a superpower in the post-war period and Ethiopia's strategic geopolitical position, and having the result that most American anthropologists focused on northern Ethiopia.[13] The Japanese tradition is undoubtedly the most distinctive. Not only is it the only Asian tradition and the most recent, but it has had a clear geographical focus on the south-west, strong linkages between researchers, and comparative group projects on specific issues relating notably to the environment and indigenous knowledge. This article has limited itself to outlining six dominant international traditions of Ethiopian studies. However, a similar analysis could be made of several other traditions, notably the Russian, Israeli, Scandinavian and Dutch traditions.[14]

Scholarly images of Ethiopia

Levine (1974) presented the following three scholarly images and their assumptions about Ethiopia: (1) an outpost of Semitic civilisation; (2) an ethnographic museum; and (3) an underdeveloped country. In geographical focus, the first was concerned with the northern Abyssinian core, the second with societies to the south, and the third with the central state and urban areas. In terms of periods, the first was dominant in the nineteenth century, the second in the mid-twentieth century, and the third in the 1960s and 1970s. Regarding subject matter, the first was concerned with written culture, the second with unique discrete cultures, and the third related Ethiopia to Western development. In terms of international research traditions, the first was dominated by German scholars, and the other two by Anglo-American traditions. The first idealised the past, the second idealised the present, and the third idealised the future.

Levine's characterisations may be considered somewhat simplistic. For instance, among anthropologists there was an early interest in the north as well as in the south,[15] and European traditions other than the German one, notably the Italian and French traditions, played an important part in the second image. However, the matrix can stimulate a consideration of what images have been prevalent during the last quarter of the twentieth century, and their characteristics in terms of disciplinary dominance, geographical focus, time period, subject interests, international research traditions and forms of idealisation.[16]

The following three images can be put forward: (1) a socialist experiment; (2) disasters (famine, war and refugees);[17] and (3) ethnic regionalism. These images were partly media-driven, and much of the literature may be considered journalistic rather than academic. In disciplinary terms, we see political science and economics becoming predominant, and increasingly sociology becoming as important as anthropology. However, there has been much disciplinary inter-penetration, some cross-fertilisation, and areas of convergence. The socialist experiment image was concerned largely with nationwide state projects – land reform, cooperatives, villagisation, resettlement – and, as such, had limited geographical focus, although there was less attention given to more remote areas, unless they became areas which the state sought to incorporate into structures of control through *encadrement* (Clapham 2002:14). As for the second image, research on famine was largely concentrated on the north, though areas of the east and south were also affected. The image of war started with a focus on the north, and most recently reverted to a concern with Eritrea, though in between, during the later Derg period, large areas of the country were affected. The image of refugees mainly focused on border areas and camps. The ethnic regionalism image concerned the process of decentralisation and the regional states. In terms of time periods, the socialist image coincides largely with the Derg period (1974–91), with some subsequent spill-over into the EPRDF period, notably regarding issues such as land redistribution. The famine image began with the media coverage of the 1973–4 famine, and resumed with the 1984–5 famine, with some subsequent concern in the 1990s.

The war and refugees image began with the war with Somalia in 1978, then focused mainly on Eritrea, and increasingly on more of the country until the defeat of the Derg, and recently was concerned with the displaced from the war with Eritrea. In terms of the main subject interests, the socialist experiment image largely related to state attempts to impose social transformation; the disasters image focused on coping strategies, entitlements, aid and dependency; and the ethnic regionalism image was concerned largely with the issues of redefining identities and relations between the federal centre and the regions, and the viability of the latter. Arguably for all three images the political element became more salient in research, and polarised and partisan views tended to become more common, sometimes hindering academic objectivity. In terms of international research traditions, the last quarter of the twentieth century witnessed a globalisation of Ethiopian studies, and, in anthropology, the emergence of a Japanese tradition. Most significantly, though, the Ethiopianisation of research on the societies and culture of Ethiopia progressed tremendously. As for forms of idealisation, the socialist experiment image tended to idealise or demonise the state, the disasters image tended to romanticise or dehumanise the victims, and the ethnic regionalism image tended to idolise or vilify ethnicity as a basis for definition of identity.

Ethiopian contributions to understanding the country's societies and cultures

The professional study of Ethiopian cultures and societies according to formal Western academic canons has been largely dominated by foreigners (A. Pankhurst 1999). Apart from three notable Ethiopian scholars, in about three decades starting from the first field-based PhD study in 1957 doctoral research was undertaken by over fifty foreign anthropologists from a variety of countries including (in alphabetical order) Britain, France, Germany, Holland, Israel, Italy, Japan, Norway, Sweden and the United States of America.[18] However, contributions of Ethiopians have not been sufficiently acknowledged in terms of (1) the influence of Ethiopians on the views of foreign scholars; (2) indigenous scholarship in the pre-war period and the contributions of Ethiopian historians; (3) studies by Ethiopian students at Addis Ababa University College and Addis Ababa University as well as abroad; and (4) the increasing role of Ethiopians at International Conferences of Ethiopian Studies and in the *Journal of Ethiopian Studies*.

The role of Ethiopian colleagues: from Gorgoryos to Aike Berinas

From the sixteenth century collaboration between Gorgoryos and Ludolf (R. Pankhurst 1969) to the late twentieth century collaboration between Aike Berinas and Strecker, the importance of Ethiopians in forming the views of their foreign partners has been considerable, although such cooperation has often been denied due recognition. Knowledge about Ethiopia was transmitted by Ethiopian monks in Rome as early as the late fifteenth century, and cases in subsequent centuries abound.[19] Anthropologists often acknowledge their main informant, friend or mentor, and may even dedicate a book to them.[20] Research colleagues may also become established anthropologists in their own right.[21] In a few cases foreign anthropologists have co-authored works with Ethiopians, notably on works relating to folklore.[22] Some anthropologists have written about collaboration with informant-friends. The most impressive example, however, is the partnership between Aike Berinas and Strecker, where an entire book (Lydall and Strecker 1979) is a verbatim account of Hamar traditions by Aike recorded and transcribed by the anthropologists, whose ongoing work consistently refers to insights derived from the former.

Ethiopians writing on society and culture: from Bahrey to Bahru

The sixteenth-century monk Bahrey provided an example of early indigenous scholarship on culture and society, a tradition that continued to some extent through the centuries in the form of royal chronicles, though these tended to treat historical and political rather then social and cultural issues.[23] The intellectual contributions of

Ethiopian scholars in the twentieth century and their views on society and culture have been studied in detail by Zewde (2002).[24]

Ethiopian historians with an anthropological interest have played an important role in the development of ethnographic knowledge (Abbink 1992: 27–8; Zewde 1991: 10), and history MA and BA theses produced at Addis Ababa University also contributed significantly (B. Shiferaw 1992). Zewde's modern history of Ethiopia (1990) takes account of social and cultural considerations.[25]

Ethiopian students' writings on anthropology and sociology
Student writings from the 1950s have remained largely ignored, perhaps because the only two student bulletins have remained relatively inaccessible, while MA theses and BA senior essays have not been published and some of the latter have not even been preserved in libraries. Moreover, the subjects covered have hitherto not been surveyed, let alone indexed. The bulletins, theses and senior essays have not only provided a starting point and basis for further research and a record of student endeavours, but have also been an important means of developing in research capacities later applied in further academic and practitioner careers.

The Ethnological Society Bulletin[26]
The Ethnological Society was founded in 1952 and produced 11 bulletins up to 1962, including over 100 articles by 55 students, who wrote on a wide range of subjects.[27] The articles contain inaccuracies, naïve statements and biases; they tend to be short and mainly descriptive rather than analytical, cultural rather than social, sometimes idealised rather than specific in time and place. They focus on a few dominant ethnic groups within the country, and sometimes use derogatory terms (A. Pankhurst 2002a). However, the nature of the *Bulletin* changed and, gradually, topics more closely related to concerns of social anthropology were addressed;[28] the articles remain of considerable interest, as a historical record and an example of student scholarship.[29] Most importantly, the society and its *Bulletin* provided a learning ground for students, some of whom went on to become prominent researchers in various fields including anthropology, sociology, history, geography, economics, language and education.[30]

BA senior essays, MA theses and the Sociology Ethnology Bulletin

More than a thousand senior essays in sociology and anthropology were produced between 1972 and 2000 by final year undergraduate students. Most of the essays were written from the 1980s onwards and numbers increased in the 1990s. Most were on urban areas and the majority of these concerned Addis Ababa, but 45 other urban areas are represented.[31] The senior essays are often based on small samples and are generally limited to a couple of weeks' research using questionnaire surveys, informant interviews or case studies. The criteria for selection of interviewees are often unclear and the attempt to draw statistical conclusions from small samples of 20 to 50 interviews is questionable. However, the senior essays provide some insights and, if catalogued and indexed, could be useful as starting points for further studies, overviews, reviews, etc. A worrying trend, as noted by Zewde (2001: 9) in the case of history, is a decline in quality over the years. With recent increases in student numbers the ability of advisers to provide meaningful advice and influence the research design and outcome is reduced and the usefulness of the senior essays, beyond providing basic training in research methods, can be questioned.

Under the MA programme in social anthropology, established in 1990, over 50 MA theses were produced by 2000. Subjects which became more popular in recent years include development, environment and social and political anthropology. More than twenty different ethnic groups were studied and a number of theses were produced on inter-ethnic relations and urban issues. There has been a move away from a more 'ethnographic' mould towards theses that address more specific issues. Recent topics include conflict resolution, agricultural extension, refugees, displacement, family planning, livelihoods, resource management and medical issues, including a couple on HIV/AIDS (A. Pankhurst and Amare 2000). The Department started a publication series and six theses have been published. They are based on up to three months' fieldwork, and tend to be largely empirical, with some attempt to relate to anthropological theory. In this respect, it can be said that Ethiopian anthropology has been moving away from the 'representative' legacy as characterised by James (1990) towards a more 'investigative' tradition.

Three issues of the *Sociology Ethnology Bulletin* were produced in the early 1990s, seeking to emulate the example of the *Ethnological Society Bulletin* of the 1950s. The articles include fieldtrip reports and thematic writings, with contributions by staff of the MA programme and visiting researchers. A departmental committee suggested upgrading the standard of the Bulletin, which spelt its demise. Student involvement in the Bulletin was also insufficient, especially compared with the Ethnological Society Bulletin.

Training of Ethiopian anthropologists abroad

Prior to the 1990s only four Ethiopian anthropologists were trained abroad, three in Britain and one in the US.[32] In contrast, during the 1990s twelve Ethiopians received PhDs: five in the US, three in the UK, two in Sweden, and one each in Canada and Germany (A. Pankhurst 2003). Five of these had conducted field studies in northern Ethiopia, and the rest in the south and east. Most of the subjects relate to development issues, notably state policies, ethnicity and identity, pastoralism, food security, and the environment.

Contributions to the Journal of Ethiopian Studies and International Conferences of Ethiopian Studies

Anthropological topics have featured in the Journal of Ethiopian Studies since its inception in 1963, representing about 10 per cent of the total over 37 years. In the pre-revolutionary period most of the anthropological papers were by Ethiopians. During the Derg period (1973–91) there was only one anthropological topic, which was by an Ethiopian historian. There was a revival of anthropology in the post-Derg period. However, although more than 70 per cent of all the papers were by Ethiopians, only two of the anthropology papers were by Ethiopians (A. Pankhurst 2003).

Anthropology's profile at the 15 International Conferences of Ethiopian Studies from 1959 to 2000 has continued to grow. The number of Ethiopian presenters increased significantly, especially at the conferences in Addis Ababa, reaching over a third at the last conference in 2000. However, despite the increase, it is clear that Ethiopian anthropology is still dominated by foreigners.

In reviewing the increasing contributions of Ethiopians to the development of the anthropology of their country, one notes the paradox that the most appropriate ways of measuring this growth seem to be in the increase in PhDs trained abroad and the number of Ethiopian participants in internationally recognised fora. This further suggests that the significance of Ethiopian anthropology can only be fully understood and evaluated in an international context, and that research traditions and cultures become more meaningful within a global context.

The teaching of anthropology, sociology and social work

The trends in teaching anthropology, sociology and social work can be reviewed by period, starting from the 1950s when formal teaching was limited, through the 1960s with the beginning of institutionalised teaching, to the revolutionary period (1974–90) with an increase in student numbers and a focus on sociology, and lastly the 1990s when an MA programme in social anthropology was developed starting from 1991.

The 1950s and the Ethnological Society

Although the University College of Addis Ababa was founded in 1950 it was only in 1958–9 that distinctly sociological courses began to be offered. In 1959 a School of Social Work was established, offering a diploma programme. Nonetheless, this was the decade of the most prolific student writing on ethnographic issues, published in the *Ethnological Society Bulletin* from 1953 to 1961. With the élitist education of the time, the students of the University College already had a high standard of English and showed a great interest in and motivation for research and writing, as reflected in the *Bulletins*. In addition to the Society's research trips and the presentation of its findings at meetings, lectures by visiting researchers must have been a major stimulus and learning ground.

The 1960s and the institutionalisation of training

In contrast to the rich output of the 1950s, student research in the 1960s seems to have been largely non-existent after the last bulletin of the Ethnological Society was produced in 1961. When Haile Selassie I University (HSIU) was formed in 1961, a sociology section, which included anthropology, was established within the Department of Social and Political Science, and in 1962–3 a separate Department of Sociology was created. In 1966 the School of Social Work began to offer a BA degree. In 1967 the Department of Sociology was renamed the Department of Anthropology and Sociology. The teachers were generally expatriate, short-term, and sometimes without formal training in the subjects taught. Although a major was apparently instituted in the following year, no student senior essays were produced or preserved until 1972. The 1960s were instead marked by student activism (Balsvik 1985).

The revolutionary period 1974–90

The 1970s were characterised by considerable instability in the university, reflecting the revolutionary conditions nationwide. Most of the expatriate staff left with the revolution and teaching was interrupted in 1974–5 as well as in 1975–6, since students were sent to the countryside to teach revolutionary doctrine in the Development through Cooperation Campaign. Teaching was resumed in 1976–7, but the political situation remained unstable. In 1977 the Commission for Higher Education was established and the University was reorganised the following year. The Department of Applied Sociology was established in 1978 under the newly formed College of Social Sciences, through the merger of the former Department of Sociology and Anthropology and the School of Social Work. The name was selected to reflect the inclusion of social work as a practical discipline. The 1970s, like the 1960s, saw limited student research on sociological issues.

The 1980s were more fertile. Undergraduate students in sociology, social work and anthropology completed around 400 field-based senior essays. The Department's name was changed in 1984 to the Department of Sociology and Social Administration, reflecting the principle of combining theoretical and applied training (Seyoum and Admassie 1989: 46; Helland 1993: 5).

The 1990s and the development of an anthropology MA programme

The 1990s witnessed the introduction of the MA programme in social anthropology within the Department of Sociology (Fecadu 1991: 22–6; A. Pankhurst 1999a: 30). This was made possible largely through the support of the Christian Michelsen Institute of Norway, which enabled the department to purchase books, journals, field vehicles and equipment, and to provide teaching support from Norway and later from Sudan. It also enabled the department to send several staff members for PhD training abroad, and to publish MA theses, bulletins, conference proceedings and staff monographs.

In the early 1990s the staff profile of the department was largely dependent on expatriate staff, and there was considerable turnover.

Only the present writer was teaching throughout the decade. Several Italian anthropologists came consecutively on the basis of a co-operative agreement; one French anthropologist was seconded to the department; and an American anthropologist came as a Fulbright fellow. Although this teaching support was important at the time, other expatriate staff came for short periods of a semester or two, and the department had limited influence in selecting seconded staff. The most sustained teaching support was by several Sudanese anthropologists sponsored by Norway and managed by the Organisation for Social Science Research in Eastern Africa (OSSREA).

The two Ethiopian anthropologists who taught in the early 1990s were among those staff members dismissed for alleged political involvement in 1993. However, a couple of Ethiopian anthropologists who had completed studies abroad joined in the mid-1990s and several who had completed MAs in the programme went for PhD training in the US, UK and Holland. Most of these returned to teach in the Department after 2000.

In 1996 the Ethiopian Society of Sociologists, Social Workers and Anthropologists held its founding conference and the society subsequently held a number of workshops on issues such as local institutions, globalisation, urban poverty and resettlement. During the early 1990s the graduate programme produced three issues of the *Sociology Ethnology Bulletin* and 54 MA theses, five of which have been published. In addition, BA students produced over 600 senior essays, with an increasing interest in development issues, and the first in-depth ethnographic studies by Ethiopian students. The number of students increased in the mid-1990s to over 50 per year, resulting in increased advising loads, which has no doubt had some negative effects on the quality of research.

Prospects for future teaching and student research

In 2001 the Department's name was again changed to Sociology and Anthropology to reflect the growing importance of anthropology. From a department that was largely composed of sociology, with some social work, the department staff profile has come to be dominated by anthropologists. At the beginning of the twenty-first century, anthropology has secured a place within the social sciences in Addis Ababa University, taking over from sociology as the lead discipline within the Department. There are now sufficient staff trained at the PhD level abroad to ensure that the MA programme in anthropology is self-reliant and sustainable. More than a dozen graduates of the MA programme have been pursuing PhD training in Germany, Holland, Norway, the UK and US, and most of these obtained scholarships largely on the merit of their MA thesis work. Half a dozen of these graduates have already obtained PhDs, and most have returned to teach in the department.

There has been a proposal that the MA programme in anthropology at Addis Ababa University should accept students from neighbouring countries, notably Sudan, Somalia, Kenya and Uganda, and that a regional programme of cooperation should be set up (A. Pankhurst and Amare 2000). Although this proposal has received endorsement from the Organisation of Social Science Research in Eastern and Southern Africa and in principle the Addis Ababa University administration has indicated a favourable response, to date the proposal has not received funding support.

It has also been suggested that given the current level of staffing the main effort should be to promote collaborative research programmes, so that staff who have returned from PhD training abroad have opportunities to engage in research and publications rather than the tendency for them to focus on teaching and consultancy work. An initial collaborative research proposal has been accepted by NORAD.

There are currently discussions about setting up an MA programme in sociology and the University is considering the possibility of relaunching social work with American support, with a view to reviving the former School of Social Work.

However, there are worrying signs that student numbers are increasing at a faster pace than staff development, in particular since the government is committed to rapidly expanding graduate studies. The MA programme has been reduced from three to two years and the BA programme is about to be reduced from four to three. The increase in self-sponsored students at the MA level, cost-sharing proposals and the introduction of student fees are also likely to affect access to higher education unless adequate scholarship schemes and affirmative action programmes are introduced. The emphasis on increasing student numbers may be at the expense of the quality of education. Although this is in line with global trends, in effect it is already resulting in a decline in standards, since there is less selection of more promising students, class sizes have increased very dramatically, and the staff is overburdened with heavy teaching and advising loads.

In terms of staff and student research, current tendencies are further limiting options for staff research and there is a decline in the standard of student BA senior essays and MA theses. Given such trends it is likely that student writing will be reduced largely to an exercise in research training rather than contributing significantly to generating knowledge. This could be detrimental to the development of anthropological and sociological research traditions within Ethiopia unless options for further graduate studies and research within Ethiopia and abroad expand in the future. Given limited opportunities within the Ethiopian academic environment, this suggests the need for greater international cooperation and initiatives in collaborative research to build bridges between local and global research cultures.

Conclusion

I began this chapter by considering reasons for the apparent dearth of anthropological research in Ethiopia. I argued that dominant perceptions underestimate the contribution of Ethiopians in shaping both the views of foreign scholars and an indigenous research culture promoted by Ethiopian intellectuals and historians. I suggest that this culture can be traced to a tradition of student writing and research from the 1950s onwards.

In the second part of the chapter I compared six contrasting research traditions within Ethiopian studies – Italian, French, German, British, American and Japanese – in relation to their historical and political interests, as well as to their specific regional and methodological and substantive interests. I then outlined the contributions of Ethiopians in shaping the views of foreign scholars, the role of Ethiopian historians, and of students in bulletins and theses – arguing that this last has been an overlooked area of local knowledge production and training in research. Finally, I explored the past and future for training and student research in anthropology, sociology and social work within Ethiopia.

I end by reiterating that the achievements of Ethiopian anthropological research can best be measured in international terms, and that vibrant domestic research and training environments require further development of contacts and exchanges between Ethiopian and international research cultures. Such a dialogue between local and global productions of knowledge points the way forward.

Notes

1 Aspects of this chapter have been covered in more detail in papers I presented at the Fourteenth International Conference of Ethiopian Studies held in Addis Ababa in November 2000 (A. Pankhurst 2000, 2003) and at the Association of Social Anthropologists of the United Kingdom and the Commonwealth conference held in Arusha in April 2002 (A. Pankhurst 2002a). I wish to thank David Mills, Mwenda Ntarangwi and Mustafa Babiker for constructive suggestions on how to rework the papers for this book.

2 Such as Conti-Rossini, Cerulli and Grotanelli (W. Tadesse 1994).

3 Notably with the Frobenius Institute expeditions to the south and Leiris and Griaule in the French Dakar–Djibouti Expedition.

4 Articles in the *Ethnological Society Bulletin* in the early years concerned mainly Amhara, Tigray and Harari cultures; however, from the mid-1950s an increasing number of articles were about Oromo culture. Ethnohistory, notably of groups from the south, began to appear from the early 1970s in history students' senior essays (B. Shiferaw 1991), and sociology students' senior essays from the 1970s dealt with cultural and social issues among over 70 groups (A. Pankhurst 2000).

5 The University College of Addis Ababa was established in 1950 and the Ethnological Society in 1952. Haile Selassie University was founded in 1961, the Institute of Ethiopian Studies in 1963, and the *Journal of Ethiopian Studies* in 1963.

6 The view that anthropology should address pressing socio-economic problems became a concern in the Ethnological Society around 1960, when the economist Stanley argued that cultural and socio-economic issues should be combined. This motion set the Society in disarray and was eventually adopted (A. Pankhurst 2002b).

7 Owing to space constraints comparative data on research centres, conference series and journal publication have been omitted (see A. Pankhurst 2003).

8 The early work of Fukui in the 1960s led to frequent Japanese research agendas involving comparative teamwork in the late 1980s and 1990s (Fukui 1997). American team projects focused on craftwork (Silverman 1999; Brandt et al. 1997) and on *enset* (Cartledge 1995).

9 Such as Donham, Hamer, Hinnant, Lewis, Olmstead, Orent, Stauder and Torry. (For references see Abbink 1991, 1996.)

10 Although Evans-Pritchard's work was largely in Sudan, he had intentions – thwarted by the Italian occupation – of studying the Oromo; his most famous work was among the Nuer, also living in Ethiopia, and he influenced a number of anthropologists who studied at Oxford to work in Ethiopia, notably James and Baxter.

11 With the notable exception of a few senior scholars such as James,

Baxter and Turton in Britain and Triulzi in Italy, and some junior researchers such as Freeman and Watson in Britain and Bassi in Italy.

12 A number of senior scholars such as Amborn, Benzing, Braukämper, Schlee and Strecker have interested younger scholars to follow in their footsteps. Strecker, for instance, has had several disciples in Hamar studies and involved a number of researchers in the context of the South Omo Museum and Research Centre, and a project to study culture contact issues. The establishment of the Max Planck Institute for Social Anthropology, with Schlee as a Director, has also involved a number of junior scholars.

13 However, a number of American anthropologists did work in the south and the Peace Corps generated an interest in studying many localities throughout Ethiopia.

14 One would note the USSR's and Israel's strategic and ideological interests in Ethiopia, and the role of missionaries and development aid in the Scandinavian and Dutch cases. It is also significant that International Conferences on Ethiopian Studies have been held in Moscow in the USSR, in Tel Aviv in Israel (as well as conferences on Bétä Esra'él Studies in this location) and in Lund in Sweden. Moreover, a number of research projects have been sponsored by Scandinavian countries, notably Norway. One might mention the Peasant Production and Development in Ethiopia project between the Institute of Development Research and the University of Trondheim, and especially a decade of support to the sociology department's MA programme in social anthropology through the Christian Michelsen Institute in Bergen. However, there is not the space to elaborate such connections further in the context of this overview.

15 In fact the earliest studies by Messing (1957), Levine (1965) and Weissleder (1965) were of Amhara culture.

16 Levine (1992) reviewed and updated his position but did not consider further images.

17 These topics are often considered together, notably in bibliographies (see for instance Abbink 1991: 195–204, and 1996: 100–7), and famine and displacement are often interrelated. However, in some respects, as we shall see, this image could be divided into two: famine on the one hand, and war and refugees on the other. There is also some overlap between this image and the other two.

18 For reviews of contributions by national traditions see Bureau (1997) for the French, Taddesse (1994) for the Italian, Haberland (1986) for the German, and Fukui (1997) for the Japanese.

19 To mention some examples: the influence of Tomas on Potken; in the seventeenth century, that of Abba Täsfa-Siyon on Gualtieri; in the nineteenth century, that of *Däbtara* Keflä Giyorgis on Guidi; and in the twentieth century, Onesimus Nesib on Cerulli, Afäwärq Gäbrä Iyyasus

on Gallina, Täsfa Sellasé on M. de Coppet, Agañähu Engeda on Cohen and Griaule and especially Abba Jérome on several generations of French scholars (Bureau 1997: 8–10).

20 For instance, Braukämper dedicates his book on Kambata to Salomon Da'emo and Anullo Cankallo, and his book on Hadiyya history to Haile Bubbamo Arficho.

21 Most notably in the case of Gemetchu Megerssa, who worked with Lambert Bartels (1983).

22 For instance, Shack and Habte-Mariam Markos (1974), Bureau with Eshetou (1994) and Braukämper with Tilahun Mishago (1999).

23 Many Ethiopian chroniclers and other writers have remained anonymous; however, the names of some early scholars, such as Abu Rumi in the late eighteenth century and Liq Atsqu in the early nineteenth century, have been preserved (R. Pankhurst 1969).

24 Writers such as Gäbrä Heywät Baykädagn, Tamrat Ammanuél and As'mä-Giyorgis, Tayyä Gäbrä-Maryam, Heruy Wäldä-Sellasé, Täklä S'adeq Mäkurya and Mahtämä-Sellasé wrote mainly on historical subjects but provide insights on issues of social and cultural importance.

25 However, Strecker (1994) notes the limited reference to ethnicity.

26 This section draws on the paper by the author at the Fourteenth International Conference of Ethiopian Studies (A. Pankhurst 2000), an overview in the Ethnological Society Bulletin Reprint (A. Pankhurst 2002b), and a paper presented at the Association of Social Anthropologists of the UK in Arusha (A. Pankhurst 2002a).

27 Including fieldtrips, life-cycle celebration and rituals, notably customs of birth, betrothal and marriage, funerals and burials; aspects of language, including dialects, forms of greeting, omens and folktales; religious and secular associations and festivals; types of food and medicine, games, etcetera.

28 Such as descriptions of associations based on age groups, religion, mutual aid, credit and burial. A number of articles also addressed issues relating to economic organisation, such as work groups, craftwork, and cultural and social aspects of certain crops; as well as ritual and religion, notably annual ceremonies and pilgrimages, and aspects of 'traditional' religion and Orthodox Christianity.

29 A reprint of the eleven issues, with author and subject indexes, has been produced (A. Pankhurst 2002b).

30 Four of the members went on to write articles in the Journal of Ethiopian Studies in the 1960s, two of which were on ethnographic topics. The two earliest professional Ethiopian anthropologists, Asmerom Legesse and Fecadu Gedamu, who were later trained abroad, were involved, the former as the last adviser and the latter attending some of the final meetings, which attempted to revive the society.

31 The essays relate to more than thirty ethnic groups, with the Oromo

representing 43 per cent, Amhara 8 per cent, Gurage 7 per cent, Sidama 5 per cent, Tigraway 4 per cent, and Wolaita and Harari 3 per cent each.
32 The first two conducted research prior to the Revolution. Asmerom Legesse (1973) published his PhD research on the Borana Gada system. Fecadu (1972) wrote his PhD (on a Gurage road-building association) at the University of London. In the 1980s Tsehai Berhane Selassie (1980) wrote a historical and cultural study (of the political and military traditions of the Ethiopia peasantry) at Oxford University, and Mekonnen Bishaw (1988) wrote his thesis (on indigenous medicine) at the University of Southern Illinois.

References

Abbink, J., 1991, *Ethiopian Society and History: a Bibliography of Ethiopian Studies 1957–1990*, Leiden: African Studies Centre.
—— 1992, 'Anthropological and Ethno-Historical Research on South-West Ethiopia: the Need for Integrative Synthesis' *Bulletin de la Maison des Etudes Ethiopiennes*, 1: 22–44.
—— 1996, *Eritreo–Ethiopian Studies in Society and History 1960–1995: A Supplementary Bibliography*, Leiden: African Studies Centre.
Arén, G., 1978, *Evangelical Pioneers in Ethiopia: Origins of the Evangelical Church Mekene Yesus*, Stockholm: Uppsala.
Asad, T. (ed.), 1973, *Anthropology and the Colonial Encounter*, London: Ithaca Press.
Asmarom, L., 1963, 'Class Systems Based on Time', *Journal of Ethiopian Studies*, 1, 2: 1–29.
—— 1973, *Gada: Three Approaches to the Study of Ethiopian Society*, New York: Free Press.
Assefa, T., 1999, *Ethnic Integration and Conflict: the Case of Indigenous Oromo and Amhara Settlers in Aaroo Addis Alem, Kiramu Area, Northeastern Wallaga*, Social Anthropology Dissertation, Series No. 5, Department of Sociology and Social Administration, Addis Ababa University, Addis Ababa.
Balsvik, R. R., 1985, *Haile Selassie's Students: the Intellectual and Social Background to Revolution, 1952–1977*, Michigan: Michigan State University Press.
Bartels, L., 1983, *Oromo Religion: Myths and Rites of the Western Oromo of Ethiopia – an Attempt to Understand*, Berlin: Dietrich Reimer.
Brandt, S. A. et al., 1997, *The 'Tree Against Hunger': Enset-based Agricultural Systems in Ethiopia*. Washington, DC: American Association for the Advancement of Science.
Braukämper, U. and Mishago, T., 1999, *Praise and Teasing: Narrative Songs of the Hadiyya in Southern Ethiopia*. Frankfurt: Frobenius Institut.
Bureau, J. (in collaboration with Eshetou Wombera), 1994, *Le Verdict du Serpent: Mythes, Contes et Recits des Gamo d'Ethiopie*. Paris/Addis Abéba: Centre de Recherche Africain/ Maison des Études Éthiopiennes.
—— 1997, *Marcel Cohen et ses successeurs ou cent ans d'études Éthiopiennes en France.*

Addis Abéba: Maison des Études Éthiopiennes.

Cartledge, D. M. 1995. 'Taming the Mountain: Human Ecology, Indigenous Knowledge, and Sustainable Resource Management in the Doko Game Society of Ethiopia', Ann Arbor, MI: UMI PhD dissertation.

Clapham, C., 1988, 'The Modes of Production Debate in Ethiopian Agriculture', Africa, 58, 3: 364–9.

—— 2002, 'Controlling Space in Ethiopia', in W. James, D. Donham, E. Kurimoto and A. Triulzi (eds.), Remapping Ethiopia: Socialism and After, Oxford: James Currey.

de Jongh, M., 1997, 'Africa Colonises Anthropology', Current Anthropology, 38, 3: 451–3.

Fecadu, G., 1972, 'Ethnic Associations in Ethiopia and the Maintenance of Urban/Rural Relationships, with Special Reference to the Alemgana-Walamo Road Construction Association', unpublished PhD thesis, University of London.

—— 1991, 'Background to the Genesis and Current Status of the MA programme in Social Anthropology, Sociology Ethnology Bulletin, 1, 1: 22–6.

Fukui, K., 1979, 'Cattle Colour Symbolism and Intertribal Homicide Among the Bodi', Senri Ethnological Studies, 3: 147–77.

—— (ed.), 1997, Comparative Studies of Northeast African Societies: Anthropology, Linguistics and History: a Review of Japanese Research Projects 1987–1997, Kyoto: Faculty of Integrated Human Studies, Kyoto University.

Haberland, E., 1986, Three Hundred Years of Ethiopian German Academic Collaboration, Stuttgart: Steiner-Verlag-Wiesbaden-GmbH.

Helland, J., 1993, 'Inventory of Anthropological and Sociological Research and Scholarship in Ethiopia', University of Stockholm.

James, W., 1990, 'Kings, Commoners, and the Ethnographic Imagination in Sudan and Ethiopia', in R. Fardon (ed.), Localising Strategies: Regional Traditions of Ethnographic Writing, Edinburgh: Scottish Academic Press, pp. 96–136.

Levine, D., 1965, Wax and Gold: Tradition and Innovation in Ethiopian Culture, Chicago: University of Chicago Press.

—— 1974, Greater Ethiopia: the Evolution of a Multiethnic Society, Chicago: University of Chicago Press.

—— 1992, 'Greater Ethiopia Reconsidered', Ethiopian Review, 2, 8: 14–16.

Lydall, J. and I. S. Strecker, 1979, The Hamar of Southern Ethiopia: I Work Journal, II Baldambe Explains, III Conversations in Dambaiti, Hohenschäftlarn: Klaus Renner Verlag.

Mekonnen, B., 1988, 'Integrating Indigenous and Cosmopolitan Medicine in Ethiopia', unpublished PhD Dissertation, Southern Illinois University at Carbondale.

Messing, S. D., 1957, 'The highland-plateau Amhara of Ethiopia', Ann Arbor, MI: UMI PhD dissertation.

Pankhurst, A., 1999a, 'Research on the Societies and Cultures of Ethiopia' in

Proceedings of the Founding Conference of the Ethiopian Society of Sociologists, Social Workers and Anthropologists, Addis Ababa: Department of Sociology and Social Administration, pp. 25–38.

—— 1999b, '"Caste" in Africa: the Evidence from Southwestern Ethiopia Reconsidered', *Africa*, 69, 4: 485–509.

—— 2000, 'A Review of University Students' Research Writings in Anthropology, Sociology and Social Work over the Past Half Century', paper presented at the Fourteenth International Conference of Ethiopian Studies, Addis Ababa.

—— 2001,'Dimensions and Conceptions of Marginalisation', in D. Freeman and A. Pankhurst (eds.), *Living on the Edge: Marginalised Minorities of Craftworkers and Hunters in Southern Ethiopia*, Addis Ababa: Addis Ababa University, pp. 1–23.

—— 2002a, 'An Age of "Cultural Renaissance"? Reviewing the Ethnological Society Bulletin of Addis Ababa University College', paper presented to the Association of Social Anthropologists of the UK and the Commonwealth, Arusha, April.

—— 2003, 'Conflict Management over Contested Natural Resources: a Case Study of Pasture, Forest and Irrigation in South Wello, Ethiopia', in P. Castro and E. Nielsen (eds.), *Power, Participation and Protected Areas: Natural Resource Conflict Management Case Studies*, Rome: Food and Agriculture Organization, pp. 59–80.

—— (ed.), 2001, *Natural Resource Management in Ethiopia*, Addis Ababa: Forum for Social Studies, Ethiopia.

—— (ed.), 2002b, *Addis Ababa University College Ethnological Society Bulletin Reprint*, Addis Ababa: Department of Sociology and Social Administration, Addis Ababa University.

Pankhurst, A. and Y. Amare 2000, 'Towards a Regional Programme? Prefeasibility Study Regarding Conditions Relevant to Including Students from Other African Countries in the MA Programme in Social Anthropology at Addis Ababa University', report submitted to the Organisation for Social Science Research in Eastern and Southern Africa.

Pankhurst, R., 1969, 'Gregorius and Ludof', *Ethiopia Observer*, 12: 287–90.

Seyoum, G. S. and Y. Admassie, 1989, 'The Teaching of Anthropology and Sociology in Ethiopia', in G. S. Seyoum and E. W. Kameir (eds.), *Teaching and Research in Anthropology and Sociology in Eastern African Universities*, New Delhi: Organisation of Social Science Research in Eastern Africa, pp. 38–55.

Shack, W., 1984, 'Social Science Research in Ethiopia: Retrospect and Prospect', in S. Rubenson (ed.), *Proceedings of the Seventh International Conference of Ethiopian Studies*, Uppsala: Scandinavian Institute of African Studies, pp.411–17.

Shack, W. and H.-M. Marcos (eds.), 1974, *Gods and Heroes: Oral Traditions of the Gurage of Ethiopia*, Oxford: Clarendon Press.

Shiferaw, B., 1991, 'Review of J. Abbink *Ethiopian Society and Culture: A Biblio-*

graphy of Ethiopian Studies 1957–1990, Leiden, African Studies Centre, 1990', *Journal of Ethiopian Studies*, 24: 133–8.

—— 1992, 'Bibliography of Senior Essays of the Department of History, Addis Ababa University, on Ethno-Historical and Related Topics', *Sociology Ethnology Bulletin*, 1, 2: 102–10.

Shiferaw, T., 2002, 'Civil Society Organisations in Poverty Alleviation, Change and Development: the Role of *Iddirs* in Collaboration with Governmental and Non-Governmental Organisations', unpublished MA thesis, Addis Ababa University.

Silverman, R. (ed.), 1999, *Ethiopia: Traditions of Creativity*, Seattle: University of Washington Press.

Strecker, I., 1994, 'Glories and Agonies of the Ethiopian Past: Review Article of Bahru Zewde 1991: *A History of Modern Ethiopia* and Bonny Holcomb and Sisai Ibssa 1990: *The Invention of Ethiopia: the Making of a Dependent Colonial State of Northeast Africa*', *Social Anthropology*, 2, 3: 303–12.

—— 1995, 'Ethno-History and Its Relevance for Ethiopian Studies', *Journal of Ethiopian Studies*, 28, 2: 39–50.

Taddesse, B., 1995, 'Agricultural and Rural Development Policies in Ethiopia: A Case Study of Villagisation policy', unpublished PhD thesis, University of Michigan.

Tadesse, W., 1994, 'Some Gamo and Konso Public Places and Their Social and Ritual Functions', in B. Zewde et al. (eds.), *Proceedings of the Eleventh International Conference of Ethiopian Studies*, Addis Ababa: Institute of Ethiopian Studies, Addis Ababa University, 2: 12–21.

—— 1999, 'Fertility and Warfare Among the Hor (Arbore) of South-Western Ethiopia', unpublished PhD thesis, London School of Economics, University of London.

Tsehai, B.-S., 1980, 'The Political and Military Traditions of the Ethiopian Peasantry', Unpublished PhD thesis, Oxford University.

Weissleder, W., 1965, 'The Political Economy of Amhara Domination', University of Chicago, PhD dissertation.

Zewde, B., 1991, *A History of Modern Ethiopia*, Addis Ababa: Addis Ababa University Press.

—— 2001, *A History of Modern Ethiopia 1850–1991*, London: James Currey.

—— 2002, *Pioneers of Change in Ethiopia: The Reformist Intellectuals of the Early Twentieth Century*, Oxford: James Currey.

Zewde, B., B. Yimam, E. Chole and A. Pankhurst, 1994, 'From Lund to Addis Ababa: A Decade of Ethiopian Studies', *Journal of Ethiopian Studies*, 27, 1: 1–28.

3

How Not to Be a 'Government House Pet'
Audrey Richards and the East African Institute for Social Research

David Mills

The 1940s and 1950s were a formative period for the academic discipline of social anthropology in the United Kingdom, but were also a period during which the future shape of African universities and their potential role in contributing to social scientific knowledge of Africa were determined. The two phenomena were intertwined. Most British anthropologists had their eyes on a future as university-based academics, and with the exception of self-proclaimed 'do-gooders' like Audrey Richards, few trained African researchers sought to foster a social research capacity in African colonial territories. In a fledgling academic discipline, research was prioritised over training and teaching. Alongside the more usual explanation of the discipline being tainted through its association with colonial rule, I suggest that this history partly explains the limited presence of anthropology in post-colonial African universities.

It is important to challenge Africa-wide generalisations about anthropology and colonialism, and country-specific analyses offer a way of exploring colonialism's very different academic and administrative cultures. In what follows, I tell the history of a post-war initiative by British social scientists to set up regional institutes of social science for research into 'colonial problems' in Africa. The anthropologist Audrey Richards was one of the key architects of this vision, and I focus on her involvement in establishing the East African Institute of Social Research (EAISR) at Makerere during the 1940s and 1950s. With funding coming from the Colonial Office, the policy was a controversial one, both within social anthropology and beyond. I begin by describing the uneasy relationship between the anthropologists and colonial authorities involved in planning the Institute. I go on to explore Audrey Richards's relationship with the colonial administrations in Uganda and Kenya, before documenting the subsequent fortunes of the Institute in the period leading up to Ugandan independence.

'Difficult folk to deal with...'

In 1940 the British Colonial Secretary Malcolm Macdonald expressed the view that 'anthropologists as a class are difficult folk to deal with' and 'I gather that it will be rather difficult to find one who has not his own personal axe to grind'. In doing so he articulated a view widely held within the Colonial Office. This suspicion had roots in the early experience of administrations employing government anthropologists, and resonated with a larger distrust of intellectual life that was part of the civil service culture of the so-called 'practical man'. In the first decade of the twentieth century, the case of Northcote Thomas was held up within the Colonial Office as a shocking example of the risk of employing scholars to do practical work; it served as a 'cautionary tale in official circles for decades' (Kuklick 1992: 201) after his removal from service in both Nigeria and Sierra Leone. He had been appointed initially to make sense of survey data collected by political officers, but on the Colonial Office's condition that 'purely scientific research ... must not interfere with his main work' (ibid.: 199). Seen as an eccentric, on both tours he had pursued his own linguistic research, seen as both impractical and as irrelevant to the practical tasks set out in his conditions of employment.

The anthropologists of the time saw his work rather differently. At the behest of the Colonial Office, a Royal Anthropological Institute (RAI) committee – consisting of distinguished scholars like Haddon, Rivers and Marrett – was set up to examine Northcote Thomas's experimental anthropological survey of Southern Nigeria in 1910, and was unanimous in its praise of Thomas's contributions.[1] During this nascent period there was little attempt at cordoning off anthropological knowledge as that produced by professional scholars. The committee declared itself 'impressed with the thoroughness of his enquiries and with the value both for administrative and scientific objects of the materials' which he had collected. His material ranged from anthropometric surveys to sociological data; in urging its publication, they suggested it would give 'utmost service to officers serving in that part of Africa'. They also proposed that he provide a 'description of the methods of enquiry so that officers who are interested in the subject may proceed on similar lines' (ibid.). The RAI report also endorsed the Colonial Office's suggestion that instruction in anthropology be given to officers of African colonies and protectors during their periods of leave.

A similar endorsement of the importance of anthropological teaching for colonial administrators was made by Sir Richard Temple three years later. In speeches presented at the British Academy for the Advancement of Science and at Birmingham University, he called for young men to 'imbibe the anthropological habit' and acquire a 'working knowledge of the habits, customs and ideas that govern the conduct of these peoples' to assist when they were entrusted in due course with the responsibilities of 'administrative, commercial and social control' (Temple 1913). These proposals were put into practice, and courses at Oxford and Cambridge for colonial probationers continued until the 1960s (Evans-Pritchard 1959). One might argue that it was through such courses, and the introduction to anthropology they presented, that the relationship between theory and practice was mediated, making important impressions on future cohorts of colonial political officers.

The anthropological ability to promote one's own usefulness was equally visible in Bronislaw Malinowski's successful grant proposal to the Rockefeller Foundation in 1926,[2] paving the way for a huge programme of research under the aegis of the International African Institute. In it, he talks of the importance of garnering respect for the 'scorned and despised science of anthropology', and pointing to the Netherlands as 'the most successful Colonial power' (sic), notes the significance of the fact that it 'recognises, uses and supports anthropology'. But amidst the bluff and flattering rhetoric, the first section's title, 'Practical Applications of Anthropology', reveals an important change in disciplinary self-conceptualisation. Anthropology is no longer a training of which anyone can partake, but is now a science to be vindicated through practical application. Malinowski is one of the first to conceptualise 'science' and its application in this separate way, a view reiterated in a paper entitled 'Practical Anthropology' (Malinowski 1929: 22) which suggested that, without a research base, the 'practical man' often merely 'gropes in the dark'. As Pels and Salemink note, 'Malinowski's definition of the "average practical man" as someone incapable of good ethnography only became influential during the second quarter of this century' (1999: 2).

If there was ever a honeymoon relationship between anthropology and British colonial authorities, it was short-lived – lasting, perhaps, the few years after the First World War. During this period the governments of the Gold Coast and Nigeria appointed administrators like Meek, Rattray and Matthews as government anthropologists. Other governments were far less enthusiastic. Mitchell, Chief Secretary of Tanganyika Office, was a prominent critic of Malinowski, and articulated the views of many about the irrelevance of academic anthropology to administrative concerns. He was of the view that the anthropologist tended 'to look out at the busy world from his laboratory window, and when he offers help, it is in terms of laboratory methods. He must learn to come down into the street and join in the life which he desires to influence.' Mitchell went on to call for some 'general practitioners of the trade' who could apply the results of scientific investigation (Mitchell 1930: 220). True to his word, he supported Gordon Brown and Bruce Hutt's 'experiment in applied anthropology' in the Iringa province of Tanganyika. Their book *Anthropology in Action* (Brown and Hutt 1935) documented an attempt to link 'specialist research to the day-to-day business of administration' on the condition that it was for the 'administrator to ask questions, and the anthropologist to answer them' (Mitchell 1930: xvii). This circumscription of research to the immediate demands of administrative rule would seem to be the direct patron–client relationship derided by anthropology's critics. But the close collaborative relationship that anthropologist Brown and administrator Hutt document was virtually unique in the discipline, and for all the rhetoric of utility, the book itself resembles a classic ethnographic monograph in genre and structure.

Relationships between anthropologists and administrators within the colonies depended partly on the local political culture, and partly on the individual personalities involved – an example here would be the prickly relationship between Max Gluckman and the Northern Rhodesian authorities. In 1948 one Kenyan native courts officer bemoaned the 'fact which should not be disregarded, however much it may be deprecated, that the District Commissioners sometimes find the presence of European anthropologists in their districts to some degree embarrassing. Each regards himself as the authority so far as authoritative European knowledge of their African community is concerned. Each feels a deep resentment at the "pretensions" of the other. And if this happens when the anthropologist's terms of reference are almost solely academic it will happen still more frequently and strongly when the academic anthropology has been written up and the anthropologist's attention turns to the application of his science to practical affairs'. Such comments need to be read in the light of the increasingly adversarial relationship that existed between the Kenyan settler community and the colonial administration.

With this level of ambivalence and mutual suspicion within the colonial territories, how did social anthropologists convince the British Colonial Office to fund such a large programme of social research after the Second World War – the first-ever direct government funding of the social sciences? By 1952 the new Colonial Office had allocated more than £1 million (£20 million at today's prices) to social science research, half of which was for the four regional research and training institutes (three of which were in Africa). This was during a period when there were fewer than 30 full-time academic posts in the discipline of social anthropology in the UK. And to what extent did this funding bridge the perceived gap between the anthropologist and the 'practical man'? By focusing on the particular case study of the East African Institute for Social Research I explore the relationship of anthropologists to colonial administration during these last years of colonial rule.

The East African Institute and a 'developmental' empire

In 1940 the Colonial Office drew up an ambitious blueprint for a new 'developmental' empire, intended to complement plans for a British welfare state. The legislation – the Colonial Development and Welfare Act (CDAW) – envisaged a grant of £50 million over ten years. This sudden munificence can be understood in the light of Britain's wartime dependence on the support of the United States, to whom a moral justification for the colonial empire now had to be made. It was also a concession to those colonial peoples who were contributing so much to the British war effort, as well as a recognition of the need to tackle the economic deprivation and growing anti-colonial movement in the West Indies.

Whilst the welfare state is one of the most lasting legacies of British socialism, comparing it to the CDAW was disingenuous – the amount initially proposed amounted to roughly £1 per head of the total population of the colonies, though it was later doubled. George Padmore, a prominent anti-colonial critic, prepared a lengthy critique of the new policy at the request of the Fifth Pan African Congress, mocking the zeal of the post-war Labour government and its 'new economic imperialism' (Padmore 1949). He pointed to the failure to consult African populations over such projects, bemoaned how much of the money would be spent on salaries for a European administrative cadre to implement such plans, and noted that it also depended on matched funding, usually in the form of large bank loans. He was also suspicious of the way that Ernest Bevin sought in parliamentary speeches to portray the CDAW as a tool of British foreign policy, by linking the Commonwealth's productive capacities to the economic growth of Western Europe.

If the bill wasn't good for Africa, it was very good indeed for anthropology. The legislation recognised that rational development planning and spending required careful preparatory research. An amount of £500,000 annually was earmarked. Only a proportion of this went to the social sciences. This was enough to provide a major multidisciplinary research agenda, a large number of research fellowships, all crowned with four high-profile regional research institutes in Africa and the Caribbean. The selection, training, supervision and support of younger scholars at these institutes were a central concern of the proposed new social sciences research council, and a significant influence on the reproduction and growth of the respective disciplines. Audrey Richards wrote retrospectively of this project as 'an important experiment in the organisation of research, on a very large scale' (Richards 1977: 33) linked into a remarkable enthusiasm for the 'great expansion of higher education in the colonies' (ibid.: 37).

Whilst the Colonial Office saw this research as targeting 'colonial social problems', the project was led by academics such as Audrey Richards and A. M. Carr Saunders, then director of the London School of Economics (LSE), who had different priorities. They envisaged a body of scientific knowledge on 'sociological and kindred matters', being heavily influenced by Lord Hailey's insistence in his African Survey (Hailey 1945) – on which Richards had worked – upon the importance of basic research.

Richards and Carr Saunders made highly effective use of the academic autonomy granted to the new council. Their initial review foresaw 'special difficulties' in carrying out such research, because of the non-existence of departments of social studies within colonial institutes of higher education. The suggested solution was to build up an independent academic research capacity within the colonial territories. The issue of 'isolation and restricted opportunities for colonial research workers' would be 'greatly mitigated if centres of research and learning could be developed in the colonies them-selves'.[3] This would also solve problems of independence and continuity. Audrey Richards was one of the keenest exponents of this policy. Makerere was at that point a government-funded technical college, and, following the precedent of the Rhodes Livingstone Institute (RLI), was cited as a place where research facilities could be built up, to go from being a centre of 'vocational training' to being a 'real centre of learning in the Colonies'.

A 'Colonial Social Research Group', made up mostly of LSE academics, was assembled to report on extant research knowledge. Its report emphasised the inadequacies and lacunae.[4] It concluded that 'the need for social research in the colonies is evident ... very few social surveys of general standards of living have been done, and of these hardly any have been in the charge of trained investigators. In some colonies no general ethnographic surveys have been made, and there are no descriptive accounts of the chief ethnic groups.' This group of 'experts' went on to recommend the founding of a Colonial Social Science Research Council (CSSRC) to play a coordinating role in the expansion of the social sciences. The limiting factor was seen as the shortage of people with 'specialised training'. Isolation, poor conditions and short-term funding contracts were also cited as pressing problems. In particular, there were 'few anthropological field workers with the qualifications necessary to undertake the conduct of one of the large-scale ethnographic or general social and economic surveys to which we give priority value'. Establishing departments of social science in Africa was seen as an 'integral part of future programmes in social research'. The report ends unequivocally with the importance of making provision for the expansion of anthro-pology and sociology departments 'if the increased demands for training envisaged' were to be met (*ibid.*).

How was the CSSRC regarded in the colonies? In one report, Richards emphasised how administrators feared that the Council's committee would try to 'dictate research policy', or that the research planned would 'be mainly concerned with problems of academic interest and would be of little value to those working in the territories concerned'. Unlike prominent anthropologists of her generation, Richards herself was very committed to the idea of making anthropological expertise available to advise on the implementation of government policies, and this made her the ideal person to act as a go-between between the immediacies of administrative demands and the longer-term approach adopted within scholarly research.

The CSSRC wasted no time in developing its ambitions, and secretary Raymond Firth produced a discussion paper proposing that 'linguistic and socio-economic studies' should be 'major aims for systematic research in the first instance'. Firth suggested that this would provide 'basic data for colonial governments and for research in other disciplines', and also rapidly secure 'a body of personnel with some knowledge of colonial conditions and local research techniques'. Minutes of the first meeting in 1944 noted that 'the Council was of the opinion that the programme of ANTHROPOLOGICAL [sic] work was most important, as it formed a basis for so many of the other sciences with which it was necessary that it should be closely associated in fieldwork'.[5]

Yet the process of setting up regional centres for social studies was far from straightforward. To whom would they be accountable? Should they be part of the university colleges, or wholly separate? Should Colonial Development and Welfare funding go into buildings and infrastructure? Could 'high quality' staff be recruited? Would the other East African colonies financially support such an institute? Establishing an institute at Makerere College involved negotiating the political and financial obstacles that reached all the way up to regional colonial policy: this was a university college for the whole of East Africa but located in Uganda, and many Ugandans were against any attempt at creating an East African federation. Much of the anti-colonial protest in Buganda during the 1940s arose from the sense of economic discrimination felt by African cotton farmers, and talk of federation with Kenya simply inflamed these issues.

To sort out the institutional politics and finances, Audrey Richards visited Uganda in 1944 with Max Gluckman, then director of the RLI, and discussed the idea of putting in an application to the CSSRC with Makerere's principal G. M. Turner. Her terms of reference included the development of social studies at Makerere (at that point African students were being taught at the LSE), the development of Makerere as a centre for research, and the possibility of collaboration between

Makerere, the RLI and the South African universities. Her final report was sweeping in its breadth, tackling likely needs of the East African governments for research into land tenure, but also making very clear the importance of establishing an autonomous research institute at Makerere.

The following year Turner wrote in his application for funding that the Institute could be compared with 'two existing Institutes, the Rhodes-Livingstone Institute (RLI) at Livingstone and the West African Institute at Achimota', adding that 'Our proposal would resemble the former in its concentration on the sociological studies, without the latter's preoccupation with technological development and the foundation of secondary industries.' Basing his costings on those supplied by Gluckman, he also noted that 'teaching at a university level in the field of social studies will be impossible until local research can provide material for it. The normal connection, therefore, of research with teaching is not yet possible at Makerere.'[6]

As it was envisaged that the Institute would 'serve the East African governments by its collection and arrangement of knowledge in various fields, and since its programme of research must be partly governed by political needs', the revised proposal was sent to all three East African governments. Responses were less than enthusiastic. The Kenyan director of education regretted the lack of attention to the 'practical and scientific aspects of development, and my fear is that by concentrating on the sociological studies only, the usefulness of the work may be limited'. Other comments were similarly deprecatory.

> I must say I oppose the proposal to set up a small institute at Makerere to do academic research only and to divorce this from the practical everyday workings of an administrative research station seems to me to be a pity if not actually a dangerous situation. It is dangerous in that it does not balance the theorist with the field worker.

A later comment confirms the distrust felt towards scholarship, noting that the 'days of the usefulness of academic anthropological study from the point of view of practical administration are past, and that the opportunity was missed about thirty years ago'. Another adds the opinion that 'we have received nothing of value from the anthropologists posted to Kenya during the last five years'.[7]

There were also tricky questions of university and regional politics to negotiate. The 1944 Asquith Commission on Higher Education had unequivocally recommended the development of such institutes, but had strongly advised against the creation of a 'semi-independent' social science unit at Makerere, which might diminish 'the authority and prestige of the university'.[8] The CSSRC, on the contrary, was of the view that developing a research agenda should be the Council's first priority. Citing the lack of literature appropriate for teaching, everyone agreed with Richards that 'emphasis should rest on research *ab initio*, as this would form the basis of the teaching of social subjects later'. After her visit to Uganda, she thus made a strong case for 'a separate institute, that the staff should be free from routine teaching duties, and that the Director should have power to frame research programmes'. Such dissension from official government policy had to be justified, and the Council developed the case that the effective teaching of social studies depended first on the accumulation of 'a body of knowledge on sociological and kindred matters in East Africa',[9] a tendentious presumption. Prioritising research was a way to avoid the danger that staff would have to 'devote an undue proportion of their time to routine teaching duties', whilst still allowing the eventual aim of merging the institute into the university.

A well-resourced research institute was envisaged, equipped with staff, dwellings and offices. After extensive consultations, William Stanner, an Australian anthropologist, was appointed as first director. On visiting Makerere in 1948, his report questioned the wisdom of establishing an institute, and made much of the financial, logistical and political complexities. He cited the capital costs of erecting permanent buildings, the looming issue of Makerere's promotion to university status, the politics of regional governance within East Africa and even the deterrent of a humid climate. In all, he felt, it would 'be a matter of years before either the Institute or Makerere could confer noticeable benefits upon one another'. More damning still, Stanner acknowledged that even he, from an administrative viewpoint, could not see the value of much anthropological material, and pointed out the error of supposing that 'the yearning for anthropological services in East Africa is as great as the desire in England to send them'.[10] This was not what the Council's committee wanted to hear. One reviewer noted 'that a man [sic] with enthusiasm for the general idea would surmount the difficulties which Dr Stanner mentions' (*ibid.*). However Max Gluckman, director of the RLI, was secretly pleased at the problems faced at Makerere, and wrote in 1948 from Oxford in 'semi-confidence' to Clyde Mitchell to say that 'Stanner has recommended, we hear, that the Makerere Institute be dropped which leaves us unique'.[11] But Audrey Richards was made of sterner stuff. In the face of her influence and a determination of Council to implement the regional centres policy, Stanner resigned in 1949.

On not being a Government house pet

Audrey Richards's appointment as director was a sensitive issue, even though she had been the original architect of the Institute. The support of the Kenyan administration was vital for the centre's regional remit, but many senior figures within the authority were disparaging, not to mention sexist, in their references about her. One talked of the 'monstrous regiment of women' who were now the experts on colonial administration (a reference also to Lucy Mair and Margery Perham), whilst another was not happy that her approach to the issues would be 'completely objective and without bias, either political or sentimental'.[12] However, Richards had influential supporters, including de Bunsen, deputy principal of Makerere, and Andrew Cohen, Governor of Uganda.

Appointed in 1949, she wasted no time in wooing the colonial administrators on whom the Institute's future and the whole policy of regional institutes depended. In one personal letter she confides that the Governor is coming to dinner: 'I have to do my best not to be a Government house pet, but of course it helps with the work.'[13] Her social confidence and sense of humour served her well in mollifying sceptics and gaining the support of the three East African administrations. En route to Kenya to take up the directorship, she wrote to the Kenyan Native Courts Officer to ask for help in what looked likely to be a 'difficult enterprise to start' and to talk about the 'way in which the work of the Institute could be planned to be of most use to you', such that it would 'enable us also to choose areas and topics of research which would be most likely to have practical value'. On arrival for her first meeting in Nairobi, she heard of the negative attitudes of the Kenyan government to anthropological investigations 'in the light of our past experiences'. With the 'present financial difficulties', the Kenyan administration had 'grave doubts of the practical usefulness of spending money unless it be for the investigation of a specific subject, such as Native customary law'. Richards replied with a note that she 'blushed to think of the crimes of my fellow tribesmen but hope we shall finally live down these and that you will soon be converted by the race of simple, hardy research workers we hope to let loose on you'.[14]

Unbowed, Richards continued her charm campaign. A separate letter sent on her arrival at Makerere promised to 'do our best to be helpful but please don't expect too much of us at first'. She went on to paint a vivid word-picture of the 'Institute' consisting 'of one house, one typewriter and one rather battered truck that has driven Stanner around East Africa for many miles. The standard of living in East Africa is so much higher than it was when I was here fifteen years ago that it seems to take much longer to live than when one sat down on packing cases in a wattle and daub hut.' Her letters to friends and colleagues alike are full of such revealing intimacies, and a testament to her own keen sense of amusement at the incongruousness of academic life.[15]

She followed up her meetings with a more formal 'scheme of cooperation' over 'actual research projects that might provide valuable information for the East African governments'. She had several ideas. One suggestion was that local commissioners could write to the Institute if they 'wanted a short paper specially prepared on some particular topic e.g. on local bride wealth'. Another was for governments to propose 'a very detailed study of some particular problem that was of purely local interest'. Richards also prepared a flyer to be circulated to all administrative officers in the three regions about the Institute, listing amongst its aims the organisation of 'studies of administrative importance' and also the 'training of African investigators and research assistants'. This was accompanied by a letter noting that 'Dr Richards is most anxious to receive any information on anthropological and sociological matters which may have been obtained by members of your staff in the course of their ordinary duties.'[16]

The first three years were characterised by a welter of activity. As well as completing the offices, library, conference facility and ten residential flats built to 'austerity standard', the Institute recruited 17 research staff. Audrey Richards participated extensively in a wide variety of research programmes, choosing research sites and training young researchers 'on the job'. The Institute held a number of conferences, including several jointly with the French Institut de Recherche Scientifique en Afrique Centrale (IRSAC) in both Astrida (Rwanda) and Makerere. At one of these Governor Cohen spoke, voicing his 'absolute opposition' to research carried out in 'academic isolation', and praising the 200 pieces of social research in progress across British Africa, including 30 being carried out by American students.

Amongst the 11 anthropologists and sociologists appointed in this early period, there were two Ugandans, Augustine Mukwaya and W. P. Tamukedde. Both were recruited as research officers to carry out surveys of immigrant labour and land tenure issues in Buganda. Out of this work, Mukwaya published a monograph on land tenure (Mukwaya 1953). He later went to do a diploma in Anthropology at the LSE, before carrying out research into the rise of African-owned businesses. He was employed by the Institute until 1958, giving a paper at its annual conference in 1957 on the rise of the Ugandan African Farmers' Union. Eridadi Mulira, whose brother Enoch was also a teacher and journalist, was also appointed in 1950, and later published a Luganda grammar and dictionary (Mulira 1952). Despite the Institute's oft-repeated aim of training African social scientists, no further African social scientists were recruited during the 1950s. Africanisation was more contested, and occurred more slowly still, in the rest of Makerere. Given the manifold political, journalistic and religious interests of scholars such as Mulira and Tamukedde it is perhaps not surprising that they did not develop university careers. Instead the Institute relied on a steady stream of young British anthropologists coming to do fieldwork en route to promising careers in UK universities.

If African research trainees were scarce in Makerere, the growing influx of American students brought a different problem. As well as regular visitors, there were an 'enormous' number of American scholars 'who come out untrained and naïve and in need of direction'. The Governor shared Richards's concerns and her dislike of the inevitably growing influence of American finance and scholarship in Africa, once announcing 'Keep the Fulbrights out of the elephant grass! That ought to be our motto.' Richards's instinctive anti-Americanism was balanced, however, by her sense of the 'academic Puritanism and lack of innovation of anthropologists' in the UK.[17]

If the aim of building local research capacity was unfulfilled, so too was Richards's desire to win over the three regional colonial authorities. When a financial crisis faced the Institute in 1952, the Kenyan treasury agreed only reluctantly to cover a third of the increased cost-of-living allowance, whilst the Tanzanian government declined to make any contribution. The Acting Secretary for Education in Kenya opposed any contribution on the grounds that the 'Institute performs a function which is of doubtful value to the three territories and should not be allowed to expand unreasonably'. For him the 'establishment of schools of Anthropology and Sociology at Universities in the UK and the USA has created a demand for jobs in this sphere which is in excess of the real need for such workers', and the expansion was the result of 'pressure from job-seekers' rather than 'the value of its services'. The Kenyan treasury continued to bemoan even its small annual contribution of £1000, and one memo noted that rather than support 'erudite papers on subjects such as the 'native authority system in Bhiaramulo' the money would be better spent on additional District Officers. The Ugandan government however was more receptive to Richards, funding surveys, publications and a whole new set of Institute buildings. How much influence did it hold as a result?

Richards took very seriously her self-professed aim to 'combine the apparently conflicting demands of fundamental and applied research' (Richards 1953: xiii). The key question for both the critics and defenders of the Institute's work was whether the Institute's own research programme was oriented primarily to the concerns of the Ugandan colonial authorities. Richards advocated a vision of relative autonomy, partly through emphasising the long-term approach to all research projects. As she commented on the Institute's study of Kampala, 'the survey is done at the request of the Government of Uganda, but it is planned on a two-year basis and we shall allow our minds to wander freely over the problems of social structure and economic differentiation in this town rather than concentrating on ad-hoc inquiries.'[18]

How freely did these scholarly minds wander? Richards openly acknowledges that the research carried out on immigrant labour in Buganda, and published in *Economic Development and Tribal Change* (Richards 1953), was instigated at the request of the Ugandan government, but this in turn was one part of a research programme originally proposed by the anthropologists Isaac Schapera and Stanner in their earlier reports on the priorities for social research in the region. This was the first major project that she led as Director of the EAISR, involving members of the administration on the steering group and working closely with a variety of government departments. Yet the resulting 'report' is a book-length collection rather than a policy document, with no recommendations or even conclusions. There is no evidence that national government policy in Uganda was directly influenced by it.

The third conference held by the Institute in 1952 was the first to which colonial administrators were invited, and was attended by 14 district commissioners and an equal number of anthropologists working in their areas, with papers being presented by both in parallel. The event also focused on issues of methodology, and agreed on a common approach to collecting case-study material. Richards did not feel that combining academic and practical inquiry was difficult, and noted that the main problem was one of publication, leading the Institute to circulate cyclostyled research reports to 'increase the practical utility of research and at the same time remove the pressure for immediate practical relevance from publications of a more academic nature'.[19]

For all her cosmopolitan sophistication, Richards was either politically naïve, or simply uninterested in the grievances of many Ugandans and Kenyans about the harsh inequalities of colonial rule. When the Acting Chief Secretary of Kenya took up her offer to carry out investigations of use to the colonial authorities, he proposed an investigation into the 'incidence of crime' committed by the Kikuyu. Her response, written in October 1950, was to suggest that a psychologist might be employed to see whether 'these habitual criminals could be reckoned to belong to definite neurotic or psychotic types'.[20] Whilst promising to 'consider this proposal very seriously, as it is of both practical and theoretical interest', she also had to stall for time, as 'we have nothing on our budget for such a post'. It may of course be that she felt obliged to be seen as willing to cooperate with the authorities at a time of growing and general civil unrest throughout Kenya, knowing full well that she was unlikely to get funding for such work. The subsequent declaration of a State of Emergency in Kenya in October 1952 in response to the Mau-Mau 'emergency' overtook any such plans to carry out criminological research.

In Uganda, a 'hear-no-evil, see-no-evil' attitude was evident in the topics of social research carried out by the Institute, none of which addressed the growing issues of political unrest or anti-colonial sentiment within Buganda, despite major episodes of unrest in Kampala in 1945 and 1949. Richards was intimately aware of the strength of Baganda feeling on the matter of independence, especially given her friendship with Governor Cohen, who expelled the Kabaka from

Uganda in 1953. The Institute instead maintained a scrupulous detachment, proclaiming its focus on 'basic ethnographic studies' on the assumption that 'background studies ... should precede more intensive work on special aspects or problems' Such studies, it was felt, 'were an excellent training for new field workers, and the best preparation for subsequent specialist studies'.[21] As well as the urban surveys and the village surveys of immigrant labour in Buganda, the Institute conducted a one-week study of 'African attitudes towards the municipal beer-hall' at the request of the Kampala municipality.[22]

Later, Richards led a comparative project into patterns of authority and social stratification in Uganda and Kenya, again with a heavy emphasis on the adaptation of 'traditional' forms of authority to modern rule. She wasn't alone in skirting around the growing strength of anti-colonial sentiment, for Hailey's huge and costly second edition of the African Survey in 1945 equally made no mention of the growing nationalist movement (Hailey 1945). It was left to writers like George Padmore and Thomas Hodgkin in Ghana to draw attention to growing African nationalism.

Instead Audrey Richards was more troubled by institutional politics. In personal letters to her friend Sally Chilver, then secretary to the CSSRC, she revealed the difficulties she faced in juggling administrative expectations and her own research plans. Writing in September 1950, she complained that the local administrators 'refuse to have anything to do with research and hand all the babies back to me to have their noses blown' (16/7B).' Elsewhere she described Entebbe's 'aggrieved' attitude that 'the Colonial Office wouldn't give them more direct grants for their own research but have financed people to do other research projects', and the fact that applications for research funds were often turned down by 'an over-worked young man of 30 who has never considered the question seriously at all'. By 1954 she was increasingly sceptical and convinced that 'it doesn't pay to try to please governments and do what they want. My reports are going to be more and more unpractical as things go on. Either governments lie to you or they don't (in neither case do they read what you write)'. She was also increasingly frustrated at the likelihood of a merger with Makerere College, which she felt was inefficiently run, and the waning support of the CSSRC. If that wasn't enough, she was also depressed by the attitudes of other anthropologists, with E. E. Evans-Pritchard in particular being 'dead-set against local institutes'.[23]

Inevitably, Richards had a strong commitment to the primacy of an anthropological approach. At one point she proposed renaming the Institute as Institute of African Studies, so to 'maintain the anthropologists' predominance without irritating people'. Ingham recalled that the Institute 'was something of a mixed blessing' for interdisciplinary work, as 'historians who were accepted into the Institute's empire had to work very much as part of the Audrey Richards team' and that 'there was a feeling in the EAISR that history was not a suitable discipline for Africa. Audrey Richards was somewhat dismissive of historians' (Ingham 1990). She wouldn't have been the only anthropologist to hold such an attitude, though in one letter to Sally Chilver she admitted her 'terrible ignorance of things historical' and that it would be 'worth retiring to learn some of this interesting stuff'.[24]

The Institute amidst winds of change

Richards finally resigned from the Director's post in 1955. She left a thriving research centre, but one increasingly uncertain about its future. The growing independence movements in Africa seemed likely to lead to the end of Colonial Office funding for the CSSRC, on the 'assumption that support will be forthcoming from the overseas governments'. This left the future of the Institute's research programme uncertain. A senior EAISR researcher, Lloyd Fallers, replaced her. Despite raised eyebrows over his nationality (American), one referee commented 'I believe that he will cooperate well with the administration.'[25]

Even after departing, Richards repeatedly challenged any idea of the Institute and the College exchanging personnel or sharing teaching, insisting that the Institute 'is an active competitor for the best research talent available', and that teaching would worsen that position. Two years of insecurity for the Institute led to new negotiations over the Institute's relationship with Makerere. Fallers was far less committed to this separation of research and teaching, noting in a College Council memorandum that 'academic research is best carried out under the direct auspices of a university and that professors and lecturers on the teaching staff should be intimately concerned with the work of the full-time research workers in their field'. This was also seen as a way of encouraging 'real' economists to take up posts attached to the Institute, which being 'dominated by sociological interests' had found it hard to attract any candidates for its posts. Fallers's proposal was for the Institute to be directed by a person with a joint appointment within the College. Despite concerns by Institute staff over the 'absorption' of the Institute and by the College over the 'feasibility of a joint-headship', the proposal was accepted, and Aidan Southall was appointed as the new director and Professorship of Sociology and Social Anthropology in 1957.[26]

With Makerere's financial support guaranteed, the CSSRC committed further funds to the Institute in 1957, partly to ensure the completion and writing-up of many of the pieces of work it had commissioned, including histories of the region. The 1957/8 CSSRC report noted with 'approval' that the completion of the basic work studying the 'major tribes of Uganda' 'has made possible a move into the sphere of studies of carefully defined comparative problems of direct administrative interest'. The research interests of the Institute were increasingly diversifying. The following year's CSSRC report recommended research on 'election studies', the 'social consequences of land consolidation' and 'changes in the civil service of countries which had received independence'. This belated change in emphasis, occurring at the time of the Lancaster House constitutional conferences of 1960, was accelerated by a large grant from the Ford Foundation for an Applied Research Unit (the title itself is revealing) within the Institute, carrying out studies on land reform and urbanisation as requested by Kenyan government ministries. Indicative of the growing influence of American foundations, the Ford Foundation also gave a grant to carry out a Ugandan education survey at the request of the Ugandan government. There was an almost 'complete change-over of research staff during 1959 and 1960', and whilst some sociological and anthropological research continued, the Institute's new incarnation was far more 'applied' than it had ever been under Richards.[27]

After leaving the East African Institute, Richards kept up a sustained campaign of lobbying and letter-writing on the importance of maintaining a 'tradition of academic research scholarship' in social science as African countries moved towards independence. Despite or perhaps because of her patrician political views, she continued to see scientific autonomy as key to the future of the social sciences in Africa. In her view nationalism in Africa was 'to be allied with an interest in African history and culture and it is important that these interests should be directed and fostered along scholarly lines', while the new governments 'sometimes have objectives beyond those of pure scholarship'. She feared that removal of CSSRC funds from the institutes would lead to a 'flood of half-baked American students and quarter-baked African politicians to be in charge of research, and that without the CSSRC umbrella there was a risk that African governments would 'attempt to censor research on social and economic problems on the grounds that it might reveal undesirable things'.[28]

These opinions were shared by many members of the CSSRC, which in 1961 declared 'great concern' about the 'break between the United Kingdom and overseas territories in the field of social science research which would ensue on the attainment of independence by colonial territories'. It called both for liaison between the UK and these 'independent territories', and for the CSSRC's reconstitution as an advisory body under the new Overseas Research Council. This Council, however, was still under Colonial Office auspices. Amongst Richards's suggestions was for the Council to be transformed into a body outside the Colonial Office, freeing it from any 'suggestion that it is motivated by older "colonial" ideas'. She proposed a 'secret meeting' about this potential future research organisation, listing likely members from a selection of universities. However, as one of her respondents noted with respect to the upcoming independence of Ghana and Nigeria, the 'general desire' was to put money that was available into the 'development of research institutions and research posts in Africa itself and in the training of Africans for such posts'.

Her idealistic plans for a new organisation to promote social science research in independent territories floundered on a number of grounds, not least financial. There was at that point no parallel organisation for social science research in Britain, making it hard to justify to the Treasury one focused on supporting overseas research. Responsibility for research also fell between administrative stools. One potential institutional home, the new Commonwealth Relations Office (CRO) also had, according to Margery Perham, an 'almost puritanical horror of the Colonial Office on the grounds that it is soaked in paternalism and that new countries would smell the taint if they took over any Colonial Office staff or traditions'. One-time reformers like Richards, Perham and Chilver now found themselves out of touch with the new post-colonial political order.

Despite the concerns Richards felt about the future of the Institute, the end of CSSRC funding and the coming of independence saw the EAISR go from strength to strength, at least until the mid-1960s. The changes in the Institute can be tracked in the shape and content of contributions to its annual conference, an event initially intended for EAISR associates. For most of the 1950s this had been a small two-day affair, dominated by anthropologists. The first economics papers were not delivered until 1959. By 1964, the conference lasted a week, with 100 participants listening to 25 papers delivered in five different streams: East African Affairs, Education, Economics, Sociology and Urban Studies. Anthropological work was being increasingly re-branded as Urban Studies or Sociology. In 1966, one of the last events to be held, 50 papers were delivered. Weighty conference proceedings were produced from each event. When added to the 33 volumes in the *East African Studies* book series, this amounts to an impressive publication record for the Institute. There is no evidence of post-independence government interference or censorship of scholarship. Indeed the opposite was true, and academic work in Uganda was affected far more by the growing lack of civil governance and worsening security situation that lead up to Idi Amin's coup in 1969.

Much of the credit for these changes goes to Derek Stenning, who replaced Aidan Southall as Director of EAISR but died in 1965 of leukaemia after four years as Director. He energetically sought to reshape the Institute in a more multi-disciplinary direction, creating directors of economic, political science and sociological research. Whilst an anthropologist by training, he sought a rapprochement with sociology, seeing anthropology's classical 1930s studies as having been conducted in a context in which 'economic depression and political inactivity' had led to 'a static view of African society'. Aware of the contradictory impulses driving academic research and the social development agenda, he introduced a number of practical measures to ensure that sociological research led to 'normative and policy' conclusions. These included requiring postgraduate researchers to teach, encouraging them to write up their research for 6 months at the Institute, setting up local steering committees for research of public interest, and helping researchers extrapolate key policy findings. Whilst aware that none of these were new ideas, he felt that they had been carried out 'unsystematically', and required 'effective middle-men, both on the academic and the action side' (Stenning 1963). During the 1960s, the Institute became a steadily more integral part of the university. It gained departmental status, and Institute members took on teaching responsibilities. The story had come full circle.

Conclusion

How, in retrospect, should we evaluate the colonial universities and research institutes? Roland Oliver points out the importance of UK–Africa links for the development of African studies in the UK, arguing that 'African history ... emerged in the university colleges of tropical Africa, where teachers of history, most of whom happened to be British, faced the problem of developing an historical education relevant to the needs of their students' (Oliver 1995: 13). Could the same be said for post-war African anthropology?

Writing in 1977, Richards was reflective about the achievements of the East African Institute. Rhetorically asking whether 'the nationals of the countries to which so much research was being directed profit from these studies, as distinct from the staff of the British universities', she suggested that the creation of universities and social science departments in countries like Uganda served to change 'attitudes of many African scholars that research was something one went overseas to do'. But she is also humble about the impact of the Institute. She admits that 'we should have made more determined efforts to speed up the training of nationals of the countries for which Great Britain was then responsible so that they could have started their own social research much sooner'. Yet she is adamant in emphasising the autonomy of the institutes – 'I never see the difficulties as having been posed by the domination of the Colonial Office' (Richards 1977: 50) – a position largely vindicated by the available evidence. If anything, the Colonial Office was a key ally of the Institute in its sometimes fraught negotiations with East African colonial administrations over funding and research access.

If the Institute's anthropological legacy was uncertain, the UK discipline of anthropology itself was more confident. Having expanded with the CSSRC's political and financial patronage, it increasingly articulated its own metropolitan intellectual agenda; a rather different agenda from the council's pragmatic focus on colonial social problems. Almost 50 anthropologists received funding or support of some sort from the CSSRC during the 1940s and 1950s – nearly all of the discipline's post-war cohort. The growth and reproduction of social anthropology as a primarily British-based university discipline depended on this colonial research base.

Richards was the exception that proves the historical rule. Richards was championing applied social research at a time when British anthropologists were distancing themselves from it. Yet her commit-ment to useful social research, and to the importance of training new generations of researchers, both African and European, was circum-scribed by her belief in the neutral, apolitical objectivity of Western social science at a time of rising nationalist sentiment and a developing sense of social and political injustice in Anglophone Africa. Ultimately the generosity of CSSRC patronage was a dangerous blessing for anthropology. The CSSRC had no real political vision for handling decolonisation, and the council largely avoided addressing the epistemological implications of anti-colonialism. The prioritisa-tion of research over teaching and training pandered to the growth of the metropolitan academic disciplines, and left the institutes vulner-able to short-term external funding decisions. Under Richards and Gluckman, the RLI and EAISR had sought to reshape the mould in which social research was carried out in Africa. Each institute was limited by the disciplinary ambitions of its founders, epistemological perspectives that had little weight in the fraught political and academic landscape of the post-colonial state.

Notes

1 Royal Anthropological Institute (RAI) House Archives, A22/3/5.
2 Oldham Mss Afrs 1829, Rhodes House, Oxford.
3 Colonial Research Council Progress Report 1942–3, LS.
4 Perham papers, file 685/9, Rhodes House.
5 CSSRC 1944 files, LSE.
6 Kenya National Archives (KNA) OP/1/459, 1ff.
7 Ibid., 4ff and 33.
8 Asquith Commission, Cmnd 6647, p. 17.
9 CSSRC, minutes of the 11th meeting, July 1945.
10 CSSRC papers LSE, CSSRC 48/42, and CSSRC 48/49.
11 Mitchell papers, Rhodes House Mss 1998 5/1 27 from Gluckman 1 July 1948.
12 KNA OP/1/459, 43ff.
13 A. I. Richards archive (AIR), LSE 16/7H .
14 KNA OP/1/459, 64–7ff.
15 Ibid., 72ff.
16 Ibid., 73–4ff.
17 AIR 16/10b.
18 Presentation at the 1953 Makerere/IRSAC conference.
19 CSSRC 12th Annual Report, p. 6.
20 KNA 94/1 99ff and 121.
21 AIR archive 16/7 B and 16/10i.

22 AIR 16/7.
23 KNA OP/1/459, 211ff, 270.
24 AIR 16/10b and KNA 590, 277/2ff.
25 CSSRC 14th, 15th and 16th reports. ·
26 AIR archives 16/7.

References

Brown, G. and B. Hutt, 1935, *Anthropology in Action: an Experiment in the Iringa Province, Tanganyika Territory*, London: Oxford University Press for the International Institute of African Languages and Cultures.

Evans-Pritchard, E. E., 1959, 'The Teaching of Social Anthropology at Oxford', *Man – The Proceedings of the Royal Anthropological Institute*, 180: 121.

Hailey, L., 1945, *An African Survey: a Study of Problems Arising in Africa South of the Sahara*, London: Oxford University Press.

Ingham, K., 1990, *Politics in Modern Africa: The Uneven Tribal Dimension*, London: Routledge.

Kuklick, H., 1991, *The Savage Within: the Social History of British Anthropology 1885–1945*, Cambridge: Cambridge University Press.

Malinowski, B., 1929, 'Practical Anthropology', *Africa*, 2: 22–38.

Mitchell, P. E., 1930, 'The Anthropologist and the Practical Man', *Africa*, 3: 217–23.

Mukwaya, A., 1953, *Land Tenure In Buganda: Present Day Tendencies*, Nairobi: Eagle Press.

Mulira, E. M. K., 1952, *A Luganda–English and English–Luganda Dictionary*, London: Society for Promoting Christian Knowledge.

Oliver, R., 1995, 'African History – SOAS and Beyond', in A. Kirk-Greene (ed.), *The Emergence of African History at British Universities: an Autobiographical Approach*, Oxford: Worldview Publications.

Padmore, G., 1949, *Africa: Britain's Third Empire*, London: Dobson.

Pels, P. and O. Salemink, 1999, 'Introduction: Locating the Colonial Subjects of Anthropology', in P. Pels and O. Salemink (eds.), *Colonial Subjects: Essays on the Practical History of Anthropology*, Ann Arbor: University of Michigan Press.

Richards, A., 1953, *Economic Development and Tribal Change: a Study of Immigrant Labour in Buganda*, Cambridge: W. Heffer and Sons.

—— 1977, 'The Colonial Office and the Organisation of Social Research', *Anthropological Forum*, Vol. 4, pp. 168–89.

Schumaker, L., 2001, *Africanising Anthropology: Fieldwork, Networks and the Making of Cultural Knowledge in Central Africa*, Durham: Duke University Press.

Stenning, D., 1963, 'Relationship of Social Research to Planning, Organisation and Evaluation of National Social Welfare and Community Development Programmes', *EAISR Annual Conference*, Makerere University, Uganda.

Stocking, G., 1996, *After Tylor: British Social Anthropology 1881–1951*, Wisconsin: University of Wisconsin Press.Temple, S. R., 1913, 'Suggestions for a School of Applied Anthropology', *Man*, 13, 102: 185–1.

Temple, S. R. 1913, 'Suggestions for a School of Applied Anthropology', *Man*, 13, 102: 185–1.

4

The Teaching of Anthropology in Zimbabwe over the Past Forty Years
Continuities and Discontinuities

Victor Ngonidzashe Muzvidziwa

The history of anthropology in Zimbabwe supports Asad's contention that it is a mistake to view the discipline simply as a reflection
of colonial ideology. This account documents this history, and in
particular the teaching of the discipline at the University of
Zimbabwe (UZ). Anthropology began to be taught at the University
of Zimbabwe whilst it was still a college of the University of London.
From the 1950s to the 1970s the discipline was marked by a preoccupation with process over time, and with the active construction
of culture and the nature of social change. Ethnographic accounts
focused on urban populations, labour migration, rural cash cropping,
peasant identities, interventions of state and church organisations,
and rural domains. Whilst tending towards the descriptive, there was
a deliberate effort to draw conclusions from both qualitative and
quantitative data. The strong ethnographic tradition was limited,
however, by a weaker theoretical base, a drawback that has
characterised the teaching of anthropology up to the present day.

The post-independence period has witnessed marked changes in
emphasis. First, there has been a strong shift towards applied anthropology; second, and more importantly, Zimbabwean anthropologists
have been caught up in the broad stream of reflective and critical
thought characteristic of the 1980s and 1990s. Themes of power and
of meaning cut across the range of studies conducted by Zimbabwean
anthropologists since independence. In this chapter I document this
history of theorising and engagement. I argue that the teaching of
anthropology in Zimbabwe has undergone significant changes and
shifts without breaking from its past.

The history of the teaching of anthropology in Zimbabwe

The history of anthropology in Zimbabwe predates its teaching in the Department of Sociology at UZ. Early-twentieth-century colonial administrators and missionaries turned to anthropology as a tool to understand native practices and systems of governance (Cheater 1994). Anthropology was one of the subjects taught under the ambit of the Department of African Studies at the fledging University College of Rhodesia and Nyasaland. The first Professor appointed to head African Studies in 1955 was the renowned anthropologist Clyde Mitchell. He obtained a doctorate in social anthropology from Oxford, though his undergraduate training had been in sociology, psychology and social work. The name of the department was subsequently changed, after discussions with staff, to Sociology rather than Social Anthropology (Cheater 1994). The 1960s was a period of sustained attack on social anthropology and its tainted association with the colonial past. In some countries there were calls to ban the discipline from university curricula. This may have swayed those deliberating on an appropriate title for the department. Today it is still a Department of Sociology, despite the strong anthropological flavour of its more recent work, marked by the renaming of the BSc in Sociology, now a BSc in Sociology and Social Anthropology.

In the 1960s teaching within the Department of Sociology straddled the two disciplines of social anthropology and sociology. Staff in the department tended to be people who had training either in social anthropology and sociology or just social anthropology. Mitchell had been trained in both disciplines and hence deliberately strove to bring the two together. The early years saw the introduction of a single honours degree in social anthropology rather than sociology. This emphasis on the teaching of anthropology to the extent of conferring a degree in the discipline was short lived, as by the late 1960s no student had specialised specifically in social anthropology. The dominance of social anthropology over sociology ended in the 1970s.

With the era of the federation and growing political tensions, the department experienced a staffing crisis in the mid- to late 1960s. Most of the white staff left for Europe. As Cheater (1994: 573) noted, the Department of Sociology's staff

> went on to much grander appointments: Clyde Mitchell to a chair at Manchester; Iowa Lewis to become professor of social anthropology at

the London School of Economics; Axel Sommerfelt (after being arrested and declared a prohibited immigrant, along with Jaap van Velsen and others protesting racial politics in 1966), to take a chair of Social Anthropology at the University of Oslo.

Desmond Reader, a Cambridge-trained anthropologist, was appointed to the Chair of Sociology in the late 1960s. It was during his tenure that the first black lecturer, Gordon Chavunduka, was recruited. He later became the first black professor in the department in 1979, rising to an appointment as the university's Vice Chancellor in 1994, a post he held till retirement in 1997, after falling out with the Minister of Higher Education.

The 1970s saw the ascendancy of sociology within the department. More and more people were recruited who had no background in anthropology. Chavunduka and A. K. H. Weinrich maintained the anthropological tradition of fieldwork. This role in the 1980s passed on to Angela Cheater and Michael Bourdillon. Cheater obtained her doctorate from Natal and Bourdillon from Oxford. By the mid-1990s Bourdillon was the sole remaining anthropologist in the Department. The 1990s saw a remarkable comeback from the doldrums by anthropology. A number of Bourdillon's graduate students, some with doctorates, joined the department as lecturers. The only regrettable thing is the inability of the department to retain the new staff. Since 1987 more than 35 full-time academic members of staff have left the department. Because of the department's strong postgraduate training it has no problem in replacing staff despite the high turnover. This is partly a reflection of the general high mobility of professional staff in the country as a whole. Sociology has remained popular with students, but the anthropologists have tended to publish more. No sociologist to date has ever attained the rank of professor in the department.

In terms of teaching, sociology has been the dominant partner, and there are more sociology-oriented courses. This was partly the result of the appointment of an American-trained sociologist when the sociology programme was revised in 1997. This led to the near decimation of anthropology courses in the revised programme. In addition to the introductory course in social anthropology, the other anthropology courses offered at second- and third-year level are qualitative research methods, rural development, race and ethnic relations, economy, society and governance, medical sociology, rituals and myths, ideas and society, and the sociology and anthropology of tourism, a course that has since been suspended because of a shortage of teaching staff. The content of courses like urban sociology and social policy and social administration depends on who teaches them. The one-year social theory course is supposed to draw its material from both disciplines; but those teaching this course have no formal training in anthropology.

The number of students majoring in sociology has risen rapidly in the post-independence period. Up to the end of the 1970s about a dozen students had majored in sociology. First-year introductory classes averaged 100 students, mostly those majoring in sociology and those from cognate departments within the Faculty of Social Sciences such as psychology, social work and politics and administration. By the late-1980s first-year introductory sociology classes attracted between 200 and 400 students, with over 100 students a year majoring in the 1990s. However, this growth rate in terms of student numbers has not been matched by a growth in teaching staff. At independence in 1980 there were about eight positions; over 20 years later in 2002 official staff number 14.

Unlike in the undergraduate programme, anthropology dominates in the Master's in Sociology and Social Anthropology programme. Nearly 30 MSc students enrolled between 1990 and 2000. Since 2001 there has been a huge increase in the number of students registering full time for the MSc programme, and in the academic year 2003/4 the Department registered 20 students in the MSc programme, the largest number since its inception. High numbers of students are enrolling in the postgraduate courses for two reasons. The general economic crisis has caused fewer students to be absorbed into the labour market on completion of the undergraduate programme, and an increased number of first degree holders means that a post-graduate degree is fast becoming a necessity to retain one's competitive edge. Thus disciplinary reproduction is no longer under threat, even though most postgraduate students do not intend to enrol for the doctorate degree and are not interested in becoming lecturers. The department also offers research degrees at Masters and doctorate levels. In the 1990s there were also six doctorates completed within the Sociology department, all trained in anthropology, the first since the department's inception.

The Master's and PhD graduate students have mostly researched in areas such as natural resource management, sex work, street children, tourism studies, crime and deviance, the anthropology of work, livelihoods, coping and survival strategies, labour studies, child labour, and rural and urban communities. Michael Bourdillon has supervised most of the work by graduate students. He has continued the tradition of the early years when there was more emphasis on in-depth analysis of case studies and collection of ethnographic data. However, as will be noted later, there has been a decided shift towards applied and policy research to meet the challenges of a post-colonial society.

The majority of the six PhD theses (Dube 1999; Galvin 1991; Magaisa 1999; Mamimine 1998; Maphosa 1996) written in the 1990s focused on people's coping, survival and livelihoods strategies. In the last decade, with the official adoption of structural adjustment programmes and increased poverty, there has been an increased academic interest in livelihood strategies. In all the studies leading to the award of the doctorate degree the students undertook extensive anthropological fieldwork as part of the initiation into the discipline. It is interesting to note that all six doctorate holders have at some point taught in the Department, though several now work outside academia in non-governmental organisations (NGOs) and the media.

Their research has led to a number of publications. Cooperation between the University of Zimbabwe and the University of Wageningen in the Netherlands in the ZIMWESI project (Zimbabwe Programme on Women's Studies, Extension, Sociology and Irrigation) has brought together senior and junior scholars trained in anthropology, sociology, soil science, irrigation, agricultural economics and agricultural extension. Amongst the resulting publications are Women, Men and Work (Bourdillon and Hebinck 2001). Two chapters focus on the tension between conserving the natural environment and gaining a livelihood from it. Another examines how women and children sometimes suffer because they do not control the profits coming out of a development project. Two other chapters examine how new technologies fail to take local needs into account. One explores how some women use sex as a survival strategy; and another looks at children's contribution to their family's livelihood. An earlier volume edited by Bourdillon (2000), entitled Earning a Life: Working Children in Zimbabwe, drew on the work of a number of scholars with anthropological training. The book is a result of case study work on children who work mainly in the informal sector: helping parents or working on their own; working in small-scale agricultural enter-prises; working for their schooling in plantations; doing domestic work; working in small-scale mining; or involved in the care of the sick and elderly. A significant amount of work has been done in the Sociology Department on child studies, rural and peri-urban livelihoods and community responses to HIV/AIDS. Much of this work is ongoing and will add to the growing body of literature published by anthropologically trained scholars in Zimbabwe.

Nonetheless, anthropology continues to be a marginal academic discipline in Zimbabwe. There is no other department teaching anthropology at UZ or at the new private and public universities. In addition, no steps have ever been taken to form a national association of anthropologists in Zimbabwe. There are no publications established to promote scholarly articles by anthropologists; publications like *Zambezia*, the UZ journal of the humanities and social sciences, are multidisciplinary in their focus. When the Zimbabwe Institute of Development Studies (ZIDS) was established in the early 1980s to act as the government's think tank, no anthropologist filled any post. The exclusion of anthropologists by the post-colonial government could have been a result of the distrust of anthropologists and a lack of understanding of what exactly anthropologists did. While the NGO community has benefited greatly from the applied research outputs of the department, the same cannot be said of the Zimbabwean government.

Trends in theory, methodology and research

Clyde Mitchell emphasised an inductive approach in his work, working towards generalising propositions on the basis of specific case studies. Empirical data provided the bedrock for theory building. This laid the basis for teaching that placed less emphasis on theory and more on the practical application of research findings. Theory has never been a key concern of academic anthropology in Zimbabwe. Nevertheless, we can still identify three theoretical phases in the teaching of anthropology in Zimbabwe. The first phase spans the early years up to the early 1970s; the second phase extends from the 1970s right through the 1980s; and the last takes us from the 1990s to the present day.

Cheater (1994) observed that, by and large, anthropology in colonial Zimbabwe had a practical orientation to dealing with the problems of colonisation and its impact on indigenous peoples. The influence of Radcliffe-Brown's structural functionalism entered the newly established college through its staff, most of whom had been trained in the English-speaking universities of South Africa. The theoretical premises of transactional and situational analysis, mostly borrowing from Gluckman's version of Marxism, served only to embellish the dominant functionalist paradigm. While some might object, I would suggest that Gluckman's work does not offer a radical break with functional analysis. I agree with Sally Moore's observation that Gluckman did not offer much as a theorist of change but made remarkable contributions as far as the study of conflict and competition in various settings is concerned (Moore 1993: 15–16).

> Gluckman was deeply interested in conflict. The outcome of conflict, as he saw it, was sociologically most interesting when it produced one of two results: when the end of a dispute reaffirmed previous social relationships and cultural norms, or when it produced radical change. He interpreted the resolution of disputes between individuals largely as normatively reaffirming, but saw political conflict and group conflict as potentially transformative and revolutionary. His vision of African society was that it was inherently 'conservative', that one chief might rebel against and assassinate another, or one ruling lineage replace another, but that once in office the new incumbent would tend to perpetuate the political system. He distinguished between rebellion and revolution in this way. Rebellion merely produced a replacement of personnel in key positions of power, but revolution actually altered the structure of the political economy.... This polar model of change both suited a structural-functional vision of pre-colonial African political systems and also accounted for the durability of the native–colonial relationship. Gluckman's was clearly a radically subversive view of the colonial situation, but a rather static conception of pre-colonial African society.

Mitchell trained under Gluckman. As the events of the early 1960s showed, functionalism could still be critical of the colonial-settler regime without predicting fundamental shifts. Some of the members of the Sociology Department rose as pioneers of a new school of thinking dubbed the Manchester School. Amongst them was Clyde Mitchell. Their notable theoretical contribution was in the form of micro-sociological social network analysis, especially of those affected by urban transformations. The early years were characterised by an eclectic theoretical approach that avoided asking questions that would lead to the restructuring of social relations. Issues of class, race and gender were conveniently ignored.

By the mid-1970s shifts towards neo-Marxist positions were discernible. However, rather than focus on state–citizen relationships, issues of governance were conveniently shelved, blunting the possible revolutionary aspects of a neo-Marxist theory. Adoption of neo-Marxist models was more a matter of practicality than conviction. The neo-Marxist teachings of the French school, drawing on the work of Balandier, Meillassoux, Godelier, Bloch, Terray, Rey, Copans and others, entered the department through the enthusiastic work of its younger members, like Cheater.

Cheater combined interactional and transactional perspectives with neo-Marxist insights. The neo-Marxist influence was short-lived and never really took root, owing partly to a lack of commitment on the part of its champions and partly to a eurocentricity that made the theory irrelevant to the lived experiences of the majority of the population. The eurocentric nature of Marxist theory was explicitly addressed by such neo-Marxists as Meillassoux (1984), Terray (1972) and Godelier. Drawing on data from their fieldwork experiences with pre-capitalist African societies, they called for the revision and refinement of Marxist models when applied to African societies and other non-Western formations.

Theoretical developments in the post-independence period also saw the complete rupture of the interface between scholarly and administrative-political interests in the country. Rightly or wrongly, most of those practising anthropology could easily be accused of having collaborated with the *ancien regime* that had been replaced by the post-colonial government. For most of the period following the uni-lateral declaration of independence (UDI) by the pre-independence government, anthropologists did not raise a critical voice against the state and therefore could not suddenly be seen to play the role of champions of individual and collective freedoms.

By the 1990s post-independence fever had died down. Michael Bourdillon's (1997: 150) reflections on his study of a Catholic parish in Harare came to the conclusion that as anthropologists we need to

> [p]ay more attention to the interests of our subjects and their under-standing of events; we should pay more respect to their point of view, and be less confident about the superiority of Western, positivist thinking; we should pay more attention to participation in the com-munity under study, and observe precisely how we interact with our informants. Post-modernists argue that such observation of our own participation is more significant than any kind of objective observation we may claim to make of others.

This is clearly a call for self-reflective critical anthropology, informed by post-modernism. The materials produced by Bourdillon and his collaborators are very refreshing in their commitment to an anthropology that is both critical and useful in its search to empower those usually sidelined by the state and other powerful agencies in society. For Bourdillon, 'Academics in less developed countries are usually more concerned with practical implications of our studies than with exotic experiences of other cultures' (1997: 151). This has led to shifts in theoretical positions to the point where issues of participation, honesty, an attention to representation and making choices are now critical to doing anthropology in Zimbabwe.

It is critical, as Michael Bourdillon would say, to have an open mind and to be prepared to accept that one's views might even be wrong. There is a serious need to re-examine the construction of 'the traditional' and by extension 'the other' in order to come up with an engaged anthropology. Anthropology in Zimbabwe is increasingly reflective and calls upon its practitioners and students to do away with binary categories such as 'modern' and 'traditional'. A question like how traditional is traditional needs to be asked. In many ways this approach shows an attempt to break from the past.

A major theme in Zimbabwe's post-colonial anthropology of the 1990s is related to notions of empowerment and disempowerment. Empowerment requires the researcher to redefine not only identities but also the methods and choice of the subject matter for investigation. It necessitates that anthropologists give a voice to the previously voiceless and less powerful such as children in the street, the elderly and the dying. While issues pertaining to globalisation have not received much attention from Zimbabwean anthropologists, those studying poverty and the impact of structural adjustment programmes, as well as the anthropology of borderlands and personal identities (Muzvidziwa 1998, 2000, 2001), are interested in knowing 'how globality behaves when it dissolves into the specific particularity' (Esteva-Fabregat 1995: 7).

What then are the methodological implications of this shift? The concern with counting, systematic observations and a scientific approach has been paramount in the department. The tendency in the department has been that of trying to combine quantitative and qualitative research techniques. Good ethnography was seen as that which approaches the study population and presents fieldwork results in a scientific manner. However, with the passage of time research in anthropology by both staff and graduate students came increasingly to reflect concerns with specific social problems and the link with social policy issues.

The kind of approach adopted in most of the anthropological research carried out by staff and students at UZ tends to be based on the collection of primary data. While ethnography has not been completely abandoned, there has been a tendency to make research fieldwork shorter, thereby reducing the cost of research in the face of limited resources. There is also a discernable move towards producing more critical, qualitative accounts.

Engaging policy makers

Anthropologists in Zimbabwe have a long established interest in observing the impact of development programmes on people's lives and relationships. However from a critical perspective constructed around Foucault's analysis of issues of 'governmentality' (the exercise of power over the population) the planning process seems to involve a mapping of people's lives, what Foucault calls 'surveillance'. Anthropological studies dating back to the 1970s tend to bring to the fore the dark side of development, and try to avoid research being an instrument of control and manipulation.

The post-colonial period has also seen the rise of donor-funded projects and donor-initiated research. Senior anthropologists have been able to access these funds but this also sometimes means compromising one's research and methodological independence, with the rise of rapid appraisal techniques adopted mainly in consultancies. While funding seems to dictate the research agenda for academics, there has always been some leeway to pursue research concerns that seek to tackle pressing social problems. Increasingly, anthropology is playing an advocacy role and speaking out as a critic of dominant views and the powerful. While it deliberately avoids *speaking for* the less powerful, it seeks to *give a voice* to such groups.

The 1990s have seen the emergence of problem-centred anthropological teaching and research. Michael Bourdillon and Marshall Murphree have been in the forefront in pursuit of a results-oriented anthropology and the politics of implementation. Michael Bourdillon became heavily involved in the work of the NGO Streets Ahead, dealing with children in the streets. He wanted change and to see an improvement in the lives of these marginalised kids as well as to change the negative attitudes of society. Bourdillon also became involved in organisations dealing with child labour. He carried out research in the eastern highlands tea estates. He became convinced that what is more productive is the need to ensure that, if ever children have to work (which is often the case), they work under safe conditions. He is also actively involved in charity work and promotes through research and active work the sustainable use of natural resources. Michael Bourdillon has been editor of *Zambezia*, the humanities and social science journal of UZ. It publishes work of a reflective nature that could have an impact on people's lives.

Marshall Murphree, former Director of the Centre of Social Sciences, has used anthropological tools to demonstrate to officials and donors such as the United States Agency for International Development (USAID), the International Development Research Centre (IDRC), the World Wildlife Fund (WWF) and the International Union for the Conservation of Nature and Natural Resources (IUCN) the need to involve communities in the sustainable use and management of wildlife resources. Local authorities, central government departments such as the Department of National Parks and Wildlife Management and the Forestry Commission, and donors have benefited from his insights. He is well known both locally and internationally for promoting CAMPFIRE – a programme interested in transferring the control and benefits that flow from local resources to local communities. This also involved strengthening participation and local institutional capacity. Murphree has been a member of public and private bodies in Zimbabwe dealing with linkages between people and wildlife particularly. In these two we clearly see the advocacy role taken to its logical conclusion. In a small way they are taking anthropology to the people and policy makers (Hulme and Murphree 2001). It is important to market anthropology and its usefulness to the wider community and society.

Anthropologists in Zimbabwe have also engaged with human rights and health policy issues. As academic anthropology made a comeback there was also a trend for anthropologists to get involved with demands from the political opposition and civil society for a more open democratic order. Research and publications specifically on human rights issues was never a concern of Zimbabwean anthropologists until the mid-1990s. The leading anthropologist in the human rights campaign is Angela Cheater. She had a brief stint in New Zealand in the mid-1990s as a professor at Waikato

University, but took early retirement at the age of fifty and came back home.

Gordon Chavunduka did his doctorate on traditional medicine. He has been actively involved with traditional medical practice over the past thirty years, for all but ten of these as president of the Zimbabwe National Association for Traditional Healers. He pioneered the setting up of a college for traditional medicinal plants and herbs. It is rumoured that he wants to raise this college to university status. Gordon Chavunduka has an independent mind: this has earned him the wrath of government and led to his recent sacking as the Chairman of the Zimbabwe AIDS Council, entrusted with the distribution of funds to AIDS orphans. Chavunduka has made significant inroads in the area of traditional medicine and indigenous knowledge systems. While his work is not necessarily political but developmental and rooted in acceptance of and respect for local cultures, he has been a critic of official policy and has consistently called for change in the way the government conducts its affairs. Chavunduka has been appointed to many commissions and quasi-governmental bodies in the 1980s and 1990s. His life is an example of an anthropologist engaged in action research: one prepared to leave the safety of a back seat and get his hands dirty.

Despite these various paths of engagement, as a discipline anthropology in Zimbabwe has throughout its history been more of an 'individualised' than an 'institutionalised' concern. Anthropology's leading luminaries have made no attempt to institutionalise the discipline through the establishment of local associations. This might be due to the conviction that anthropology thrives best where no attempt is made to assert its identity.

Conclusion: Change and continuity in Zimbabwean anthropology

The picture painted above is of a discipline that started with promise but for various reasons lost ground, became marginalised, and went underground for nearly thirty years. There is evidence that the 1990s have seen the comeback of the discipline in Zimbabwe. Paul Nkwi (1998) noted that the future of the discipline everywhere on the continent is rooted in Africans understanding themselves. The survival of the discipline, according to Nkwi, depends not on isolation but on demonstrating the usefulness and relevance of one's work, and of networking with others. In other words, the discipline should be seen as practically relevant in tackling social problems and inter- as well as intra-group relations.

I have argued in this chapter that the teaching of anthropology in Zimbabwe has undergone significant changes and shifts without completely breaking from its past traditions. Concerns with process over time, social change and differentiation, and indigenous know-ledge have remained. Issues of power and representation are being tackled as new areas of concern. It is my hope that identity politics will also soon receive the attention of academic anthropologists.

While there have been changes in the way research and teaching are carried out, the areas of focus have not changed. New questions are being asked of old problems. Graduates in anthropology continue to be absorbed in both the private and public sectors. Many are called to participate in the construction of a new society in view of the land reform programme. The fundamental changes sweeping across the country signal the tasks that anthropologists will be called upon to undertake. In the light of all the changes Zimbabwe is going through, it appears that there is a need for more rather than fewer anthro-pologists, at least in the foreseeable future. But the burden extends beyond a response to structural change: the HIV/AIDS pandemic, growing unemployment, increasing poverty levels and deepening social problems all point to the need for in-depth studies by anthropologists or those with anthropological training. Hence the future of and need for anthropology are not in doubt. The survival of the discipline appears assured given the recent developments in Zimbabwean anthropology and the country at large. Anthropologists are strategically positioned to study the impact and consequences of globalisation on societies such as Zimbabwe's. One can only hope that the discipline in its specific local context can build on the past as it engages with present issues of societal concern.

References

Boonzaier, E., 1998, 'Doing Anthropology "at Home": Local Responses to Anthropologists in a Changing South Africa', *African Anthropologist*, 5, 2: 172–91.

Bourdillon, M. F. C., 1993, 'Anthropological Approaches to the Study of Religion', *Numen*, 40: 217–39.

—— 1996, 'On the Theology of Anthropology: A Response to Stephen Buckland', *Studies in World Christianity*, Vol. 2.1.

—— 1997, 'Studying Thy Neighbour: Reflections on Participation', *Anthro-*

pology and Humanism, 22, 2: 150–8.

—— (ed.), 2000, *Earning a Life: Working Children in Zimbabwe*, Harare: Weaver Press.

Bourdillon, M. F. C. and P. Hebnick, 2001, *Women, Men, and Work: Rural Livelihoods in South-Eastern Zimbabwe*, Harare: Weaver Press.

Chavunduka, G. L., 1979, *A Shona Urban Court*, Gweru: Mambo Press.

Chavunduka, G. L. and M. Last (eds.), 1986, *The Professionalisation of African Medicine*, Manchester: Manchester University Press.

Cheater, A. P., 1986, *Social Anthropology: an Alternative Introduction*, Gweru: Mambo Press.

—— 1994, 'Contemporary Sociology in Zimbabwe', in P. Mohan and A. Wilke (eds.), *International Handbook of Contemporary Developments in Sociology*, Westport: Greenwood Press, pp. 567–82.

Dube, L., 1999, 'Street Children: a Part of Organised Society', unpublished PhD thesis, University of Zimbabwe.

Esteva-Fabregat, C., 1995, 'Interview with the Doyen of Catalan Anthropology: Claudio Esteva-Fabregat', *EASA Newsletter*, 16: 6–9.

Galvin, T., 1991, 'Socio-Cultural Sources of Stress in Marital Decision Making Among Zimbabweans Married to Foreigners', unpublished PhD thesis, University of Zimbabwe.

Godelier, M., 1986, *The Mental and the Material*, London: Verso.

Herzfeld, M., 1997, 'Anthropology: a Practice of Theory', *International Social Science Journal*, 153: 301–18.

Hulme, D. and M. Murphree (eds.), 2001, *African Wildlife and Livelihoods: the Promise and Performance of Community Conservation*, Oxford: James Currey.

Magaisa, I. T., 1999, 'Prostitution in Zimbabwe: a Study of Black Female Prostitutes in Harare', unpublished PhD thesis, University of Zimbabwe.

Mamimine, P. W., 1998, 'Tourism and Culture: a Case Study of Chapungu Sculpture Park', unpublished PhD thesis, University of Zimbabwe.

Maphosa, F., 1996, 'The Role of Kinship in Indigenous Businesses in Zimbabwe', unpublished PhD thesis, University of Zimbabwe.

Meillassoux, C., 1984, *Maidens, Meal and Money*, Cambridge: Cambridge University Press.

Mitchell, C., 1956, 'The Kalela Dance', Rhodes-Livingstone Institute Papers, No. 27.

—— (ed.), 1969, *Social Networks in Urban Situations*, Manchester: Manchester University Press.

Moore, S. F., 1993, 'Changing Perspectives on a Changing Africa: the Work of Anthropology', in R. H. Bates, V. Y. Mudimbe and J. O'Barr (eds.), *Africa and the Disciplines*, Chicago: University of Chicago Press, pp. 3–57.

Muzvidziwa, V. N., 1998, 'Cross-Border Trade: a Strategy for Climbing Out of Poverty in Masvingo, Zimbabwe', *Zambezia*, 25, 1: 29–58.

—— 2000a, 'Survival of Urban Women under ESAP in Masvingo, Zimbabwe', *Review of Human Factor Studies*, 5, 1 and 2: 115–29.

——— 2000b, 'Confronting Difficult Circumstances: the Case of Masvingo Widows', *Southern African Feminist Review*, 5, 1: 73–92.

——— 2001, 'Forging New Identities: Globalisation, Cross-border Women Traders and Regional Integration', in S. K. B. Asante, F. O. C. Nwonwu and V. N. Muzvidziwa (eds.), *Towards an African Economic Community*, Pretoria: Africa Institute of South Africa, pp. 42–9.

Nkwi, P. N., 1998, 'An African Anthropology? Historical Landmarks and Trends', *African Anthropologist*, 2: 192–217.

Pelissier, C., 1991, 'The Anthropology of Teaching and Learning', *Annual Review of Anthropology*, 20: 75–95.

Smyth, J., 1992, 'Teachers' Work and the Politics of Reflection', *American Educational Research Journal*, 29, 2: 267–300.

Terray, E., 1972, *Marxism and Primitive Societies*, New York: Monthly Review Press.

5

The Practice of Anthropology in Francophone Africa
The Case of Cameroon

Séverin Cécile Abega

Today, it is difficult to discuss how anthropology is practised in French-speaking Africa. National statistics, even when they exist, are poorly disseminated. Moreover, unlike some historians such as Ki–Zerbo, or philosophers such as Towa or Hountondji (who have gained academic prominence beyond their national borders), or sometimes a controversial celebrity like the late Senegalese scholar Cheikh Anta Diop or the Congolese linguist Theophile Obenga, African anthropologists have a surprisingly discreet profile in both regional and international spheres, as if their works have been classified as confidential. It is important, therefore, to attempt a general overview of the practice of anthropology in Francophone Africa, even though its characteristics, I must admit, will be difficult to summarise. Some specific examples derived from Cameroon will be used in support of some of the issues raised, while a general overview of the practice of anthropology in other Francophone countries will be brought to bear intermittently. I will first discuss the contexts within which anthropological work has emerged before talking about training, publication, working conditions and, finally, the content of these studies.

Anthropology has three originating contexts in much of Francophone Africa: academic, religious and administrative. The role of these three is critical in understanding the shape and practice of anthropology today. It is thus important to investigate these contexts first in order to understand the discipline's current developments and the main orientations that are peculiar to it.

The academic context

The factors that have shaped anthropology in Francophone Africa give the discipline an essentially ambiguous history. Anthropology flourished mainly in countries that were part of a colonial empire (see, however, Alula Pankhurst's contribution in this volume for a discussion of the development of anthropology in a non-colonised Ethiopia) where anthropological traditions in the colonies evolved from existing or developing traditions in the colonising states. In this respect, I can name Germany and the work of Frobenius as an example; Britain, where the publications of Malinowski, Radcliff-Brown, Evans-Pritchard, Mary Douglas, Nadel and Meyer Fortes have retained their authority; and France, with Griaule, Leiris, Balandier, Bastide, Mauss and Gurvitch. American anthropology, lacking a colonial empire, looked to its indigenous populations (predominantly Native Americans) to provide the subject of anthropological study. The Asian populations of the Soviet Union attracted the Russians, whereas Brazil's Black and Indian populations were the subject of several university studies in that country. Very often the objective was/is to understand how these populations live so as to dominate and govern them, and to penetrate them economically. However, there are studies that followed a purely intellectual approach, as is the case with Marcel Griaule's work among the Dogon of Mali and Georges Balandier's work among the Fang of Gabon or the Ba-Kongo of Congo-Brazzaville.

These works served as a source of inspiration to Francophone African anthropologists in two ways. On the one hand, they provided them with a precious theoretical and methodological contribution, while, on the other, in the absence of written documents and historical studies, they allowed them to see how the peoples under study lived at a certain period in their history. Nevertheless, they are poorly disseminated and remain within university libraries, or in the hands of a small élite able to purchase and read them.

Access to these works by future anthropologists only occurs later, when they become university students, and when the university they attend has a good and up-to-date documentary reserve library; that this is not always the case is evident in some Cameroonian universities. The central library of the University of Yaoundé is a good example. Because of the way the lists are managed it is very difficult to get access to a document, even if this document is recorded in the files. Newly published books are also very scarce, even when they are published by lecturers in the same university.

These studies are carried on locally by institutions that were started in the 1930s. The first research on the prehistory of the African continent, for example, started with the initiative of Theodore Monod, founder of the Institut Français d'Afrique Noire (IFAN) in Dakar, Senegal on the eve on the Second World War. Through this initiative, Senegal can be regarded as one of the first West African countries to be the subject of research in this period. IFAN was also associated with renowned scholars such as Hampaté Bâ or Cheikh Anta Diop. In 1944, towards the end of the Second World War, the Organisation Recherche Scientifique et Technique Outre Mer (ORSTOM) was created. It is a French parastatal structure specialised in fundamental research applied to inter-tropical areas. Today it is the Institut de Recherche pour le Développement (IRD). Its twofold mission is to improve scientific knowledge on inter-tropical areas, promoting their development and the implementation of such knowledge. Many African researchers begin their careers within ORSTOM-IRD teams. Experienced researchers receive credits from this institution and work with their French colleagues in joint teams. They may also receive scholarships and research grants that allow them to travel and work in French universities and research institutions. Some are even employed as local representatives of the Institute in Mali and Congo-Brazzaville. It is often their only chance of finding funding for their research, as this is no longer provided by all governments.

Nevertheless, it must be noted that the studies carried out by ORSTOM-IRD researchers take place within the framework of a partnership with the countries in which they occur, the initial impulse coming always from France and the French researchers. The contribution of African researchers is thus sometimes reduced to that of mere raw data collectors or informants.

The role of administration

Assimilation was the ideology of the French colonial administration; it obliged local populations in the colonies to adopt the French language and behaviour. The French colonial administration's role was to lead these overseas populations towards a French destiny. Their way of living therefore had to be investigated and understood in order to measure the extent of the task the colonial administrators would have in converting them to Francophiles. Several books were published on the 'customs and traditions' of the colonised peoples, including many by famous administrators such as Leon Faidherbe, who was governor in Senegal. Others include Marcel Chailley, who was a commander and a historian in French West Africa. Besides monographs, there were ethnographic films on the peculiarities of these peoples that were also produced. These documents were ethnocentric and thus condescending to local cultures, whose practices they often condemned. Moreover, several publications were just like novels, as administrators did not always have time to observe what they described, often relying on the narrative of a janitor or a houseboy to provide their work with a 'native's' perspective. Chailley is at the heart of such a practice as he gives an account of his achievements, identifying himself with France and her colonial mission, as Hubert Deschamps writes in his preface to the soldier-historian's work on French West Africa (1968: 8): 'Chailley, officier français, ne peut s'empêcher de dire : "nous ... notre pays ... nos troupes" et de s'identifier à la France et à son oeuvre, bien qu'il la juge parfois rudement'.[1]

Eldridge Mohamadou (1963: 156) gives us an eloquent analysis of such works in his critique of a book on African Muslims by Froelich (1962), a former colonial administrator:

> Force est de constater qu'il est un certain nombre d'africanistes européens de la vieille école à qui il est impossible de s'adapter à leur époque et au renouveau de la pensée qu'elle a entraînée sur la plupart des problèmes du continent noir. Beaucoup d'entre eux ont été trop longtemps convaincus de l'infériorité du noir, de la faiblesse quantitative et qualitative de l'apport de l'Afrique à l'histoire, à l'art, aux sciences et à la pensée universelle pour qu'il ne leur soit pas intolérable de faire peau neuve et d'examiner les réalités avec des critères nouveaux.[2]

While such works on Islam, which have been vigorously questioned by Western scholars, remain interesting to read as one view of the dawn of independence, they are particularly relevant today in reference to issues of religious pluralism. Today, these works are still consulted in spite of the disrepute now surrounding the auspices under which they were published – in a period when the ideology of racial superiority over local cultures prevailed among the writers and, moreover, data collection methods were suspect in their objectivity, and analysis was flawed by the administrative and political concerns motivated more by colonial directives from the metropolis than by realities in the field. Despite such doubts, it remains true that these earlier works are often the only available testimony on the social and cultural life of the people at this period, and thus continue to be a source of information and inspiration for contemporary studies.

Religious influences

In French colonies, religious leaders were key actors in the mission to bring 'civilisation' to the colonised. They brought the light of Christ as part of the cultural indoctrination of indigenous populations. Disseminating the gospel was also conceived as a fight against the savage and barbarous manners of the indigenes. Christian administrators produced a plethora of publications to reflect these missionary objectives. Father David Boilat gives an example of this in his *Esquisses sénégalaises* (Senegalese sketches). His declared ambition is evangelisation and the facilitation of the colonial mission, as is the case in the publications of Fridoil, Kobès, de Martrou or Raponda-Walker.

The French or Belgian priest who writes is often the hero of his own story, and through writing what he discovers about the peoples he studies, he tells his own adventures in the manner of Hergé's Tintin. Trilles (1912), for example, fills his book with scenes of cannibalism, sorcery and cruelty to which the writer claims to have been an eye witness. The acknowledged aim was to show the indigenous person as a mentally retarded being, somebody whose behaviour is deviant to say the least and who needs to be taken in charge and supervised by the envoy of a superior culture who can offer reassuring guidance, mediated through the light of Christ. The work undertaken through evangelisation is also recalled, to show, on the one hand, the extent of the task to be achieved and the merits of those who achieve it, and, on the other, to call for the political and financial support of the state and charitable organisations.

These works are disseminated through edited anthologies as well as through journals published by Catholic congregations or Protestant churches. They can easily be found – they are sometimes available in churches, while missionaries disseminate them and make them available to those who can read. The motive of conversion that brought missionaries into local cultures led to monographs and field studies based on suspect data collection methods. However, these works are not all together useless; many of them are accepted as dissertation theses in universities. In a word, therefore, the development of anthropology as a discipline enjoyed mixed fortunes in Franco-phone Africa, benefiting from colonial administration and missionary work undertaken with a specific agenda of domination. It is in this context that we can start to see and understand the enduring links between the post-colonial state and the former colonisers.

Training

Many French Africanists have studied in seminaries, and some have even been in the priesthood. Anthropologists like Philippe Laburthe-Tolra,[3] Louis Mallart-Guimera,[4] Réné Bureau,[5] Claude Pairault[6] and Eric de Rosny[7] are cases in point, among many others. There are also publications that were produced by Africans who were trained by these missionaries. Members of the indigenous clergy who produced studies on local cultures include Theodore Tsala and Pierre Mviena. Indigenous scholars who were trained within the framework of the church include Cameroonian anthropologists such as Jean Calvin Bahoken, Jean Pierre Ombolo, Jean Marc Ela and Pierre Titi Nwell.

There is also the role played by scholars such as the European and American anthropologists who have worked in Francophone Africa, a role sustained by their African colleagues who took over from them and kept the flame of anthropology burning. The first generation of African anthropologists was trained in Europe: mainly in French, but also in British, American, German and Soviet universities. Scholarships or stipends were granted by their European countries of residence within the framework of cooperation agreements, but also by their own countries, in a bid to train an African élite that would replace foreign staff.

This is particularly noticeable in the case of Cameroon, a bilingual country in which English and French have an equal status and in which the official policy is to break down barriers between Franco-phones and Anglophones. For a long time, Yaoundé was the only uni-versity that welcomed students who were initially trained in the two languages. The even-handed rule was that the lecturer communicated in the language of her choice, while the student expressed himself in his chosen language. The current head of the Department of Sociology and Anthropology, Jean Mfoulou, is a Francophone Cameroonian with a PhD in sociology from an American university. The other members of this department with doctorates are Joseph Mboui, a perfect heir of the French university tradition (he was trained in the French system and obtained all his degrees at French institutions), and Paul Nkwi, the Anglophone holder of a doctorate obtained in Sweden. Nevertheless, they have all studied in seminaries.

Africans who have taken over the leadership of universities and research institutes have been trained in the same institutions as their European colleagues. It can be said that they have the same competencies, having received the same education and having been taught by the same masters. However, they don't work in the same material conditions as regards their salaries, research budgets, academic framework, access to documentary resources, and general intellectual environment. This has an effect on academic production, for example, that I will use as evidence. Nevertheless, it is difficult to arrive at a really objective evaluation, since the numbers and perspectives necessary for sectorial comparisons are scarce.

In fact, this generation of anthropologists is made up of dissidents from philosophy. Training in philosophy has a central place in the curriculum of several great French anthropologists: Claude Lévi-Strauss, Roger Bastide and Pierre Bourdieu are all examples. The tutelage exercised by philosophy departments will only disappear gradually, and Africans who choose anthropology or sociology have often received a philosophical training first. Until the 1970s, in some universities it was necessary to have a first degree in philosophy before undertaking a course in anthropology, and the latter was often a speciality that could only be undertaken in connection with research. The situation has completely altered now, but training in philosophy has continued to be important.

The new generation has followed more classical courses. They have obtained their qualifications, partly or completely, in their countries' universities. In Cameroon, we have the examples of Emmanuel Vubo Yenshu (BA and PhD in Yaoundé), now a lecturer at the Buea University; David Nkweti (BA and MA in Yaoundé, PhD in the US), now retired; John Mope Simo, a senior researcher in Yaoundé (BA and MA in Yaoundé, PhD in the UK); Flavien Ndonko Tiokou (BA in Yaoundé, PhD in Germany) and Antoine Socpa (BA and MA in Yaoundé, PhD in the Netherlands), all of them lecturers at the University of Yaoundé I. However, the academic links to Europe are not completely severed, and those who belong to wealthy families can go abroad for their studies. They also differ from their elders as they have followed courses in anthropology and sociology right from the first year, and are less influenced by the teaching of philosophy and more oriented towards fieldwork. These are fundamental elements that will be important when it comes to scientific publications, as we will see later. The situation is not the same in some former French colonies. In countries like Gabon, the Central African Republic or Chad, to date the local universities do not award doctorate degrees. A student whose wish is to prepare for a doctorate degree is obliged to go abroad, mainly to France because of bilateral conventions and also because of the language barrier. Most of them are awarded scholarships by their governments or by the French cooperation services.

It is also important to say a word here on female sociologists and anthropologists. Until the mid-1980s, there were hardly any indigenous female anthropologists in French-speaking Africa. Since then, a small number have emerged in countries like Burkina Faso, where we have the case of Fatou Ouattara; Cameroon, with Paulette Beat Songue, Marie Thérèse Mengue, Solange Ngo Yebga and Njikam Savage;[8] Gabon, with Claudine Angoue; Mali, with Aïssa Diarra, a medical doctor who is also trained in social anthropology; Niger, with Hadiza Moussa. They have been trained under the same conditions as their male colleagues, and follow the same paths, but the going is tougher and lonelier for them since only a small percentage of women have access to higher education in Africa. Their arrival has brought many positive changes such as a more holistic approach to ethnography, now including insights by female scholars with new and deep perspectives on the human condition.

Publication

As regards publication, it is difficult to assess its role in the development of anthropology. Goróg (1981: 386–94) points out that there has been an increase in the publication of socio-cultural studies in Africa since independence. The liberation of the continent seems to have had a positive effect since at the time she was writing (1980), the total of Africanist publications produced in the previous 20 years had just equalled the total produced between 1860 and 1960. She adds that in French-speaking countries the rise in Africanist publications is particularly remarkable in sociology, anthropology and ethnology, history and literary history. This author also notices that subjects such as ethnology, linguistics or history, which belong or are close to anthropology, are only a tiny part of the studies listed, whereas the number of literary studies has risen more sharply. There has been a progressive decline in the number of anthropology-related publications: 27 per cent before 1921, 24 per cent between 1921 and 1940, 17 per cent between 1941 and 1960, 15 per cent between 1960 and 1970, and 9 per cent between 1970 and 1980. The contribution of French-speaking Africa to these publications is 21.4 per cent. Although these are old figures, it is obvious that the publication of such studies has been undergoing a permanent crisis, shown by such a continuous drop.

It would be difficult to assert that this drop has been stopped or even stabilised. From the mid-1970s, African countries faced an economic crisis resulting from their high indebtedness. Structural adjustment programmes were adopted, eliminating a number of budgetary provisions for academic work. Research in the human sciences was the first to be sacrificed as it was regarded as contributing little to productivity. Research programmes were abandoned and no longer received funding. Researchers hardly received their salaries, and publications slowed to a trickle. The impoverishment was not only quantitative, but also qualitative.

Researchers lacked the means to undertake fieldwork, even when they were not under suspicion as enemies of the government. In the 1970s and 1980s one-party systems and authoritarianism were still the rule. As the subject matter of sociology and anthropology is the society itself, it is difficult to undertake a study based on field data in cultural, social, economic or political anthropology without perceiving the multifaceted crisis which affects the continent. Some of the visible effects of this crisis are corruption, a progressive impoverishment of the population, the resurgence of endemic diseases (malaria, for instance), an exponential increase of AIDS since the mid-1980s, the excessive brutality of the administrative authorities and the forces of law and order, and a widening gap between the preoccupations of an arrogantly rich minority and the actions of the government authorities, on the one hand, and the needs of a majority made up of miserable people on the other. In describing such a reality and in showing its underlying mechanisms, the researcher automatically comes to be regarded as a subversive, a dangerous person within a society that permits only praise, chanting and the worship of political and government leaders. In a country where the continuous echo resounds that all is good thanks to the wisdom and perspicacity of the government and the unique party, it is difficult to picture publicly what is really happening. Censorship is there to check and control intellectual publications. Yet the anthropologist cannot undertake fieldwork without describing this field; he cannot reasonably practise his profession without carrying out detailed ethnographic descriptions. He is therefore obliged either to pretend not to see what is really happening, or to stop undertaking and publishing his work, or to go into exile. Many have chosen one of the first two courses, to the detriment of the discipline.

Working conditions

As for salaries, even when they are still being paid – since many African countries (Niger, Mali, Central African Republic, Cameroon, Democratic Republic of Congo, etcetera) have accumulated salary arrears for civil servants – they cannot support the funding of field or even documentary research (purchasing books, photocopying materials, study trips to consult archives). There is also a fear of saying what will not be well-received, and in so doing putting one's life in danger. Pressure from the socio-political environment obliges the scholar to avoid inconveniencing the powerful, and so avoid being arrested, as this can be regarded as an irresponsible attitude on the part of a father or a husband. In Cameroon, this period was marked by the brutal murder of several renowned scholars, such as Bernard Nanga, a writer and philosopher, Father Mbassi, a Catholic priest and renowned journalist, and Engelbert Mveng, a historian. Even though the government and political authorities cannot be accused of these crimes, since they have not been properly investigated, these murders have created a climate of fear among scholars. Persistent rumours designating him as the next victim of these murders because of his steady stream of intellectual publications led Jean Marc Ela, a renowned sociologist, to go into exile in Canada.

It is not only the powerful who can make the scholar's life difficult. The researcher who goes into the field on his own, and who addresses informants according to the classical fashion, is suspected as a government spy, since he is a government employee and the bearer of a mission order signed by an administrative authority. He is unlikely to overcome the conspiracy of silence and the formulaic responses to authority figures used by the grassroots population to avert the abuses of power. He is more likely to lose his own credibility and conduct his field study in an atmosphere of suspicion and fear that will plague the resulting data collection. I can mention here my own experience in fieldwork conducted in 1989 in Mbandjock, a small town in the Central Cameroon region, where the mayor invited me into his office after a few days of data collection and asked me abruptly why I wanted him to be fired from his position as a mayor and as a member of the central committee of the governing political party. During the same field trip, some of my collaborators were kept under custody for more than two hours by zealous citizens because they were suspected of having been sent by a clandestine political party to recruit activists secretly. They were released only after my personal intervention. More recently, a colleague working in the Central African Republic was obliged to conduct his fieldwork under the supervision, for his own protection, of two soldiers of the national army.

But, certainly, this unwilling idleness has caused a lot of criticism of local researchers who have been accused of not working, not showing concern for the problems of their society, and of not being worthy of the profession for which they received a salary. So they have found themselves within the jaws of a merciless vice. Should they publish and find themselves at the fringes of their society, provoking the anger of authorities who wield the formidable weapons of money and administrative power and police violence, or face the accusation of idleness and laziness? The researcher's room to manoeuvre is thus too narrow, and only a small number of researchers have been able to escape this terrible trap.

Those who try to continue working are in fact a small élite who benefit from foreign funding, namely French funding, through the local programmes of the Agence Universitaire de la Francophonie (AUF, previously AUPELF-UREF), ORSTOM-IRD, or sometimes the local Centre Pasteur. These researchers are less of a threat to the establishment because they address seemingly less controversial fields such as reproductive health, food, local communities, environmental concerns, the recovery of the past, and cultural symbolism. They, however, run the risk of depending too much on programmes conceived and funded outside the country. This risk is manifested in two ways: there is no follow-up in programmes from outside, as these reflect the policies of the donor country. The researcher is therefore obliged to constantly change his focus, stopping when funds are dried up and moving in new directions when he has an opportunity of contributing to a new project. In such changing conditions, the field reports are written mainly to fulfil the administrative requirements, even if they also give an ethnographic record of the data collected. The researcher is also poorly specialised as he keeps changing his areas of specialisation according to the funding of projects. He cannot hope to navigate a long-term route in this ocean that lacks fixed points of reference.

Moreover, objectives, methods and data collection instruments are conceived elsewhere, and the local researcher is obliged to insert himself within a ready-made project. His contribution in drawing up programmes and projects is really negligible, and only begins when the basic elements have already been fixed. Sometimes, he is even reduced to the role of a mere collector of raw data, since his European colleagues never require serious input from him on the issues and hypotheses that underlie fieldwork and analysis, and seldom inform him of the opportunities for disseminating results (colloquia, seminars, conferences, topical reviews) that link his project to others.

Finally, he constantly gives the impression of being a student because the power relationships within the project are advantageous, not to those who are qualified or experienced, but to those who provide funds or who provided the opportunity to insert him into a financed programme. There are cases where high-ranking and middle-ranking university professors found themselves under the supervision of doctorate students from France or Belgium, just because the latter earned a grant from the donor institution. So his qualification matters very little; he is treated with a lot of condescension and excluded from the decisions and discussions that have an impact on the advancement of the project. The funding allocated to him is hardly significant and always smaller than the one of his European counterparts, even though he is expected to provide an equal if not greater output and has the same obligations as regards the purchase of documents, communication and travelling.

Consequently, research is poorly institutionalised locally. Even if there exists a partnership that binds local institutions in collaborative programmes, they have little say in the actual operations of the project because they can no longer contribute to the funding. Moreover, since they are hardly functional because of the burden of their administrative and financial hardships, they are no longer regarded as host structures for national or international scientific projects. Thus these projects function autonomously, or with minimal local administrative supervision. This results in poor integration of local structures in the international funding of research, which is geared instead towards the project-beneficiary countries and is sometimes even financed by credits which the home government will have to reimburse. The results of these studies are not always available to the home country through reports and publications, and it loses ownership of the research because local researchers are reduced to a minor role.

The researcher who negotiates a research contract with Western partners in this context of poor institutionalisation cannot benefit in return from the framework provided by such a situation. Therefore, some of the funding eludes him, on the one hand, and, on the other, there is no policy conceived beforehand that would allow him to defend some options. Since he is often regarded as part of the Western team, or as a member of a laboratory or a small team, he cannot reverse the imbalance thus created.

The new international context that has emerged since the late 1980s has boosted the anthropological profession. With the development of new communication tools, it has become possible to receive international funding from sources other than specialised government institutions. At the same time, an urgent need for field studies has been created by the implementation of HIV/AIDS or poverty alleviation programmes funded by the World Bank, the United Nations specialised institutions, leading international NGOs, and other bilateral and multilateral institutions. Anthropologists and sociologists have been called upon to respond to this need. Even if most of these studies are short, circumscribed and superficial in terms of the traditional methods of these disciplines, they have allowed scholars to renew and continue their fieldwork experience. Here I can cite the example of my own research on the behavioural aspects of the HIV/AIDS epidemic, funded by institutions like the World Health Organisation (WHO), the Joint United Nations Programme on HIV/AIDS (UNAIDS), Wellcome Trust and Cooperation for Assistance Relief Everywhere (CARE).

However, this applied research has not enrolled only qualified and experienced researchers, nor has it involved only specialised institutions. Several persons, qualified or not, from different fields of specialisation and belonging sometimes to organisations with no more than a letterhead as evidence of their existence, rushed at the opportunity to carry out so-called anthropological studies. As the sleeping partners themselves were poorly qualified or were seeking a favourable share of the financial allocation to the beneficiaries, the selection has not always been objective. So professionalism has broken down, and specialists in the discipline must share the label 'researcher in anthropology' with others who have not been trained in ethno-graphic methods, a practice previously observed under colonisation when the roles of missionaries and administrators were conflated. If these facts are not specific to anthropology, it remains true that anthropology regularly faces them and that no evaluation of research capacity can be achieved without referring to them.

The content of publications

I shall now attempt an evaluation of the works by concentrating on their content, considering not so much its value as the ideas and topics which derive from it. I shall point to a strong emphasis on the teaching of philosophy, a weak empiricism, poor fieldwork, a strong tendency to confine studies to one's own group, a lot of emphasis on symbolism, a reconstitution of the past – and then, recently, greater attention to issues such as poverty, government politics and sexuality.

The influence of philosophy

The importance attached to speculative approaches can be explained by the history of the subject, which was marked by the training of the first specialists in philosophy departments. It can also be explained by the presence of former seminary students and religious leaders within their ranks. Moreover, African philosophers often undertake analyses based on the collection of ethnographic data referring to local cultural topics. So philosophy is invoked in tandem with anthropology and this relationship influences the analysis.[9] This was evident in the emergence of ethno-philosophy. Francophone African thinkers have for long been influenced by the Negritude movement. Taking inspiration from the works of Frobenius, a German anthropologist, since the 1930s they have described the Negro as he who looks for harmony with natural rhythms instead of putting them into question. As an emotional being, Senghor's Negro, because he abandoned rationality to the Greek, has suffered the world more than he has managed it. This position has been strongly criticised by Nkolo Foe who borrowed the term 'parascientific epistemology' from Piaget to discuss it (Nkolo 1992).

Another source of inspiration has been the 'Bantu Philosophy' of Placide Tempels (1948). For him, the Bantu regard the universe as a combination of graded vital forces, those of the White being superior to those of the Black. In this way, this writer legitimises the colonial undertaking, presenting the colonised as themselves considering it normal in this philosophical framework. Still, according to this author, one can take ownership of the vital forces of other peoples: as a result, there is fetishism and cannibalism, which in fact means irrationality. This publication, which the writer explicitly addresses to Bantu people (who were an essentially illiterate population at that time), was also and perhaps mainly directed at colonial administrators and missionaries: it provided them with a way to affirm their control over the colonised and had a considerable impact in Zaïre (now the Democratic Republic of Congo), for example, where scholars came to be classified as pre-tempelsians, tempelsians and post-tempelsians (without forgetting pro-tempelsians and anti-tempelsians). Philosophy in Cameroon took a different route, one which did not reflect these divisions; it was shaped by the research of such scholars as Marcien Towa (1989), who drew the discipline in the direction of ethno-philosophy. This development engaged contributions from ethnologists, theologians and philosophers that explained elements of African cultures, not in terms of what is intrinsic to them, but as a representation of what exists, or what happens elsewhere – for example, as an intuition preceding and preparing the arrival of Christianity. This is an approach that implicitly presents the nature of African thinking as decaying and confused. The most recurrent names in this trend of thought are the Rwandan Alexis Kagame (1956), the Kenyan John Mbiti (1972), and the Zaïrians Mulago (1965) and Lufualuabo (1962), in a bid to legitimise Tempels's works within the Bantu tradition. Meanwhile the Cameroonians Bahoken (1967), Basile Fouda (1967) and Manga Bihina (1992), and the Senegalese A. Diop (1949) and Senghor (1964) have all celebrated the genius and the vital forces of a specific African social form. All these works are halfway between ethnology and philosophy, and would very easily pass for anthropological works. C. R. Mbele (1992) relates ethno-philosophy to Tempels's thinking, and summarises Bayart's position in qualifying the essence of post–colonialism in Africa as 'la politique du ventre avec ses miasmes: la corruption, l'improductivité, la cupidité et la prédation des élites incapables d'exploiter les forces productives africaine'.[10] As Mbele points out (1992: 96), the most damaging judgement is to consider, as does Bayart, that all these shortcomings are the fruits of a historical continuity described by an anthropology that refers only to the negative aspects of Africa.

The weakness of empirical studies

Weak empirical studies result from the fact that researchers do not let the facts speak for themselves. The analyses are all inspired by *a priori* theories and explanatory matrices taken from literature. The researcher uses many quotations to show well how loyal he is to an established and undisputed master. Consequently, there is a lack of originality and advance in theory as well as in the quest for explanations, since everything is deduced from analogies with data similar to the ones analysed by others elsewhere. I mention here that Arab, Japanese and Indian anthropologists are already being quoted in studies and synthetic summaries, whereas African anthropologists, and particularly the French-speaking ones, are surprisingly absent. Yet African thinkers inspire the analyses of anthropologists. So Georges Balandier in his political anthropology took inspiration from *Le Roi miraculé*, a novel by Mongo Beti, to explain the fission of lineages and the building up of new lineage entities. Thus, too, *L'Aventure ambiguë*, a novel by Cheikh Ahmidou Kane, is used to facilitate studies of acculturation. Laburthe-Tolra often refers to Mongo Beti and Jean Pierre Warnier, among other Cameroonian indigene authors. This reliance on literary works, and a tendency to take models of comprehension from second-hand sources, inevitably reflects the weakness of field studies.

In French-speaking Africa, few anthropological studies are documented by exhaustive fieldwork. This situation continues to pad out anthropological analyses with poorly observed generalisations. Several authors continue to fill lengthy paragraphs with very general terms such as *pensée/cultures africaines, noires/nègres, mentalité, authentique, traditions, valeurs propres, l'âme, la personnalité*,[11] when really such concepts are of no practical use if not generated by extensive cross-cultural fieldwork. To that should be added the much-chorused hymn of 'adapting' abstract general notions to local realities. One example of this is the notion of 'Bantu civilisation', which led to the creation of the Centre International des Civilisations Bantu (CICIBA) in Libreville, Gabon, a centre which was for a long time run by Theophile Obenga, a Congolese. Though linguists have been able to identify a group of Bantu languages and to give it a precise description, it would be difficult, from an anthropological point of view, to specify the element allowing one to differentiate between a Bantu and a non-Bantu, as neither the kinship system, nor the social and political organisation, nor the material and non-material systems of production allow such a distinction.

In addition to the philosophical training of most of the first researchers, the weakness of empirical studies can also be explained by the fact that few researchers attended universities where there were enough lecturers to cover this aspect of the subject adequately. Spending a long time on fieldwork would seriously penalise students and the good conduct of classes in general. University administrations did not wish to give them free time to carry out ethnographic investigations. Another reason is the scarcity and paucity of funding to facilitate long spells of fieldwork. Data collection can only be brief, with a necessarily limited scope. Here one must acknowledge the fact that most researchers work on their own cultures. However, data originating in this way are ambivalent and their explanatory value must be handled with care. A researcher working in his village has the impression that he already knows the truth about what he is supposed to investigate, and that for this reason he no longer needs lengthy observation to understand the population under study. The observation period is seriously shortened and he identifies too readily the data to be collected or the most interesting informants. A researcher who is denied fieldwork opportunities will use vacation time or a trip to the home village to collect data, which he will then use as the basis for an analytic study. Instead of failing to publish, he will offer the analysis of his own culture. This situation has many different outcomes: a researcher working on his own culture may arrive at a fine observation of the data. He can speak the language and language idiosyncrasies are not a problem for him. He participates intimately in the life of the group whose values he shares, and he can offer an inside knowledge. Yet he lacks a certain distance, which may result in his missing the importance of some phenomena or issues because they look too banal to offer useful material for analysis. By the same token, he may take notions for granted because they are familiar to him, though they may need careful discussion.

Symbolism and the reconstitution of the past

The emphasis on symbolism comes from several sources. On the one hand, it is a major orientation of French anthropology, and it is certain that its influence will have affected those educated in this tradition. On the other hand, the strong influence of religion,[12] omnipresent in the studies and training of university researchers, has not failed to orientate further studies on topics with a religious bearing. Finally, we have seen that researchers work in difficult circumstances and that, even today, it is still not easy to give an independent account of field observations. The observation of rituals and ceremonies, of ancient artistic productions or productions inspired by cultural traditions, gives one an opportunity to set oneself free from this constraint. One can then freely analyse what one has observed in the field, even if such observation has been short.

The attraction to the reconstitution of the past relates to several factors. One is that the identity crisis faced by peoples of African origin, due to colonisation and subsequent Westernisation, has caused many to look for their roots and a redefinition of self, thus explaining the popularity and/or legacy of Negritude and nationalism. In addition, when confronted with the surge of models of the past from outside and mainly from Western countries, African researchers try to identify which ones were 'theirs' and can serve as the rationale for a re-foundation. Such an effort is laudable but may be useless, since it is difficult to predict how this return to the past will be effected. However, it facilitates the understanding of notions which are still encountered nowadays, but which no longer occur in a context which facilitates their proper understanding. The return-to-the-roots approach can be seen as a useful way of doing anthropological work without having to face censorship and compromise oneself in confrontations with paranoid administrative and political authorities. Yet such studies have often been criticised for academicism or élitism, because they appear to be geared more towards a certain university audience than towards clarifying social realities. Consequently, such an anthropology gives the impression of being cut off from the real world, and only interested in documents for rhetorical exercises in amphitheatres.

A new context
The liberalisation of the political context in the last decade has facilitated the reappearance of an active concern with current issues. The need for studies allowing a better understanding of the social and cultural context of the rise of the AIDS pandemic or more accurate targeting of poverty alleviation policies, and international funding for the support of these studies, has facilitated this reappearance. As regards research in political sociology, Claude Aké (2004) has found abundant evidence of 'statolatry' and of the poverty of African research in an area such as political sociology and anthropology. This analysis can be extended to other areas of interest. But there has also

been an emerging interest in topics such as sexuality, gender, health, civil society and corruption. This can easily be seen in journals such as *Politique Africaine, Cahiers d'Études Africaines* and *le Bulletin de l'APAD*, in which there are from time to time, but more often now than in the past, articles written by Africans. Nevertheless, we cannot affirm that the decline noted in Gorög's study, referred to earlier, has been reversed. In examining some specialised journals, such as *l'Homme, Cahiers d'Études Africaines* and *Cahiers africains*, one does not discover a strong presence of Francophone African anthropologists. Even the few that are there are questionable, as the identities of the authors are not always presented, their speciality is not always mentioned, and even if their name is what is taken into account, one is not sure whether it is a European married to an African and hence the African-sounding name. Also, in only considering articles in French, one may have put aside studies published in English by Francophone scholars. However, even in accepting a good margin of error, it remains true that the presence of indigenous anthropologists from French speaking African countries still looks modest. From issue 121 (June/March 1992) to 170 (April/May 2004), the *Cahiers de l'Homme* seems to have published only three studies by this group of researchers in a total of 351 articles. From issue 1–2 in 1992 to 61–2 in 2004, the *Cahiers africains* published 10 such articles out of 117; from issue 105 in 1987 to 172 in 2004, the *Cahiers d'Études Africaines* published 50 out of 401. These figures do not give the true picture of scientific publications by these researchers, since I was unable to include journals published in different countries, as well as books, unpublished texts and dissertations. They nevertheless show the weight of these scholars at the international level, because these journals publish a high proportion of Africanist studies in the social sciences field.

Conclusion

It is difficult to draw conclusions from this study. The glimpse it has offered has been too scanty and too brief. Yet it enlightens us to some facts: the weakness of anthropological publication in French-speaking Africa and the difficulty of carrying out field studies due to constraints that include the problem of funding, the problem of institutional tutelage, the suspicion of administrative and political authorities, and even the distrust of the populations studied. To this must be added the influence of a philosophical orientation, and a very strong subordination to foreign countries at the material and ideological levels. However, there is an emerging new context, though it is still weak and is impossible to consolidate in the absence of a clear policy from government authorities to support and value the efforts of researchers. The expectations are nevertheless high, as since the late 1980s, African countries have been experiencing both political and economic changes and a major cultural and social change: globalisation.

Notes

1 Translation: 'Chailley, a French officer cannot avoid saying : "us ..., our country ..., our troops" and to identify himself to France, even though he sometimes judges her severely.'

2 Translation: 'It ought to be noticed that a good number of European Africanists of the old school find it impossible to adapt to the present, and to revise the views that they put forward on most problems of black Africa. Many of them have believed for so long in the inferiority of the black man, and in the qualitative and quantitative weakness of the African contribution to history, the arts, the sciences and universal thinking that they cannot bring themselves to examine the facts in the light of new criteria.'

3 Now in retirement, Lobarthe-Tolva taught in Cameroon, Burkina Faso and at the René Descartes Paris V University.

4 Also now retired, Mallart-Guimara was a professor of anthropology at the University of Nanterre, France.

5 Bureau worked in Cameroon, Gabon and Côte d'Ivoire.

6 The late Claude Pairault wrote four books and many articles based on data collected in Chad and Côte d'Ivoire. He also worked in Mali, Burkina Faso and Cameroon.

7 Now in Cameroon, de Rosny is known for his books on Cameroonian traditional healers.

8 Njikam Savage is of Nigerian origin, but teaches at the University of Douala.

9 A good example here is Chindji Kouleu's book *Négritude, Philosophie et Mondialisation* (Yaoundé: Editions Clé, 2001). Chindji Kouleu is a Cameroonian anthropologist.

10 Translation: 'the policy of the belly and its miasma: corruption, lack of productivity, cupidity and the predatoriness of an élite that is unable to exploit African productive forces'.

11 Translation: 'African thought/cultures, blacks or Negro, mentality, authentic, traditions, own values, the soul, the personality'.

12 It is really difficult to find books written by French-speaking African

anthropologists. But of the few I was able to gather, most focused on religion, or on symbolism with a religious orientation: Edouard Gasarabwe, *la Geste Rwanda* (Paris: Union Générale d'Editions 10/18, 1978); Paulin Nguema Obam, *Aspects de la Religion Fang* (Paris: Karthala, 1983); Jean Calvin Bahoken, *Clairières Métaphysiques* (Paris: Présence Africaine, 1967); the work of Pierre Titi Nwell and Thong Likeng; most of the ethnographic work of Amadou Hampaté Ba.

References

Aké, C., 2004, 'L'Espace Public entre le Proche et le Lointain', unpublished PhD thesis, Université de Paris XIII.

Arnould, J., 1996, 'Le Débat Contemporain entre Sociobiologie et Théologie', *Revue des Sciences Philosophiques et Théologiques*, 80, 2: 221–42.

Bahoken, J. C., 1967, *Clairières Métaphysiques Africaines*, Paris: Présence Africaine.

Balandier, G., 1955, *Sociologie Actuelle de l'Afrique Noire*, Paris: PUF.

Beti, M., 1958, *Le Roi Miraculé*, Paris: Buchet-Chastel.

Boilat, D., 1984, *Esquisses Sénégalaises*, Paris: Karthala.

Chailley, M., 1968, *Histoire de l'Afrique Occidentale Française, 1638–1959*, Paris: Berger-Levrault.

Deschamps, H., 1968, Préface, in M. Chailley (ed.), *Histoire de l'Afrique Occidentale Française, 1638–1959*, Paris: Berger-Levrault, pp. 284–301.

Diop, A. N., 1949, *Préface à la Philosophie Bantoue*, Paris: Présence Africaine.

Evouna Mfomo, G., 1994, 'La Formation de l'esprit Rationnel dans la Perspective du Développement des Peuples', *Syllabus*, 1, 4, pp. 92–109.

Fouda, B. J., 1967, 'La Philosophie Négro-Africaine de l'Existence', unpublished PhD thesis, Université de Paris, Lille III.

Frobenius, L., 1925, 1987, *Peuples et Sociétés Traditionnelles du Nord Cameroun*, Stuttgart: Franz Steiner Verlag Wiesbaden.

—— 1933, 1987a, *La Civilisation Africaine*, Paris: Le Rocher.

Froelich, J. C., 1962, *Les Musulmans d'Afrique Noire*, Paris: Orante.

Geary, C., and A. Njoya, 1985, *Mandou Yénou*, München: Trickster Verlag.

Gorög, V., 1981, *Littérature Orale d'Afrique Noire. Bibliographie Analytique*, Paris: Maisonneuve et Larose.

Kagame, A., 1956, 'La Philosophie Bantu Rwandaise de l'Être', unpublished PhD thesis, Université de Bruxelles.

Laburthe-Tolra, P., 1981, *Les Seigneurs de la Forêt*, Paris: Publications de la Sorbonne.

Lufuluabo, F. M., 1962, *Vers une Théodicée Bantoue*, Tournai: Casterman.

Manga Bihina, A., 1992, 'L'ethnophilosophie sans Complexe', *Syllabus*, 1, 4: 162–73.

Mbele, C. R., 1992, 'L'École Bayart ou la Mise en place d'une Nouvelle Doctrine de la Domination de l'Afrique Noire', *Zeén*, 2, 4: 88–102.

Mbiti, J. S., 1972, *Religions et Philosophie Africaine*, Yaoundé: Clé.

Mohamadou, E., 1963, 'Recension de "Les mulmans d'Afrique noire par J. C. Froelich', *Abbia*, 2: 153–9.

Mulago, V., 1965, *Un Visage Africain du Christianisme*, Paris: Présence Africaine.

Nkolo, F., 1992, 'Leo Frobenius: aux Sources de l'Épistémologie Parasicentifique Africaine', *Zeén*, 3, 4: 53–82.

Senghor, L. S. 1964, *Liberté I: Négritude et humanisme*, Paris: Seuil.

Tata Cissé, Y. 1994, *La Confrérie des Chasseurs Malinké et Bambara*, Paris: Nouvelles du Sud.

Tempels, P., 1948, *La Philosophie Bantoue*, Paris: Présence Africaine.

Towa, M., 1989, 'Pour une Histoire de la Pensée Africaine', *Zeén*, 1: 19–48.

Trilles, R. P., 1912, *Chez les Fang, ou Quinze Années de Séjour au Congo Français*, Lille: Desclée de Brouwer.

PART II

Acknowledging Critiques, Debunking the Myths

6
Forgetting Africa

Johannes Fabian

'Forgetting Africa', simple as it may sound at first, quickly turns out to be an incredibly complex phrase and topic. To begin with, it comes as a performative contradiction; the phrase negating what it seems to state. Reflecting on forgetting Africa implies not forgetting Africa. Logically and generally speaking there is something general in the notion of forgetting, general enough to predicate it on an entire continent. At the same time, the idea is apparently convincing enough (rhetorically rather than logically) to make us feel that forgetting Africa is a 'problem' that needs to be addressed. What does it mean to issue a statement deploring such forgetfulness and demanding that something could be done about it?

Can one assert that Africa is being forgotten at a time when, for instance, the Congo has been rediscovered by the media, reported on by the press, re-imagined and re-presented by the retelling of its gruesome early history (Hochschild 1998), and made the subject of great literary evocations of the events around independence (Kingsolver 1998) or of travel in the post-colonial tropics (O'Hanlon 1996)? Docudramas of the passion of Lumumba run on television and in movie theatres. The Belgian parliament is forced to conduct an inquiry and publicly debate Lumumba's assassination. And while these lines are being written in 2001 an Anti-Racism Conference takes place in South Africa calling on the West to take responsibility for centuries of enslaving Africans.

Are these exceptions that confirm the rule? Perhaps, but there must be something else that still keeps us feeling that forgetting Africa remains a problem. Is the question so tenacious because forgetting is not only something we do but also something that happens to us? Once, when Africa was discovered, it took a while realise that – at least before exploration turned into colonisation – this was an intellectual event in Western history. Is that not also the case with forgetting Africa? Is such forgetting not more of a threat to those who forget than to those who are being forgotten? I think there is need to assert this and make this assertion critically productive, precisely at a time when the end of the Cold War and the brute facts of global economics cause the continent to descend into seemingly bottomless pauperisation and, were it not for the gruesome stories of rebellions, civil war and genocide, into political oblivion. Which brings us back to complexity and detail. The contribution I hope to make is to show, in as many ways as I am capable of, what 'forgetting Africa' could mean.

The politics of forgetting

Much as we may think that forgetting Africa is something that happens now, or has reached an unprecedented degree or scope in recent years, we should remind ourselves that remembering Africa and forgetting Africa – in the sense of recognising and denying its presence – have always gone together, often in such a way that the latter has been a condition of the former.[1] Concern with forgetting Africa may overlook that the situation we have now has a long history, even if we let it begin only in the second half of the nineteenth century – the time of the colonial 'scramble for Africa' that, if anything, ought to have been a time of remembering Africa (in the sense of recognising its presence). Governments were in search of empire, missions got organised to save souls. Capitalists were on the look-out for profitable investments in the exploitation of natural and human resources, and learned societies had resolved to fill the gaps on the maps of geography, ethnography and natural science. A broad public was eager to read about the heroic accomplishments of all of the above. Africa was 'on our minds'.

But we know (or ought to know) better. Political, economic and scientific appropriation of Africa was based on denial of recognition and therefore on suppression of memory. Just how deeply engrained denial of recognition for Africa and Africans has been in Western history has recently been shown by Susan Buck-Morss in a remarkable essay on 'Hegel and Haiti'. Focusing on slavery as a 'root metaphor of

Western political philosophy' (2000: 821), she sets out to show how political interests and academic specialisation and compartmental-isation have resulted in obscuring or completely blotting out the role that real Africans played in the rise of ideas we count among our highest theoretical achievements. Her first example concerns the 'the paradox between the discourse of freedom and the practice of slavery' (822):

> Freedom ... was considered by Enlightenment thinkers as the highest and universal political value. Yet this political metaphor began to take root at precisely the time that the economic practice of slavery ... was increasing quantitatively and intensifying qualitatively to the point that by the mid-eighteenth century it came to underwrite the entire economic system of the West, paradoxically facilitating the global spread of the very Enlighten-ment ideals that were in such fundamental contradiction to it (821).

As we know, some Enlightenment thinkers rejected slavery; others found theoretical and practical justifications that could be upheld only while forgetting real African slaves. To me, this existential contradic-tion (not just a paradox) found its most striking monument in the lay-out and architecture of Monticello. This residence near Charlottes-ville, Virginia, was built, after his own plans, by President Jefferson. Slave lodgings and semi-subterranean workshops were located so that they stayed out of sight for residents and visitors, while underground passages to the main building made it possible for the owner and his guests to have discreet access to their slave paramours.

Buck-Morss goes on to assemble convincing evidence for an astounding example of forgetting. It concerns the origin of Hegel's idea of lordship and bondage, undoubtedly one of the most influential figures of thought in the history of Western philosophy. Hegel was aware of the slave uprising in St. Domingue/Haiti, widely reported and discussed in the German press he read. In her words:

> Either Hegel was the blindest of all the blind philosophers of freedom in Enlightenment Europe, surpassing Locke and Rousseau by far in his ability to block out reality right before his nose (the print right in front of his nose at the breakfast table); or Hegel knew – knew about real slaves revolting successfully against real masters, and he elaborated his dialectic of lordship and bondage deliberately within this contemporary context (844).

Blindness, I would argue, is too easy a metaphor for what was in fact an act of forgetting as denial of recognition (which, remember, was the issue Hegel tried to develop by means of the master–slave trope). But the concluding sentences of her essay show that her metaphor did not make Buck-Morss miss the core of the issue. What counted then and counts now are those 'moments of clarity in action' achieved by African slaves rising up against their lords:

> What if every time constellations of power in perceiving the concrete meaning of freedom, this were valued as a moment, however transitory, of the realisation of absolute spirit? What other silences would need to be broken? What un-disciplined stories would be told (865)?

Slavery is no longer a colonial institution. Post-colonial Africans continue their fight for survival through, among other things, cultural creations that result in 'moments of freedom' – an 'un-disciplined story' that counts among the most blatant targets and examples of Western forgetfulness and will have our attention later.

Travelogues and forgetting Africa

Is 'forgetting Africa' a cognitive, a moral, or a political issue? Granted, all three aspects are connected, perhaps even so much so that any attempt to separate them will never be quite successful. Still, these distinctions should be made and I want, whenever possible, to concentrate on the first one, intellectual failure. There is a kind of forgetfulness that impairs reason and knowledge because it prevents recognition.

This is an insight I gained from a study of travelogues reporting on the exploration of Central Africa, roughly between 1878 and 1910 (Fabian 2000, see also 1999). What struck me first was how often the African countryside through which they travelled would remind explorers of landscapes, often of specific features, shapes and places 'at home'. Not always, yet with surprising frequency, knowledge (cognition) of physical Africa would come to them through memories (re-cognition); by making the strange look familiar they appropriated 'geography' and tropical nature. This kind of remembering Africa was imaginative and poetic rather than purposeful or instrumental; travellers were 'overcome' by memories. Yet it resembled in many ways the operation of scientific method in that the latter – under the paradigm of 'natural history' that governed exploration – also was designed to make the strange familiar by means of mapping and collecting specimens to be placed in existing rubrics and pigeonholes of classification.

Then I made another, disconcerting, discovery. The same explorers whom a rainy day in Africa reminded of a *vraie pluie de Belgique* consistently failed to see, say, in the faces and demeanour of African 'savages', those of hard-working peasants at home. Ritual processions accompanied by drumming and dancing, drunken celebrations of important events would strike them as 'primitive' rather than remind them of the village festivals or the raucous drinking parties they must have been familiar with (many travellers had small-town or rural origins and most of them were military officers). As far as human Africa was concerned, exploration depended on forgetting as denial of re-cognition. To be exact, even more frequent than outright denial were statements that paired recognition with denial. A typical example, since we mentioned drinking parties, is the following observation made by Camille Coquilhat:

> Les cercles de libation prennent quelquefois des proportions gargan-tuesques, et dans ce cas, au lieu de se terminer comme une scène d'un tableau de Teniers, ils finissent fréquemment par des querelles, dégénerant en luttes sanglantes (1888: 267).

As if the Flemish peasant scenes Teniers had in mind had always been as peaceful as they were made to appear in genre painting.

But there were remarkable exceptions to this rule that prevented the story from becoming totally depressing. There were moments of forgetting prejudice and preconceived ideas when these explorers actually 'remembered' the other they encountered in Africa. A most remarkable and moving example of this was noted down by Hermann von Wissmann, an explorer who later became one of the toughest proponents of German colonial rule in East Africa. This is how he recalled his encounter with an African woman:

> [She had something] *that made us forget* that we had before us just a half-clothed negro woman from the savage interior, something that uncon-sciously made us behave toward her as to an elderly lady from our home country (1889: 151, my emphasis).

In the end, the 'unconscious' – memory as it overcomes us – lost out to purposeful forgetting required by the enterprise of exploration and later colonial domination. The latter we may find expressed in a statement that, it must be said, was typical of one of the 'greatest Africanists', Leo Frobenius. The context is one of his disquisitions on ethnographic collecting.

Trading ethnographic stuff (*Kram*) is, as it were, the great highway that leads to a community of interest, to a common understanding with the negro. *One should never forget*, the Negro is by all means a materialist and a positivist of the worst kind. (1907: 355, my emphasis)

Perhaps one should not read too much into this remark. However, it was not the casual slur (possibly even meant 'humorously') that made me quote it; it was Frobenius's exhortation 'never [to] forget'- never to let what we think we know be overcome by remembering what we know better.

Critiques

Should great ethnographers and 'Africanists' like Frobenius not be given credit for having assembled the knowledge and achieved the understanding of Africa that makes 'forgetting Africa' impossible to imagine?

Post-colonial critique has been tempted by a seemingly inescapable conclusion: since all African ethnography was conducted, somehow and at some point, in collusion with colonial domination, it should be discarded. Let us forget the Africa of the Africanists. Another argument is less crude but leads to much the same result: even if they worked with the best intentions and scientific methods, ethnographers could only study African societies and cultures as they had been (de)formed by centuries of slavery and modern colonisation. To those who would argue that ethnographers were conscious of the historical conditions affecting their research, some critics respond that the Africa ethnographers considered authentic was an 'invented' Africa, not the Africans' Africa (Mudimbe 1988).

This sort of radical critique had to be formulated; its logic was inescapable. Yet it was not radical enough because it tended to dismiss what it should have confronted: for better or worse, our ethnographic, anthropological ways of producing knowledge about Africa were practices that were real even though they may have been guided by ideology and directed at an invented Africa. The most fateful mistake or shortcoming of the anthropological study of Africa before the end of direct colonial rule was not so much that it worked with concepts (such as kinship, magic, ritual) that, while producing large numbers of knowledgeable ethnographies, reified 'tradition'. It would be silly to deny that we owe to these efforts a huge archive of African culture that, used with the precautions with which all archives must be approached, will make it possible to remember Africa.

At the same time it must be said that this sort of 'classic' ethnography thrived on forgetting Africa, that is, refusing to recognise 'traditional' Africa's contemporaneity. Enacting tropes that go back at least to the Enlightenment origins of anthropology, ethnographers pursued their work as the study of a vanishing Africa, of traditions crumbling under the impact of colonisation. Africa's modernity, the move of masses of peasants into an urban-industrial world of wage labour, commerce, employment in the military, in administration, and education and the concomitant adoption of 'Western' lifestyles (including the use of European languages) were more often than not deplored, sometimes ridiculed, as 'deracination' or as pathetic mimesis. It was not until the intra-disciplinary critique of anthropology's culturalism (and functionalism) had prepared us to 'remember the present' that we began to perceive and appreciate African contemporary culture in its many creative expressions (in music, theatre and painting, but also in urban storytelling, grassroots literacy, and historiography). Forgetting Africa is not a fate. At stake, when Africanists began to study 'popular' culture, was to recognise its vigour and contemporaneity, not to construct it in contrast to 'high' culture.[2]

Just how much 'forgetting Africa' was asked of African writers and artists who (often by the choice of their literary language and genre, by the styles they adopted and the content they expressed) gained admission to global high culture at the price of separation from the masses, is for them to consider. My impression is that many are beginning to use the bridges built by popular culture to return to the people where they find readers, audiences and clients – as long as living in Africa is not reduced to sheer survival.

Remembering forgetfulness

Anthropologists working in and on Africa under colonial rule were not the only ones whose projects demanded forgetfulness. They were a minute minority among 'colonials' whom we cannot imagine getting through their careers – or just through the day – without 'forgetting Africa'. Expressions of fascination, even infatuation, with Africa notwithstanding, establishing and maintaining distance to Africa has been a principle of 'tropical hygiene' since the days of exploration. And there is little reason to assume that this has changed for expatriates who live in post-colonial Africa. Racial and certain social barriers may no longer exist but development workers, technical and health experts, NGO personnel, and so forth, spend relatively brief periods in one place, are seldom motivated to learn local languages or socialise with the population. AIDS and tropical diseases such as malaria are more threatening then ever. It is not hard to imagine that forgetting Africa becomes an ever-present longing *while* living in Africa.

That some kind of distance is required by all bureaucratic organisations, by scientific and even by missionary work, is one thing; that, going on testimony by colonisers as well as colonised, so many intelligent and honest agents of colonisation thought, or were forced to think, that their work could be carried out only by forgetting their own humanity and that of their subjects, is another. Once again, the point to be made here is not (or not only) one of moral indictment. It is forgetfulness as intellectual failure, damage done to reason, which in the end deprives us of the possibility to pull ourselves out of the morass of our colonial past.

We begin to get studies of testimony by colonisers that, as may be expected, find more expressions of 'imperialist nostalgia' than reflections on forgetfulness.[3] This is different when we turn to testimony by the colonised. Remembering forgetfulness – that is, making forgetting a topic – has been a preoccupation I found everywhere in the 'memory work' that makes up an important part of popular culture. I will briefly discuss examples from a number of different expressions but first I want to be sure that we do not lose sight of the significance of forgetting in situations where the intellectual challenge is to make sense of life under oppressive regimes.[4]

A few years ago, David William Cohen, a historian of Africa, quoted in the Preface to a collection of his critical essays the novelist Milan Kundera (from his *Book of Laughter and Forgetting*): '[The] struggle of man against power is the struggle of memory against forgetting' (Cohen 1994: xiii). Reflecting the problems of writing African history mainly based on 'oral tradition', on what people remember, he says: 'Kundera's story reopens this ground in an important way, calling one to recognise not only the fragility of memory but also how complex and challenging the notion of "forgetting" is' (xiv).[5]

Remembering through popular historiography

When I now turn to documents of African popular thought that I have found in the course of my own research since the mid-1960s, it is important to keep in mind that, as an anthropologist, I was not on the look-out (at least not initially) for 'oral traditions' as sources for writing the academic history of a place or region in Africa. What I will have to say has a bearing on the topic of this essay in the sense that may help us to expose yet another unexpected twist of the story: 'forgetting that Africa remembers'.

Ironically, 'forgetting that Africa remembers' has been a danger especially for those historians of Africa who placed all their bets on a doubly constricted view of 'oral tradition': they counted as tradition only those oral sources that could be treated methodologically as equivalents of the written documents of Western historiography and resolved to consider as sources only those verbalisations of memory that enacted what a given 'tradition' had defined as ways of remembering and contents to be remembered. More recently, African historians have learned from developments in folklore studies and the 'ethnography of speaking' that there is more to 'oral tradition' than its being a substitute for written documents.[6] They are only beginning to come to grips with the vanishing boundaries between orality and literacy that characterise contemporary African memory work, which is no longer restricted to enactments of traditional forms of remembrance. Everywhere in Africa we have become aware of popular, grassroots historiography – belatedly, because its origins go back to the adoption of literacy at the beginnings of colonisation a century and a half, or so, ago.

Documents of popular historiography show a high level of theoretical awareness. There is meta-history in the reflections that authors address to their work, in the ways they consciously employ poetic and performative modes of narration, in their dialectical approaches to historical 'truth', and in the explicitness with which they take positions when their accounts and those of academic history come into conflict. It is also true that the fervour applied to narrating the past concentrates on memory, which means that in the examples to be discussed remembering will be in the foreground, whereas what I can say about forgetting comes, with few exceptions, from evidence *e contrario*, from memory work directed against forgetting.

In the Shaba/Katanga[7] region of the Congo popular discourses of memory are expressed in local varieties of Swahili. However, these discourses – religious doctrine, historical narratives, song lyrics and dialogue in theatrical performances are instances I studied – are not limited to talk about memory; though spoken language remains central, they appear in other media such as written texts, televised performances and, most impressively, in popular painting. Lexically, considering the words that are available in Shaba/Katanga Swahili, the semantic field of remembrance is mapped by four verbs (and corresponding nouns):

-kumbuka, to remember, but used also as a synonym for to think (of), in expressions introducing statements, such as nakumbuka, I think (that); with a causative form, -kumbusha, to make one remember, to remind, and an abstract noun, ukumbusho, a reminder.

-waza, to think; with the noun wazo, thought, idea, most often in the plural form mawazo.

-saha(b)u, to forget; without a corresponding noun.

-pote(z)a, to lose, but also used as a synonym for to forget.

Shaba/Katanga Swahili is characterised by a high incidence of code-switching (to French and, to a lesser degree, to local Bantu languages). I think it worth noting that French terms and phrases are conspicuously absent in talk about remembering and forgetting. A recent linguistic study (de Rooij 1996) found that code-switching to French must be understood as a stylistic-rhetorical practice (rather than as a device to fill lexical gaps). This allows us to hypothesise that the absence of French in memory discourses may have rhetorical and, indeed, political significance in a context of colonisation.

That the terms I listed belong to one and the same semantic field can be demonstrated by associations that are not just logical or specu-lative. They are reflected in their actual co-occurrence in the different memory discourses I mentioned earlier. For instance, ukumbusho, reminder, was a current term that both artists and their customers used when they spoke about the meaning or purpose of genre painting that had become a spectacular expression of popular culture in Katanga/Shaba in the 1960s and 1970s. More explicitly, a painting was valued for its capacity to remind the viewer of past events and present predicaments, specifically for its becoming the occasion to tell a story.

In the course of intensive conversations I had in the Autumn of 1974 with Tshibumba Kanda Matulu, who was to become the most prominent of the genre painters, he insisted that his work as both a painter and a historian was in essence to think, -waza, to express ideas, mawazo, rather than simply to depict. A central idea in his monumental History of Zaïre (told in more than one hundred paintings and corresponding narratives) was that colonial history was a story of loss, -potea, loss of sovereignty, of knowledge, of trust and dignity, of 'everything', as he sometimes put it. Tshibumba frequently used the verb -sahabu, but only to say that he personally had forgotten specific names, places, or events; whenever he wanted to describe collective forgetting that came as a result of oppression he used the stronger – potea.[8]

Ten years before Tshibumba completed his History of Zaïre, in 1965, a certain André Yav had published the Vocabulaire de ville de Elisabethville. The text, typed in Swahili and mimeographed, was a history of the town of Elisabethville/Lubumbashi, the capital of Katanga. Though separation by a decade made for a noticeable difference in perspective, the two documents resemble each other in many respects, including in the concepts they apply to the work of memory. The Vocabulaire also designates its content as mawazo, thoughts, and its purpose as -kumbusha, to make (its readers) remember/think. As I noted before, in these documents the task of remembering/ reminding (here also designated, more explicitly than in Tshibumba's work, as knowing, -jua, and explaining, -elezea) tends to overshadow reflections on forgetting. In fact I found only one occurrence each for -pote(z)a and -sahabu (with opposed meanings, one positive and the other negative) that make statements about 'forgetting Africa'. In the first one, the Vocabulaire praises the white pioneers as people who took care of their African helpers 'pasipo kupoteza mtu wao, without losing/ forgetting their man (servant)'. The second one appears in a fable of colonisation where the protagonists are a human Belgian husband and his animal African wife. It is a story of mistreatment and humiliation and the wife brings what went wrong to this powerful point: 'yule wangu bwana mutu amesahabu kwake kwa kunifahamu, this human husband of mine forgot who I am'.

Another decade earlier, in the mid-1950s, a religious movement, the Jamaa, had emerged among many social thinkers in Lumbashi, in response to the teachings of a Belgian Franciscan missionary, Placide Tempels.[9] It started among mineworkers in the Kolwezi and quickly spread throughout Katanga and beyond. Jamaa doctrine, documented in instructions (oral and written) to candidates for initiation into the movement, had made –*waza*, to think, and *mawazo*, thoughts, the pivot of its discourse and ritual. As in the other examples we briefly examined, Katanga/Shaba Swahili was the linguistic medium it shared with other expressions of popular culture. It differed from later phenomena such as historiography and painting in that its doctrine, though formulated as a universal, was hermetic, reserved to the movement's members who considered themselves 'guardians of *mawazo*'.

It is impossible here even to sketch the essentials of Jamaa thought as it is developed in a coherent system. What counts for our purposes is the finding that the semantic field of thinking-remembering-forgetting was, in this discourse, intensified and elevated to a level that entitles us to translate *mawazo* as gnosis, knowledge as salvation. Specifically, salvation was to be attained by remembering, –*kumbuka*. Remembering what? *Umuntu*, best paraphrased as all and everything it takes to be human. This is what mankind has lost/forgotten, -*potea*, -*saha(b)u*; such forgetfulness is *kushindwa kujua*, failing to know: for instance, failing to know a fellow human being because of distinctions of gender, age, race or ethnic affiliation. The mission of the Jamaa was *kukumbushana*, to make each other remember. This expression had its negative counterpart in *kujisahauna*, a complex reflexive-reciprocal derivation from -*sahau*, literally 'to make each other forget oneself'. Forgetting, far from being just something that happens, was conceived as a social act, of commission rather than omission; the 'victim' of the act is the one who commits it, the one who forgets.[10]

Reflections

Is there a need to spell out in more detail, beyond what was quoted from texts documenting popular thought, how much we stand to lose when we forget that Africa remembers? Among all the other instances of forgetting Africa mentioned and discussed, this one may appear as the least obvious. Yet it may be the most important one. If making 'forgetting Africa' a topic is a call for remembering Africa, the goal can be reached only if and when memory becomes one.

Probably I should end my reflections here: this is what I can say as an anthropologist and ethnographer of contemporary Africa in the short space of an essay. I have only touched on language, and the really interesting question remains: does forgetting speak a language? The best I can do by way of a hunch, a mere *vignette*, is to leave the reader with a sentence from Patrice Lumumba's famous speech that scandalised the assembled Belgian dignitaries during the ceremonies of Congolese independence:

> We were insulted, we had to suffer beatings, morning, noon and evening because we were niggers. Who is going to forget that a black person would be addressed *tu*, not, of course, because that is how one addresses a friend but rather because the respectful *vous* was reserved to Whites only? (cited in Willame 1990: 110)

Notes

1 That acknowledging the other's theoretical presence (in disciplines such as Oriental studies and anthropology) demanded the other's real absence (as our coeval) was Edward Said's thesis in his *Orientalism* (1979) and mine in *Time and the Other* (1983).

2 See my account of this (Fabian 1998).

3 See, for instance, Dembour 2000, an ethnography, not of memories but of ways of remembering, based on conversations with Belgian former territorial administrators.

4 To readers who are interested in connections between memory and power in pre- and post-colonial times I recommend Werbner 1998, the writings of Bogumil Jewsiewicki (for example 1988), and Roberts and Roberts 1996.

5 Cohen's sensibility to forgetting is in marked contrast to that of his colleague, the eminent historian of Africa and premier authority on oral tradition, Jan Vansina. The index to his *Oral Tradition as History* (1985, a thorough revision of his classic *De la tradition orale*, 1961) has entries on 'Memory, collective', 'Memory, process', 'Remembering', 'Remembrance', 'Reminiscence', but nothing on 'forgetting'.

6 A striking example of this, already cited, is the revision that occurred between Vansina's two books on oral tradition (1961, 1985).

7 The awkward double designation of the region and the local variety of Swahili reflects the changes of names that were imposed by Mobutu (Congo became Zaïre).

8 Incidentally, the French term *oubli* occurred only once in our conversations – when he chose to read to me from a newspaper article: 'On se souviendra d'un certain John Panda qui dans les années vingt publiait déjà dans les journaux de Kinshasa des écrits absolummement

révolutionnaires. Même celui là est tombé dans l'oubli.'

9 Author of *La philosophie bantoue* (1959, orig. 1945), one of the most influential calls for 'remembering Africa' then and still debated today.

10 So as not to burden the text with notes I have refrained from referencing specific statements and examples. Here I offer a comprehensive guide that, though far from being complete, will be useful to readers who want more information. Of the principal documents on popular historiography, the *Vocabulaire de Ville de Elisabethville* was published in Fabian 1990a. As to Tshibumba's History of Zaïre, the complete series of paintings and excerpts of his narrative and our conversations (in English) may be found in Fabian 1996. All the texts of the *Vocabulaire*, a text related to this work and a commentary, the complete Swahili transcript and English translation of Tshibumba's narrative and our conversations, and the Swahili transcript and translation of a theatre play (first published in Fabian 1990b) can now be found on a website devoted to 'Language and Popular Culture in Africa' (www.pscw.uva.nl/lpca). In the future, this site will also contain a collection of texts documenting the teachings of the Jamaa movement. Meanwhile see Fabian 1971 on the Jamaa in general and Fabian 1969 on its gnostic character.

References

Buck-Morss, S., 2000, 'Hegel and Haiti', *Critical Inquiry*, 26, 4: 821–63.

Cohen, D. W., 1994, *The Combing of History*, Chicago: University of Chicago Press.

Coquilhat, C., 1888, *Sur le Haut-Congo*, Paris: J. Lebègue.

Dembour, M., 2000, *Recalling the Belgian Congo. Conversations and Introspection*, Oxford: Berghahn.

Fabian, J., 1969, 'An African Gnosis: for a Reconsideration of an Authoritative Definition', *History of Religions*, 9: 42–58.

—— 1971, *Jamaa: a Charismatic Movement in Katanga*, Evanston: Northwestern University Press.

—— 1983, *Time and the Other: how Anthropology Makes its Object*, New York: Columbia University Press.

—— 1990a, *History from Below: the 'Vocabulary of Elisabethville' by André Yav. texts, Translation and Interpretive Essay*, Amsterdam and Philadelphia: John Benjamins Publishers.

—— 1990b, *Power and Performance. Ethnographic Explorations through Proverbial Wisdom and Theatre in Shaba (Zaïre)*, Madison: University of Wisconsin Press.

—— 1996, *Remembering the Present: Painting and Popular History in Zaïre*, Berkeley: University of California Press.

—— 1998, *Moments of Freedom: Anthropology and Popular Culture*, Charlottesville:

University Press of Virginia.

—— 1999, 'Remembering the Other: Knowledge and Recognition in the Exploration of Central Africa', *Critical Inquiry*, 26, 4: 821–63.

—— 2000, *Out of Our Minds: reason and Madness in the Exploration of Central Africa*, Berkeley: University of California Press.

—— 2001, *Anthropology with an Attitude: Critical Essays*, Stanford: Stanford University Press.

Frobenius, L., 1907, *Im Schatten des Kongostaates. Bericht über den Verlauf der Ersten Reisen der D. I. A. F. E. von 1904-1906, über deren Forschungen und Beobachtungen auf Geographischem und Kolonialwirtschaftlichem Gebiet*, Berlin: Georg Reimer.

Hochschild, A., 1998, *King Leopold's Ghost*, Boston: Houghton Mifflin.

Jewsiewiski, B., 1988, 'Mémoire Collective et Passé Présent dans les Discours Historiques Populares Zaïrois', in B. Jewsiewicki and H. Moniot (eds.), *Dialoguer avec le Léopard?*, Paris: L'Harmattan, pp. 218–68.

Kingsolver, B., 1998, *The Poisonwood Bible*, New York: Harper Flamingo.

Mudimbe, V. Y., 1988, *The Invention of Africa: Gnosis, Philosophy, and the Order of Knowledge*, Bloomington: Indiana University Press.

O'Hanlon, R., 1996, *Congo Journey*, London: Penguin Books.

Roberts, A. F. and M. N. Roberts, 1996, *Memory: Luba art and the Making of History*, Munich: Prestel.

Rooij, V. A. de, 1996, *Cohesion through Contrast: Discourse Structure in Shaba Swahili / French Conversations*, Amsterdam: Ifott.

Said, E., 1979, *Orientalism*, New York: Vintage Books.

Tempels, P., 1959, *La Philosophie Bantoue*, Paris: Présence Africaine.

Vansina, J., 1961, *De la Tradition Orale. Essai de Méthode Historique*, Tervuren: Musée Royal de l'Afrique Centrale.

—— 1985, *Oral Tradition as History*, Madison: University of Wisconsin Press.

Werbner, P. 1998, 'Diasporic Political Imaginaries: a Sphere of Freedom or a Sphere of Illusions?' *Communal/Plural*, 6, 1:11–31.

Willame, J. C., 1990, *Patrice Lumumba. La Crise Congolaise Revisitée*, Paris: Karthala.

Wissmann, H., 1889, *Unter Deutscher Flagge quer durch Afrika von West nach Ost. Von 1880 bis 1883 Ausgeführt von Paul Pogge und Hermann Wissmann*, Berlin: Walther and Apolant (fourth printing).

7

But We Know It All!
African Perspectives on Anthropological Knowledge

Christine Obbo

When I mention anthropology to educated Africans, I perennially receive an exasperated, and exasperating, reaction: 'But we know it all!' It is a refrain I have also heard from North Americans. But what exactly do we, or rather they, know? The majority of people usually associate anthropology with digging up bones. This is not surprising given the long history of Western involvement with Roman, Greek and Egyptian archaeology. In recent decades palaeontologists have dazzled people with their findings regarding the ancestry of modern peoples. African findings in Kenya and Ethiopia have held centre stage. But this exotic imagery, eagerly and skilfully evoked by *National Geographic* and the global media, makes it all the harder to convey an understanding of anthropology as a social science engaged with contemporary concerns and dilemmas.

African scholars currently practising anthropology feel it is time to move their discipline to the heart of the much-vaunted African Renaissance. As ever, power is key to ownership of the knowledge production process. Contemporary problems of development, health and indigenous knowledge demand that we define the theoretical agendas and practical issues that are of concern to us. Too often hitherto, we have been involved as junior partners (though some more flattered and financially rewarded than others) in research enterprises engineered by Northern scholars. At the same time, in as far as Western education is part of our history and an inescapable global force, we must be actively engaged in the research, teaching and theoretical debates developed by such scholars.

During the 1980s, when teaching with a colleague in an American university, we used to begin our introductory course on Africa with a slide show. Our aim was to problematise the tourist brochure imagery of Africa, imagery which inhibits observers from appreciating African social lives. The slides were made from the *National Geographic*, tourist brochures and Disney-style theme park advertisements. They revealed that, whereas other continents were often represented by images of people involved in social and cultural activities, Africa was always predominantly represented by nature – lush savannah with beautiful animals, stunning deserts and waterfalls.

What irritates Africans most is that when they are acknowledged as being part of the African landscape, they are represented either as nomads or pastoralists; they are depicted as either dancing or starving; and they are shown emerging from the ultimate badge of poverty – the hut. During the 1970s, as part of the outreach activities of the African Studies programme at the University of Wisconsin, aimed at increasing knowledge of Africa among Americans, African students used to be invited to talk to community groups and schools. In one such talk, to the surprise of everyone, a Nigerian student presented a slide show consisting exclusively of the skyscrapers in downtown Lagos. He insisted that he was showing the image of Africa that was never displayed.

Recently, I also took pictures of multi-storey buildings in five African cities. In all the pictures – of banks, government offices, Houses of Parliament – it was difficult to avoid images of street children, beggars, hawkers of newspapers and snacks, and ordinary people going to work. Of course there were also pictures of the élite emerging from their luxury cars or luxury hotels, though frequently such hotels were walled off to seclude tourists from the poor or the sight of nearby slums. That Nigerian student had wished to provide a corrective to the Western gaze that selected its African imagery, ignoring skyscrapers, a familiar part of the Western urban imagination. He could have shown beautiful indigenous architecture or naturalised non-indigenous architecture from many parts of Africa. In my view the Nigerian was seeking to articulate the voice of an African élite that was ashamed of the smells, flies and mud huts, images through which Africa is essentialised. His slides were seeking to show how Western banking, schooling and medical institutions – not to mention expatriate labour – made Africa part of the global community; and not the isolated, deprived and exotic other.

'Super modern man'

The 1960s were a momentous period. The majority of African countries achieved political independence and entered the development decade, dominated by Western economists and political scientists. Modernisation was the catchphrase in academic theories and public discourse. With the help of Western aid, expertise and advice, the transformation of Africa would be achieved by modernising traditional political, economic and social practices. In East Africa, in the late 1960s, a popular song introduced by the Moral Rearmament Movement[1] went as follows:

> We say Yes! to the land of Africa
> We need every man in Africa
> We want to send from the land of Africa
> SUPER MODERN MAN!

Those promoting the rapid modernisation of Africa felt that this would be achieved through the creation of a 'middle class' imbued with 'Western' values. In the early 1960s European and American foundations sponsored international travel for the educated few to expose them to the social and political milieus of the 'modernised' world. The élite became the representatives of Africanity, the face of Africa to the outside world. Meantime the majority of the people became 'the masses' to be harnessed for votes and to continue to provide the backbone of predominantly agriculture-based economies. Over- emphasis on the 'modern' African man had a profound effect upon many aspects of thinking. African cultures were reduced to the occasional wearing of batik shirts and the promotion of dance groups.

Yet this had contradictory effects, particularly for gender relations. As the men became more comfortable in woollen suits and ties, censorious attitudes and, in some countries, laws deemed contemporary Western dress unsuitable for African women, who were the guardians of culture. On the whole, the modern men could nod to token aspects of this culture, and women in general were responsible for observing the rest. The cultural traditions that were being forced on women as their preserve were rural, and educated men were ashamed of them. Women in towns were portrayed in novels and popular discourse as prostitutes.

The ambivalent attitude of Anglophone African men towards Western culture was visible in the underestimation of the positive contributions of women to African modernity. Francophone African men of the Negritude movement used poetry to innovate an aesthetic centred on women as the embodiment of the African continent. The most valuable women were seen as those operating in the traditional mode and regarded as somehow closer to nature. These sentiments were in contradiction to the reality of the economic, legal and educational changes that were affecting women as well as men. In fact, élite men wanted modern women but they wanted them to accept the same old standards of male domination. It is not surprising that soon after independence it was common for élite men to abandon their 'traditional wives' to the villages, and to marry educated urban younger wives. This was true even of the intellectuals who exhorted the celebration of African culture. A case in point is Okot p'Bitek, whose unforgettable heroine Lawino excoriatingly exposed the shallow modernity of Acoli men (1968).

Anthropology, seen as the only discipline giving voice to 'non-modern' people residing predominantly in rural areas, came under fire. Educated men were embarrassed by pictures taken before people adopted Western dress, or capturing rituals that involved the stripping off of clothing.[2] What, it was asked, was the point of concentrating on the peasants when the élite could provide answers to any queries? Because they studied the activities and thoughts of the majority in a social or cultural group anthropologists were seen as being part of a conspiracy to discredit the modern Africans who were described in colonial policy reports as 'detribalised'. The detribalised Africans had been seen in colonial times as the thin end of the urbanisation wedge, the trend that would ultimately destroy the traditional ways of life. Some anthropologists, however, consistently condemned the label 'detribalisation', which was usually used evaluatively to suggest a 'pathology' of 'disintegration' and 'demoralisation' (Fortes 1938: 61); they suggested that this was a 'mistaken and exaggerated mis-apprehension of the nature of social relations' (Watson [1959] 1970: 46). In fact, they argued, being exposed to elements of Western culture in urban life was not an obstacle to settling back into tradi-tional rural living (Schapera 1947:171; Watson 1970: 47). Gluck-man's assertion is appropriate here: 'An African townsman is a townsman, an African miner is a miner' – but this does not mean that they do not have other identities (1961: 68–9).

In contrast to the many colonial whites who did not want natives to be alienated from their traditions and who probably despised those who were, advocates of the modern African after independence saw detribalised men as the hope for the future. The 'detribalised' African was in fact the success story of the colonial educational system. The education project was to produce an élite driven by new cultural rules. The ideal sites for such a project were boarding schools, where students were removed from the rural and traditional environment and harnessed with the trappings of European schooling. Colonial education took place in Christian missionary schools. All instructions were in English and the speaking of vernacular at school was a punishable offence. In some schools students did not go home for holidays but stayed at school to catch up on their studies and perfect their English. The end result was Africans who were unable to face sitting on mats, entering smoke-filled kitchens or hoeing for hours in the sun. Manual work was despised, even by those who had not been to boarding schools and who may have had only a few years of schooling. This pattern continues today.

But what has this to do with anthropology? Plenty. The educated saw themselves as the proper representatives of Africa to the outside world and their voices as the authentic conduits of social and cultural truth. An anthropologist who has worked in Zaïre once told me of a prominent African intellectual who had become very upset when the anthropologist visited his village and stayed with his relatives. The African intellectual had received a good Jesuit missionary education and he saw his vocation as writing about African ideas. For him, fieldwork to collect empirical evidence was a waste of time. Villagers, in his mind, had no theories, let alone the luxury of philosophical thinking.

My own relatives have never understood why I go to live in my fieldwork site when I say I am doing ethnographic fieldwork. In 1989 a colleague at the Makerere Institute for Social Research admonished me: 'Why do you waste so much time in Rakai? Surely, you already know what those people are saying and could write it in your sleep.' I protested and pointed to the poor-quality reports people at the Institute were writing, with information often gleaned from coffee-break conversations. His answer was: 'Well, they are being paid by the research tourists, who have no time or language skills to do fieldwork. You and I know this stuff. Go to the village for a day but why stay there for weeks on end?'

In the 1980s AIDS created an urgency among foreign researchers to get information out as quickly as possible. On arriving in Uganda, foreigners went for short periods on scouting tours with hired local research assistants who were to return later, collect data and write reports. The reports of the research assistants were poor and the principal researchers were in a hurry because they were teaching or conducting projects in different countries. As a result the hypotheses that were supposed to be tested by the research exercise turned into confirmed theses. This was a case of library research and travel as bonus. Yet even under these circumstances some researchers deluded themselves that surveys could yield quantitatively meaningful results. A research assistant told me in 1990 that the principal investigators in his project did not want to hear 'gossip' until they had finished the research. The assistant accordingly kept quiet and the banal findings (minus the rich nuances) were transformed into models and hard data. Such exercises in futility defeated the expectations of those who waited impatiently for information relevant to the promotion of development or curbing the AIDS epidemic.

'We are in trouble if we stop smelling the poor'

Anthropological input was desperately needed in the early days of the AIDS epidemic but there were no anthropologists on the spot. Departments of anthropology have failed to produce anthropologists in large enough numbers to make their work relevant. Even in South Africa, which has four active departments of anthropology, the number of African anthropologists is low. It was, however, encouraging to see so many students at the 2002 annual conference of South African anthropologists at Rhodes University. Departments of anthropology were casualties of the African economic and political crises of the 1970s and 1980s. The few trained anthropologists sought work outside universities. Those with overseas anthropology degrees could only work, on returning to Africa, in departments of sociology or general social science faculties. At Makerere, anthropology slowly died as we fled into exile during the years of Amin. When political stability returned, heads of social work and psychology refused to invite anthropologists back because they claimed to be teaching the courses that would normally be listed under anthropology. In one department where I served on several occasions as external examiner, I always recommended that they hire an anthropologist. Each time one or two faculty members would say that they were anthropologists, and had obtained their degrees overseas. My point was that there was no evidence that the students had been exposed to anthropological concepts, a lack that was reflected in the teaching syllabuses.

Once when I conducted a one-day seminar for the Ugandan students I was examining, there was great enthusiasm to understand the anthropological approach to doing research and making sense of the world out there. We discussed the anthropological project of participant observation. The tools needed for the project were looking and listening for extended lengths of time, asking for clarification and posing questions relevant to the topic of research. Being there and doing things with the people also required knowledge of the languages of the people studied. Yet there was consternation at the suggestion that even if one was a native speaker of the language, it was important to ask people what they meant rather than assume that knowledge.

Anthropologists access the world of others through the humble apprenticeship of becoming participant observers. In this way we collect data, examine how people act, what they believe and try to figure out the connections between their acts and beliefs. People are all the time interpreting the world and acting on those interpretations. The anthropologists need to access people's interpretation through participating in their world. It is only through participation that one can begin to understand people's subjective experiences and make any sense of the meanings they ascribe and the purposes they embrace in their lives. The issue here was that any anthropological study had to contend not only with the interpretations of the researcher but also with the interpretations of the people.

When a student in the seminar pointed out that the most important thing he was learning was that facts were not just sitting there waiting for them to collect them and write them up, I knew we were making progress. This was the point to discuss allowing different truths to emerge. We noted the government's neglect and even abuse of the rights of individuals when politicians regard the views of other ethnic groups or those not in power as divisive. They define the problems and assume that they are providing the right solutions. This led to the discussion of how privileged people, including students, constantly ignore and refuse to hear what ordinary people are saying. They seemed to be reluctant to engage in the time-consuming exercise of allowing other voices to emerge. Essentialising and generalising were so instinctively attractive that deconstructing it took some time. It was pointed out that when one talks in universal terms ('We do such and such'; 'We believe') it is usually with pride and sounds positive. The next question was what happens when different people in the same group or situation insist that their way is the authentic way, or when others just keep quiet. This revealed the issues of contested truths and muted voices. It is not only non-anthropologists who are attracted to universal models of society. Ardener (1972) pointed out that for a while anthropologists were attracted to the generalised models presented by the men in the societies they studied, and that they found the women's answers based on their particularistic experiences cumbersome for constructing analytical models. Thus women's voices became muted by their own men and the anthropologists. The students stressed the need to make extra effort to hear women because when meetings take place they sit at the back; in most societies, they are socialised to speak softly, especially in the presence of men; and often, even if they have something to say, they are pressed for time to complete chores before it gets dark. This remained true despite the efforts of the Ugandan government to push for women's political involvement. Vocal women in Parliament are provoked by male colleagues, and asked who is minding their children and husbands. During election campaigns, men are seen as rightful political aspirants but women are asked whether they are married, whether they are married to foreigners, and whether they are foreigners. Most women thus avoid politics because it is rough terrain.

Past and present memories

The students were asked to say something about the anthropological monographs they had read. Some carried well-thumbed copies of John Beattie's Bunyoro, John Middleton's The Lugbara, and Aidan Southall's The Alur. Apparently these students had gone to a lot of trouble to get these books and I noticed that they treated them like Bibles of truth about their societies. The changes that had taken place since the late 1940s when those studies were done they regarded as irrelevant and a distraction from the timeless truths these monographs represented. Reluctantly, the students agreed that societies were constantly changing as people responded to the social, political and economic situations they found themselves within. For example, I suggested for a start that religious ideas about rainmaking, social rules about sex and marriage and reciprocal labour needed to be restudied and assessed. They were not easily convinced because, as Jones notes about colonial anthropology in Nigeria, 'any monograph written by an anthropologist on a particular tribe and accessible to its literate members becomes the tribal Bible, the charter of its traditional history and culture' (1974: 287).

It is partly because we have not reproduced ourselves by training new generations of anthropologists that monographs take on lives of their own, although we cannot deny the power of the 'shallow modernity' noted by p'Bitek. I am not denying that some monographs are classics (I for one am not willing to dismiss a century of anthropology), but they are only part of specific cultural histories, and never the last word. In 1993, George Bond talked about the strange experience he had when he returned to Zambia and found that his study was being cited in a court case by the Yombe, a ciTumbuka-speaking people of Isaka Province. Parties in the dispute used sections of his book (Bond 1976) to assert the legitimacy of their claims. Elsewhere, too, anthropological writings take on a life of their own as arbiters of cultural truths. Among most of the overseas Baganda, especially those in North America, Apolo Kagwa's *Mpisa Za Baganda* is the cultural reference book of choice when, for example, in doubt about the details of proper marriage practices. *Mpisa* was first published in 1905, reissued in 1934 and reprinted in 1952. Kagwa was John Roscoe's research assistant or, in current parlance, colleague. If Roscoe's *The Baganda* (1911) had been translated into Luganda it would also have become a cultural reference book. I remember, in my village during the late 1950s, people coming to consult my father's Luganda library on what Kagwa had to offer on twin rituals, and how to settle disputes, including rape fines. In 1992 I interviewed two diviners who had independently hired readers and memorised sections from Kagwa's *Empisa* and *Bassekabaka be Buganda*. One of the diviners liked to recite quotations that were fundamental to his practice of creating princely fetishes used in healing. I only realised that he could not read when he tried to read a book held upside down.

Kagwa recorded oral history as he heard it from those close to him. He was then the Prime Minister of Buganda. Perhaps his study was an élite view of Kiganda culture, even then.[3] Perhaps society was not greatly differentiated, and cultural practices were uniform for the élite and the peasants. When the AIDS epidemic forced people to find culturally appropriate words for education and prevention, they did not find Kagwa's Christian and sanitised language helpful. For example, *kulabagana* (to see each other) is ambiguous, and has a double meaning when asking people about having sex. After a century of exposure to Christianity, many words were consigned to the dustbin of rude cultural practices.

It has taken Uganda two decades of aggressive prevention campaigns, lots of money and the efforts of many to reach a point where there is a decline in the numbers of infected urban youths and pregnant women. UNAIDS is citing it as an example of the 'good practices' that should be followed by other countries. The delay in achieving positive change has been due primarily to ignorance and inability to address the social and economic causes fuelling the AIDS epidemic. The widespread shame and denial the educated display about the lives of the rural and urban poor does not promote awareness. From the beginning politicians who did not want to promote condoms would say that they were not opposed to condoms but that the uneducated people would not know how to use them. An urban myth, which I failed to verify with any villager, was that they would wash and reuse the condom. In my conversations people went to pains to point out their aversion to body fluids and doubted that anyone would reuse a condom. Often in fora discussing the factors that made people vulnerable to HIV transmission, the causes would be placed not only in distant geographical areas but in the distant historical past. Polygyny, the practice of having several wives, was identified as a risky practice perpetuated by village and Muslim men. The informal polygyny of élite men with several girlfriends or mistresses was not perceived as dangerous. There was much talk about rural practices associated with promiscuous behaviour that leads to HIV infection. At Makerere and at the AIDS Control Programme offices at Entebbe people cited the dangerous practice of *Kisiki*, the all-night gatherings (in the past around a log fire in the middle of the compound) for a bachelor party or a wake for a funeral. At the local level the political leadership issues half-hearted bans on *Kisiki* parties, late weddings and disco dances. Predictably, people continued to hold their parties, arguing that promiscuous people have many other opportunities to do what they want to do but most people just enjoy themselves and then go home. Remarks on the banning of discos and dances were most telling for what they revealed about colonial memories. People kept saying: 'The missionaries prevented us from dancing.' One man noted 'I find it incredible that our own people are also stopping us from dancing even the modern disco.' Dancing also means having sex. In one sense the missionaries had found some of the Kiganda dances seductive and had discouraged their performances.[4] In another sense, the missionaries' push for monogamy was an attempt to control the promiscuity of natives by limiting the number of men's sexual partners. In the late 1980s and early 1990s there was resistance to the preventive thinking coming from the élite in the capital and it took time for many young people to accept the life-saving preventive measures of safer sex. In 1986 in neighbouring Zaïre, élite urban young men constructed a metaphor from the acronym SIDA as 'an Imaginary Syndrome invented to Discourage Lovers' (Schoepf 1995: 36). Apparently, there is no telling the lengths to which white people will go in order to control blacks.

Anthropology and the study of the 'other'

While other Western disciplines initially proceeded confidently on the assumption that all non-European politics and history could be framed in relation to the activities of European colonials, anthropology established itself as a metropolitan discipline specialising in the 'other': non-Western peoples. This is no longer so: since then, anthropologists have tried to make sense of their own cultures and societies as well. The endogenous critiques[5] within the discipline have led to a diversity of approaches. The criticisms often reached us belatedly in Africa. For example the criticism of anthropology as the handmaiden of colonialism in the late 1960s was picked up by politically motivated élites and used to rationalise their denial of their humble rural roots. Personally I think that anthropologists in general are brave and that some early ones behaved in radical ways that sometimes did not endear them to the colonial administrators. It is ironic that the colonial administrators were suspicious of anthropologists because they lived too close to the 'native', while the modern African élite resented them for keeping alive the beliefs and practices of the masses. With regard to the masses, the information in most of the early studies seems to have come from the male élite of the time in those societies. It is also important to remember that anthropologists were involved in studying people in the changed situation of labour migration to mines and cities. The colonial official view tended to confine itself to Africans as urban villagers. In the mid-

1950s the Institute of Social Research at Makerere focused on the African residential areas of Mulago, Kisenyi and Mengo because, in the words of the Urban Affairs Administrator, 'We want to know what goes on behind the bananas.'

Despite the trappings of globalisation in many aspects of urban life in Africa, local cultures still matter; they are the lived experiences of the majority of people.[6] We need to reintroduce anthropology to the universities but before we can do so, there will have to be a drastic change of attitudes. In the first instance we have to bring anthropology to centre stage, demonstrating its vital contribution to understanding the way things 'really' work. The failure of the development decade can be blamed in part on relegating anthropology to the outhouse. Development aid made us deaf to what the masses, who were to bring about development, were saying. We did not have time to listen to them because we were no longer capable of sitting on mats or bare floor or stooping to enter smoke-filled kitchens. Ironically, the forces that had hitherto promoted 'the modern African Man' were by the late 1980s urging that instead of wasting money on higher education, it might be wise to educate Africans just to be good farmers.[7] In 1989, President Museveni, opening the brand-new Department of Technology and Commerce, urged students not to take useless subjects like history, and generally gestured negatively in the direction of the arts and social sciences. Yet such utilitarian rhetoric is risky – a diverse training in different disciplines will produce people with a broad education to help solve Africa's problems.

Anthropology must contribute to the understanding of and solutions to development and human rights issues in Africa. Ethnographies can bear witness in contexts where the poor human rights record inhibits political and cultural criticism. It is instructive to look at the African Charter of Human and People's Rights, also known as the Banjul Charter, adopted in 1986 and by 1991 ratified by 41 of the 51 member states of the Organisation for African Unity. The charter emphasises 'second generation' economic rights as opposed to 'first generation' civil and political rights. Globally, the document is unique in its emphasis on 'third generation' collective rights; hence the inclusion of 'peoples' and 'human' in the title. However, by the 1990s the widespread abuses of human rights through dictatorial regimes, genocide and communal violence eroded the belief hitherto popular among academic and political élites that economic security must precede the establishment of civil and political rights. Widespread poverty means that the fundamental economic rights of food, shelter, health care and basic education are denied to many. It is now widely acknowledged that political and civil rights are necessary for the protection of economic rights. Women, people living with HIV/AIDS and activists are leading the human rights movement in Africa and have argued that the Banjul Charter's stress on group rights encourages governments to ignore human rights issues.

No topic lies outside the potential remit of the discipline. It is not possible to understand African development without knowledge of the culture of foreign aid and how it props up corrupt dictators and encourages kleptocracy. In nearly all African countries since independence different waves of élites have acquired great wealth for themselves while denying economic opportunities to those not in power. It is undeniable that colonial policies underdeveloped African entrepreneurial and industrial capacities (Rodney 1972), but this argument sounds false today when even the peasants know that politicians are corrupt, that they are underpaid for cash and food crops, and that all investments go to the state-owned prestige projects run and milked by politicians. The African economic crises have been partly due to the highly competitive world markets that our export-oriented agriculture encountered. The challenge to the much-talked-about African Renaissance is to eat 'humble pie', and to base policies on well-grounded, in-depth research that will promote the ownership of African development by all sectors of the population. This is, in fact, an admission that industrialisation projects failed because we lacked expertise, infrastructure and technology.

Anthropology is still the best way to get at the opportunities and constraints that influence people's actions and thus give shape to the design for living which we call culture. Some problems are indeed intractable and anthropology may not always provide answers, but much can be learned in the process of asking questions about them. This is because culture is the result of human actions and thoughts. It acts as a catalyst for further action as people debate, contest and reinterpret previous actions. Anthropology is time-consuming, frustrating and an imperfect art. Yet if we stick with the project we meet philosophers who elucidate for us ideas about religion, how time and space are embodied in memories of places and things,[8] about the social construction of individuals,[9] surviving wars[10] and other misfortunes,[11] and even about evil.[12]

The anthropological project of intensive and extensive participatory research is still the best way to study individuals in groups and organisations, and to teach the students the necessity of humility before 'facts'. First we must arm African anthropology students with these skills; without them the present malaise will continue. Development agencies and non-governmental organisations since the 1970s have employed African university graduates to do policy-oriented, short-term research projects. Often carried out in multiple sites, these exercises have often been described as collaborative and applied. However, the collaboration has been mostly in name, as the employees have not been empowered or given analytical or grounded research skills. Many social science graduates can claim to be able to do anthropological research because 'what people do is so self-evident that it does not take much to understand it'. However, this mere declaration of 'understanding' inhibits us from translating everyday, as well as extraordinary, information into knowledge. The African Renaissance will be bogus without a grounded anthropological base.

Notes

1   This secular morality preaching movement began in Switzerland but was exported and popularised in Africa by Americans.
2   The revival of breast-exposing rituals among the Zulu and Swazi is interesting. In recent decades women in Kenya have used stripping as an effective public protest. The practice has been reported all over Africa at different times.
3   See note 4.
4   Melodious singing of hymns replaced dancing for the Christians. An eighty-year-old woman told me in 1974 that her mother had been a singer/dancer at the king's palace at the turn of the century. There is no mention of such professional women or of the mother, despite the fact that Kagwa fostered her young girl at his home with the intention of marrying her to his son, who was abroad. As it turned out he violated her at age twelve and added her to his collection of women. They had three children who are still alive.
5   See, for example, Fabian 1991.
6   Sometimes anthropologists are so focused on their research speciality that they deny the experiences of other local realities. Once I attended a conference in which the Zambians present time and again reported that in their research and personal experiences people valued and depended on rural links. Each time, these rural–urban linkages were denied and ridiculed by an expert on Zambia. I think that it is one thing to say that

a high percentage of Zambians live in towns but to take at face value the words of informants alienated from the rural areas seems strange. Even in Zambia the rural serve as the ultimate safety net for many urban problems.

7   See World Bank 1995.
8   See, for example, Griaule 1965 (1970); Caplan 1997; Stoller 1997; Parkin 1991.
9   See, for example, La Fontaine 1985; Lienhardt 1985; Heald 1999.
10 Hutchinson 1996.
11 Whyte 1997.
12 Parkin 1985; Willis 1985.

References

Ardener, E., 1972, 'Belief and the Problem of Women', in J. S. La Fontaine (ed.), The Interpretation of Ritual, London: Tavistock.

Bond, G. C., 1976, Politics of Change in a Zambian Community, Chicago: University of Chicago Press.

Caplan, P., 1997, African Voices, African Lives: Personal Narratives from a Swahili Village, New York: Routledge.

Cohen, D. W. and E. S. Atieno Odhiambo, 1989, Siaya: The Historical Anthropology of an African Landscape, London: James Currey.

Fabian, J., 1991, Time and the Work of Anthropology: Critical Essays, Reading: Harwood.

Fortes, M., 1938, 'Culture Contact as a Dynamic Process', in Methods of Study of Culture Contact in Africa (Memorandum 15), London: International African Institute.

Gluckman, M., 1961, 'Anthropological Problems arising from the African Industrial Revolution', in A. Southall (ed.), Social Change in Modern Africa, London: Oxford University Press, pp. 67–82.

Griaule, M., 1965, 1970, Conversations with Ogotomelli: an Introduction to Dogon Religious Ideas, London: Oxford University Press.

Heald, S., 1999, Manhood and Morality: Sex, Violence and Ritual in Gisu Society, New York: Routledge.

Hutchinson, S. E., 1996, Nuer Dilemmas: Coping with Money, War and State, Berkeley: University of California Press.

Jones, G. I., 1974, 'Social Anthropology in Nigeria during the Colonial Period', Africa, 44, 3: 280–9.

La Fontaine, J. S., 1985, 'Person and Individual: Some Anthropological Reflections', in M. Carrithers, S. Collins and S. Lukes (eds.), The Category of the Person: Anthropology, Philosophy and History, Cambridge: Cambridge University Press.

Lienhardt, G., 1985, 'Self: Public, Private: Some African Interpretations', in

M. Carrithers, S. Collins and S. Lukes (eds.), *The Category of the Person: Anthropology, Philosophy and History*, Cambridge: Cambridge University Press.

Mphahlele, E., 1962, *The African Image*, London: Faber.

Mudimbe, V. Y., 1988, *The Invention of Africa*, Bloomington: Indiana University Press.

Okot p'Bitek, 1968, *Song of Lawino*, Nairobi: Heinemann.

Parkin, D., 1985, 'Entitling Evil: Muslims and non-Muslims in Coastal Kenya', in D. Parkin (ed.), *The Anthropology of Evil*, London: Basil Blackwell.

Parkin, D., 1991, *Sacred Void*, Cambridge: Cambridge University Press.

Rodney, W., 1972, *How Europe Underdeveloped Africa*, Dar es Salaam: Tanzania Publishing House.

Roscoe, J., 1911, *The Baganda*, London: Macmillan.

Schapera, I., 1947, *Migrant Labour and Tribal Life*, London: Oxford University Press.

Schoepf, B. G., 1995, 'Culture, Sex Research and AIDS Prevention in Africa', in H. Brummelhuis and G. Herdt (eds.), *Culture and Sexual Risk*, Amsterdam: Gordon Breach Publishers.

Stoller, P., 1997, *Sensuous Scholarship*, Philadelphia: University of Pennsylvania Press.

Watson, W., 1959, 1970, 'Migrant Labour and Detribalisation', in J. Middleton (ed.), *Black Africa*, Toronto: Macmillan.

Whyte, S., 1997, *Questioning Misfortune: the Pragmatics of Uncertainty in Eastern Uganda*, Cambridge: Cambridge University Press.

Willis, R., 1985, 'Do the Fipa have a word for it?' in D. Parkin (ed.), *The Anthropology of Evil*, London: Basil Blackwell.

World Bank, 1995, *A Continent in Transition: Sub-Saharan Africa in the mid-1990s*, Washington, DC: World Bank.

8

African Pastoralism through Anthropological Eyes
Whose Crisis?

Mustafa Babiker

The driving force behind much of the anthropological research on African pastoralism is a set of powerful, widely circulated and, at times, emotional images about its future. Many anthropologists, compassionate to pastoral peoples, have repeatedly and persistently mourned the approaching end of pastoralism. In this context, any trend towards integrating herding with farming is viewed as leading to a loss of the resources necessary for the survival of pastoralism. However, such despondent predictions and the associated apprehensions about the future of pastoralism are, of course, not without precedent. In the Sudan, for example, the 1944 Soil Conservation Committee had recommended that 'where herders are in direct competition for land with cultivators, it should be the policy that the rights of the cultivator be considered paramount because his crops yield a bigger return per unit area' (cited in El Tayeb 1985: 35). This view in turn echoes that of Sir Charles Eliot, then High Commissioner to the East African Protectorate, who, more than 50 years earlier, strongly announced the demise of pastoral people in Eastern Africa, predicting that their way of life would not be sustained in the face of the advance of Western ideas and technologies; the future, Eliot firmly believed, lay with the cultivator, not with the herder (cited in Anderson 1993: 121).

Moreover, worries about the future of pastoralism were further consolidated by the observed tendency in post-colonial development policies that invariably displayed a strong bias in favour of arable cropping in terms of jurisdictional, technical and economic assistance. Official engrossment in the question of how to restrict pastoral mobility and the associated settlement plans added a further dimension to concern over the future of pastoralism. The implications of such developments for the 'traditional' systems of pastoral production and resource management were posited as critical: it was a 'crisis in survival'. The recurrence of droughts and famines in recent decades has lent great support to the prediction that pastoralism is on the verge of extinction (Baker 1977; Carr 1977; Morton 1988, 1993).

This chapter attempts to contribute to the ongoing effort to challenge what are perhaps the two major hurdles in the progress of our understanding of the dynamics of human adaptation in the African drylands. These are the persistence of 'crisis scenarios' and the insistence on a 'herder/farmer' dichotomy when the future of pastoralism is considered in the context of a resource competition and conflict problematic. The first section of the chapter questions the methodological foundations of the 'crisis scenarios'. The second section examines the processual character of the relationship between farming and herding and demonstrates how it is far too complex to be captured in a simple 'herder/farmer' dichotomy. However, I think my point will be much clearer if the reader is told how I came to be involved, and what research I have been doing, in the field of pastoral studies. It is within this autobiographical context that the issues I am raising and the arguments I am advancing can be appreciated.

The story goes back to 1982, when I was employed as a research assistant by a group of researchers (an anthropologist, a human geographer and an economist) from the University of Khartoum, commissioned by the Regional Minister of Finance (an agricultural economist) of Kordofan region to prepare a study for the establishment of a credit institution for small farmers. My assignment was confined to the collection, on the basis of a checklist prepared by the researchers, of information in the western district of Kordofan region, popularly known as Dar Hamar (that is, the home of the Hamar tribe). The checklist used for the collection of the required information displayed a clear bias towards one aspect of the Hamar livelihood strategies: farming. I completed my task by visiting a number of villages, interviewing household heads about their farming activities on the basis of that checklist. Since the senior researchers, after a one-day visit to the district, returned home with all the vehicles that had brought us, data collection was confined to those villages that are close to the highly unreliable means of public transport. Although the experience was personally enriching, I was totally deceived by my assignment, believing I was working among communities who drew their livelihoods exclusively from farming. Pastoralism was excluded from the picture. That was the time when the district was suffering the burden of below-average rainfall and successive seasons of near-total crop failure.

However, that experience encouraged me two years later (in 1984) to select Dar Hamar as a site for my proposed PhD research topic, initially framed as an investigation of the problems and prospects of agricultural cooperatives. I began fieldwork in the middle of a period when Dar Hamar was on the verge of a disaster with famine looming on the horizon. Since most households had already lost their flocks of sheep and goats through mortality and distress sales, livestock was not a topic in daily discourse. Rather, they were totally preoccupied with the issue of how to secure their staple food grain. However, the total suspension of all farming activities during that season enticed me to shift my research focus from agricultural cooperatives to the issue of desertification and its historical link with the introduction of cash crops (mainly peanuts) for export.

After completing my PhD dissertation early in 1988, I immediately had the chance to go back into the field as a consultant with a bilateral donor in the context of the burgeoning effort for rehabilitation and development that gained momentum in the wake of the drought. During that visit I met with representatives and consultants of a multilateral donor who were already conducting an appraisal exercise for a project on cooperative credit. Interestingly, that project was emphasising the revival of the production of export crops (mainly peanuts), which had been totally abandoned by local people in their post-drought strategy of directing their meagre resources to the production of their staple grains (mainly millet and sorghum). Up to that point it had never occurred to me to question my earlier characterisation of Dar Hamar households as predominantly agriculturalists. However, over the next 10 years I became a frequent visitor to Dar Hamar, participating in various commissioned studies and short-term consultancies. One of these visits was especially memorable as it was the first time I was able to travel all over the district and during the peak of the rainy season. For the first time in my association with Dar Hamar, thanks to an assignment by the West Kordofan state Minister of Agriculture, I enjoyed the use of a very reliable four-wheel-drive vehicle, without which travel in the district during the rainy season is totally impossible. During this visit I observed phenomena in the natural world and events in the social world that encouraged me to question all my earlier perceptions about the Hamar and their homeland. For example, the thick and lusty tree cover and the rich pasture associated with the successive years of above-average precipitation were reason enough to question the received wisdom concerning the irreversibility of desertification and environmental degradation. More significant to my argument, I was listening to conversations between local people of all walks of life who were discussing issues related to animal husbandry rather than crop production. Not only that, but also the cooperative credit project referred to earlier, which had emphasised export crop production, now changed its philosophy and began massive livestock restocking operations. These observations and encounters stayed in the back of my mind for a while, waiting for the opportunity to be articulated into a coherent argument.

That opportunity came in 1997 when I was invited to join a research project on resource competition and conflict between herders and farmers. In the summer of 1998, I had to visit the Institute of Social Studies in The Hague to write and present a paper to a workshop organised in conjunction with that project. I spent almost six weeks reading and reviewing the literature written on pastoralism all over the world. Two dominant themes in the literature were particularly difficult for me to subscribe to in the context of my case study: the persistence of crisis scenarios and the insistence on a herder/ farmer dichotomy when the future of pastoralism is considered in the context of resource competition and a conflict problematic. My determination not to join the bandwagon and mourn pastoralism's impending extinction delayed the completion of my paper. The fear of being thought odd during the workshop and my failure to find any inspiring ideas in the literature to articulate my argument intensified the agony of writer's block. During the weekend before the beginning of the workshop I almost lost hope of completing my paper. Luckily, that sense of despair did not last very long. The breakthrough came via an encounter in a bank in The Hague, rather than in the library. Having failed to complete my paper, I had decided to go to the bank to withdraw some money for shopping. I filled in the necessary form and gave it to the lady behind the glass window together with my passport. After having a look at my confusing bilingual passport, since all the entries are written in both English and Arabic, the lady, still looking into the passport, said: 'I can't read this!' I replied: 'Strange language, isn't it!' The lady responded: 'No! Just different!' That was the magic phrase: 'Just different.' I rushed back to my accommodation and in a few hours completed the draft of a paper entitled 'Resource Competition and Conflict: Herder/Farmer or Pastoralism-Agriculture', in which I questioned the empirical validity, the analytical utility, and the policy relevance of the herder/farmer distinction (Mustafa 2001). Encouraged, I went on to prepare a paper for the project's second workshop. In 'Dar Hamar Pastoralism: from "Crisis in Survival" to "Survival in Crisis"' I tried to chart the history of Dar Hamar pastoralism over the past two centuries, explaining why Dar Hamar at some times appeared more pastoral and at other times more agricultural and, in the process, to question the dominant, but emotional, characterisation of pastoralism in the literature as a form of production on the verge of extinction (Mustafa, forthcoming). In the remainder of this chapter I shall show how this characterisation relates to a more fundamental methodological problem associated with the very way in which anthropological research among pastoral societies has been practised in Africa.

The crisis scenarios

In recent decades increasingly optimistic scenarios about the future of pastoralism have begun to emerge. This is especially true in the case of research inspired by the revival of 'actor-oriented' perspectives and the academic reinvention of the so-called 'indigenous knowledge' systems, as opposed to different brands of structuralism, which dominated research in the 1970s. Although it is admitted that the 'pastoralists have historically experienced many cycles of herd growth and collapse, good weather and bad weather, and high and low prices for their products' (Barfield 1993: 216), the 'pastoralists have proved remarkably resilient in the face of both natural and man-made disasters and there is no reason to believe that the end of pastoralism is near' (Hogg 1992:135). Despite this optimism, gloomy scenarios are persistently adhered to by many students of pastoral societies: 'Many an anthropologist is deeply concerned about the fate of the people among who her or his work was done but still say that those people can take care of themselves. This view is nonsense: in every case that I know of, pastoralism is losing ground' (Aronson 1984: 74).

Many of the crisis scenarios are rooted in a narrative that tells how things were in earlier times when the pastoralists lived in harmony with their environments; how the state (both colonial and post-colonial), aid agencies and the herders themselves have undermined that harmony. Talk of 'harmony' is misleading, for large parts of the pastoral habitats in Africa are characterised by extremely harsh and unstable natural and social environments. The incidence of rainfall is particularly irregular in amount and is characterised by high degrees of both spatial and temporal variability. More often than not, the recurrence of droughts, epidemics and civil strife are associated with total crop failures, livestock losses and general human suffering. It is thus easy to discredit the portrayal of the African rural communities at any point in their history as completely self-sufficient and living in absolute harmony with their natural environment. African pastoral and agricultural forms of production are essentially systems characterised by incestuous instability (cf. Gartrell 1985). Their apparent persistence and survival in the face of climatic hazards and socio-political adversities is not so much dependent on the establishment of equilibrium, as on the dynamic responses facilitated by the flexibility of their resource base. These include: dynamically shifting emphasis between various forms of production; variable mobility to expand, both quantitatively and qualitatively, the scale of resource utilisation; and protean ethnic identities. Such dynamism is predicated on the exploitation of a broad resource base and the maintenance of extensive trade and trans-ethnic relationships (Niemeijer 1996: 100f.). Thus, in the rush and haste to make despondent predictions, many a student of pastoral communities has failed to notice certain processes, such as the temporary disappearance of social forms. In this way, the observed phenomena are totally depleted of their temporality and richness. This involves carefully orchestrated conditions to generate data that yield internally consistent prophesies but lack empirical reference.

The perseverance of the crisis scenarios may be attributed to the fact that they suited the interest of donor agencies and national governments to 'eternalise' various forms of planned development interventions: 'The dependence of weak African government departments on official development assistance; and the political and moral pressures on donors to be seen to respond to their domestic constituencies and to act quickly ... create a policy-making environment within which ... "crisis narratives" ... can flourish' (Leach and Mearns 1996: 23). Moreover, the herders themselves, in their attempts to secure development benefits and relief assistance, were seen by many commentators as contributing to the crisis discourse by exaggerating their actual or assumed predicament.

However, the reasons why the crisis scenarios have proved so resistant to change have to do with much more than the priorities of national government departments, the interests of the donors, or the aspirations of the herders. Rather, the reasons are rooted in a particular approach to the generation of knowledge, including the timing of observations, procedures for investigation and objectives of research: 'In virtually any discipline particular methods come to acquire credibility and authority, and it can be the inheritance of such methods ... that explains the persistence of some received ideas. By defining what is acceptable as evidence, certain privileged methods also act to exclude other sorts of data. It is in this way that certain questions remain unasked, and certain types of evidence are ignored or dismissed as invalid' (Leach and Mearns 1996: 14).

A common methodological problem in much of the literature on African drylands derives from making assumptions about the future of pastoralism on the basis of short-term observations and taking these as evidence of long-term trends, when they may simply describe one phase or a low point of some climatic cycle of aridity. In some ways, this is symptomatic of most development-oriented and donor-driven research which, based on such techniques as the so-called rapid rural appraisal (RRA), participatory rural appraisal (PRA) or participatory action research (PAR), operates within too short a time-span to be able to capture such long-term processes. As Barfield (1993: 216) puts it: 'The focus has been on what is observable in the short term and using that data to extrapolate current trends into the future.' Thus, one major methodological trap associated with the crisis scenarios is rooted in attempts to discern processes from some combination of short-term observations that give convenient and emotional, but highly misleading impressions about the destiny of pastoralism.

Another methodological trap encountered in the crisis scenarios is the tendency towards a general preoccupation with the fate of the pastoralists rather than the future of pastoralism: 'The collective future of traditional pastoralists is ... at risk in East Africa. By the end of the century [20th] they may belong merely to memory, as traditional African hunter-gatherer populations do' (Dyson-Hudson and Dyson-Hudson 1982: 213). In this way the herders are 'too easily made the symbol of a past world, representing ... a romanticist ideal of Africa's pre-modern values and aspirations, as people whose way of life should be protected against the assault of modernisation' (Anderson 1993: 122). It is therefore not particularly surprising that the anthropological defence of the herders in this context has been scornfully described as an 'ethnic preservationism' since it sounds like a call for 'a tribal reserve system in which the ethnic group is kept in a kind of living museum status' (Bennett 1988: 46). Of course, no one would agree to deliberate extinction of traditional pastoralism. This would challenge the rights of minorities for self-determination and cultural survival, and individual human rights to opportunity and freedom in respect of career preference. Yet by the same logic it would be naïve, if not hypocritical, to insist that everyone borne into a pastoral society should inevitably remain a herder. Less than 200 years ago, more than half the American population lived on farms and now less than 3 per cent do, but no one considers this to be evidence of an agricultural crisis or decline (Barfield 1993: 218).

A further methodological trap in the crisis scenarios relates to the use of the term pastoralism to designate a way of life rather than an economic activity. This designation, it has been argued, 'bears the danger of misleading the non-specialist into the belief that animal production and husbandry – herding, broadly – is all that pastoralists do. The trap is then set for outsiders to focus entirely on herding activities as they think about pastoralists' future' (Aronson 1980: 175). The fact that most rural societies in Africa have agricultural and pastoral, mainly agro-pastoral, groups, and that changing from one mode to another has been more common than believed, provides yet a further justification for our earlier call for abandoning the preoccupation with the fate of pastoral people in favour of a focus on the future of pastoralism. In this fashion it would be possible to ask questions about the ways in which pastoralism has changed to make it more or less competitive in the modern world. There is ample evidence to suggest that, rather than being static, pastoralism has adapted to new socio-economic and biophysical conditions and found a niche in the modern world. Perhaps the most significant change pastoralism is experiencing in many parts of the world is the increasing importance of raising animals for exchange rather than for sheer subsistence (Barfield 1993; Behnke 1983; Kavoori 1996).

Finally, while the anthropological literature is very rich on the various aspects of time in the societies studied, the implication of temporality for anthropologists' own findings and predictions is to some extent overlooked. In most cases the analysis tends to focus on the particular conditions of the *moment*, and is not concerned with *preceding* and *succeeding* events (Firth 1964a). Therefore many statements on the future of pastoralism, to borrow Firth's words, tend to 'rest on short-period study of what may be only a temporary, casual association; they have not been tested in terms of their observed co-variation over time' (Firth 1964b: 54).

Thus, if one reads the anthropological literature on the future of pastoralism carefully, one realises that many groups at the time of observation displayed imbalances in their local systems, and that in only a few cases have anthropologists been able to stay around long enough, or to reconstruct history adequately, to obtain evidence showing how these imbalances evolved and for how long they will persist in the future (Niemeijer 1996). Most observations were of relatively short duration and there is no detailed information available on the stability of findings over time. In this way, predicted social phenomena are considered 'as occurring empirically in a certain manner when they have not been actually observed' (Firth 1964b: 54). As Bennett once argued, 'generalisations about stability and instability in human societies need to consider the factor of time in order to obtain an accurate perspective. The tendency in cultural evolutionary thought to consider states of being at particular moments in time as sufficient evidence for generalisations about process leads to erroneous judgments' (Bennett 1976: 147f.). Thus, the credibility of predictions is enhanced by prolonged engagement and persistent observation.

Even the work of those who have been able to use a sequence of long-spaced visits to a field or setting has methodological limitations. As Firth put it: 'It is apt to be dual *synchronic* rather than truly *diachronic*, comparative at separate periods and ignorant of intervening events which might modify the interpretation of trends' (Firth 1964b: 54f., emphasis added). This is perhaps one of the reasons why Frederik Barth long ago argued that '[b]ecause of our general unwillingness to abandon well-established routines, studies explicitly addressed to the investigation of change have been prone to contain descriptions of a social system at two points in time – or even at one point in time! – and then to rely on extrapolation between the two states, or from the one state, to indicate the course of change'. Thus, 'if we want to understand social change, we need concepts that allow us to observe and describe the events of change. Our contribution as social anthropologists must lie in providing such primary materials for understanding the processes; it lies in our powers of observation out there where change is happening today, and not in producing secondary data by deduction and extrapolation' (Barth 1981: 106).

Anthropologists, therefore, need to expand their perceptual time horizons in order to make their analyses more perceptive of slow and gradual transformations as well as of very rapid change processes. Physical or social phenomena are events that take place in the world, which are more clearly explained or understood when placed in the appropriate context that brings them into sharp relief. In other words, physical and social phenomena are episodes that unfold and recur in the flow of time and are only meaningful when understood in that context; they are processes, not forms (Cupchik 2001). Thus, the fundamental goal of social science research on issues related to the future of African pastoralism should be to reveal the processes that underlie observed social phenomena.

The farming-herding continuum

The presence of the cultivating and trading pastoralists, the trading and herding farmers, and the herding and farming traders presents a challenge to the category-bound worldview that dominates the social (and natural) sciences. It is a common feature of the modern scientific enterprise to put simple labels on natural and social phenomena: to divide into classes and to separate into stages (Niemeijer 1996: 97f.). This propensity is, of course, rooted in the pervasive human tendency toward the classification of all phenomena, the general inclination 'to impose order on aspects of nature, on people's relation to nature, and on relations between people' (Kottak 1997: 342). According to Edmund Leach, '[o]ne very important feature of this ordering process is that we cut up the continua of space and time with which we are surrounded into segments' (Leach 1978: 21). Thus, we are predisposed 'to think of the environment as consisting of vast numbers of separate things belonging to named classes, and to think of the passage of time as consisting of sequences of separate events. Correspondingly, when … we construct artificial things (artefacts of all kind) … or write histories of the past, we imitate our apprehension of Nature' (ibid.). Although many phenomena are continuous rather than discrete, it is precisely because of the general tendency to impose order that we treat them as being more different than they actually are. Thus, things that are quantitatively rather than qualitatively different are made to seem absolutely dissimilar (Kottak 1997: 342). In this way, 'the flow of events in everyday life is stopped or segmented off and turned into an object or subject of inquiry' (Cupchik 2001). This act of segmentation and classification, however, is always selective: it involves breaking the flow of events in the real world and selectively focusing on this or that episode. This selectivity is therefore an immediate source of bias and distortion, since it accounts for a derived, not a real world. This path of vitalising and stereotyping description leads to concrete and limited knowledge because it does not provide an account of underlying recursive processes. Alternatively, a coherent account of the dynamics of social and physical processes is the one that accommodates the greatest number of single but interconnected episodes (*ibid.*).

The 'herder/farmer' dichotomy is an example of oppositions that reflect the general tendency to convert differences of degree into differences of kind. However, in most parts of Africa the herder/farmer distinction is progressively breaking down: farmers are investing more of their surpluses in livestock and herders are relying more on farming; they are becoming 'herder-farmers' or 'farmer-herders', terms used to describe the blurring of occupational categories previously assumed to be distinct (Toulmin 1983). In this sense herding and farming might be perceived not as sharply segmented aspects of social reality, but as processes in a continuum the polar opposites (or *ideal types*) of which are pastoralism and agriculture. In this framework, one should view herding and farming as adjustments to particular sets of ecological conditions, at given technological levels, ranging from a completely agricultural life with no herding at one extreme to pastoralism with no farming at the other. Along this continuum an infinite variety of different forms of agro-pastoralism with varying combinations of herding and farming could be found, each form adjusted to particular conditions in specific places at definite points in time, although in practice the actual number of forms would undoubtedly be substantially smaller. While individual households and groups of households located at any point in this conceptual continuum might represent stable adaptations, these adjustments should be viewed as dynamic ones that allow an individual or a group to move from point to point along the continuum as conditions change. At no time does an individual or a group cease to be a pastoralist/agriculturalist unless they give up herding/farming altogether. Thus, at the agricultural end of the continuum some individuals and groups are always dropping out of pastoralism and becoming farmers, while others are increasing the size of their herds and spending more time as pastoralists. Similarly, at the pastoral end of the continuum some individuals and groups are dropping out of agriculture and becoming herders while others are increasing the size of their land and spending more time farming.

Moreover, the recent droughts in most parts of Africa have drawn insistent new development initiatives that are invariably geared toward the revival of agriculture (seed provision programmes, animal traction, agricultural credit schemes, etcetera). In such endeavours, pastoralism is totally left out. Whether such bias is deliberate or based on false assumptions about the actual and potential economic contribution of pastoralism, both locally and nationally, the strategic reality for most rural communities in Africa is to attempt to combine herding with farming, and to sustain the linkages between the two.

One really wonders if this is an entirely new and recent phenomenon. Ibn Khaldun's *Muqqaddimah* aside, there is ample historical and ethnographic evidence to suggest that groups, and individuals within these groups, have shifted between herding and farming where and when the ecological and political-economic conditions demanded and allowed (Anderson 1988, 1989; Mustafa 2001; Haaland 1972; Khazanov 1984; Mace 1993; Spaulding 1979). This tendency contradicts the commonly held conception that man gradually but steadily moved from one form of production to another in a phased, progressive evolutionary path from hunter-gatherer to herder to farmer (Niemeijer 1996). Perhaps, however, the tendency may be better understood by reference to the distinction between what Raymond Firth (1964a: 9) calls *non-emergent* and *emergent* dynamics: the former describes a social system maintaining itself in essentially the same form, the latter one that is in process of alteration. In most cases the process of change involves the operation of forces with partial disintegrative or disruptive effects on the existing society, tending to the creation of social forms blending old and new elements (Firth 1964a). Repressed social forms never disappear completely; they continue to exist, to operate and present themselves, but in disguised forms (Godelier 2000). Moreover, the movement from one social condition to another may be reversible or irreversible, gradual or rapid; it may occur in one major institution only or in several at the same time (Firth 1964a: 7ff.). Changes in subsistence patterns occur regularly, but not in a single direction. The shift from herding to farming, for example, has been neither inevitable nor irreversible. Thus, rather than extrapolated prophesies, it is the complex interaction of natural, social, economic and political factors, operating at a specific time and in a given geographical setting, that should inform our comprehension of the dynamics of human adaptation in the African countryside.

Pastoralism and cultivation, on the ground, are therefore not discrete and static objects for academic analysis. Rather, they are dynamically interrelated and it is this very dynamism that determines the forms and outcomes of the processes of transition between herding and farming over time and in different socio-ecological settings. Groups assumed to be radically different in terms of their resource base interact with each other in a manner that enhances the survival capacity of each. They also serve to demonstrate that the movement of individuals and groups between different productive regimes is an integral part of the dynamics of African rural societies. Such processes are not immediately apparent to the anthropologists or ecologists who have only a limited-time experience of the societies and cultures they study. Their bewilderment is clearly due to the fact that the cultures they confront during fieldwork need not necessarily be adapting to conditions that prevail at the time of their visit but to more limiting conditions which have occurred, probably many times, during the past. The value of intermittent fieldwork stretching over as long a period of time as possible lies in the opportunity not only to study temporal processes, such as social and cultural change, but also to understanding the rationality of those seemingly timeless cultural arrangements embodied in ritual, belief and symbolism (Holy 1988: 150).

The position taken here should by no means be construed as a total negation of the importance of the herder/farmer dimension when one analyses issues of resource competition and conflict and their implications for the future of pastoralism. On the contrary, distinctions of this kind are legitimate enough and indeed necessary heuristic devices to some stages of inquiry, provided that they are taken as conceptual images to aid analysis, and not as representations of empirical situations (Firth 1964a). The point is that the complexity of interaction between pastoralism and farming cannot be understood adequately by basing one's inquiry on a herder/farmer dichotomy. Much of the semantic problem in this regard results from a desire to fit every group in a livelihood form that is inherently diverse into a neat pigeonhole (Johnson 1969: 17). Thus, it is clear that labels such as herder and farmer are out of place in the broad-based subsistence of many African rural communities. That is, in the African context the terms herder and farmer, like the terms rural and urban, 'are more remarkable for their ability to confuse than for their power to illuminate' (Pahl 1966: 299).

Of course, no one would dispute the right to use these terms in everyday discourse to denote different patterns of land use, which are easily discernible; what is contestable is the sociological relevance of these occupational labels, especially in societies characterised by high degrees of fluidity in their social division of labour. However, the notion of a herding-farming continuum introduced here is no more than a response to the nearly universal academic romance with polar distinctions. This should by no means be construed as a total negation of the existence of discontinuities in some instances, but these should be empirically demonstrated rather than extrapolated from predetermined narratives.

Concluding remarks

The foregoing discussion calls for a focus on disclosing disguised assumptions, especially those informing key conclusions and predictions, exposing their inconsistencies and their deficiencies, and developing new, more systematic postulates for improving our understanding of the dynamics of human adaptation in the African drylands. As Maurice Godelier argues: 'Searching out the implicit exclusions in an analysis, the silences in an argument, the omissions in an observation are necessary steps in the unfolding of any knowledge-seeking activity' (Godelier 2000: 309, *emphasis added*). Thus revealing the elements implicitly excluded from analysis, the silences in a reasoning process, and the blind spots in observation, is indispensable if we are 'to flush out any lurking prejudices … that might have influenced the choice of data, their interpretation and their formulation' (Godelier 2000: 308f.).

In laboratories, scientists can eliminate the effects of intruding exogenous variables and carefully simplify the complexity of real processes. The real world of social life offers no such control and opportunity. This is simply because, in the social world, phenomena are difficult to observe as they are not restricted to sense data but involve the application of judgment (Cupchik 2001). Thus, the partial character of many accounts of the future of pastoralism could be attributed to the conscious or unconscious exclusions of phenomena or people observed: the repression, silencing, displacement and disguising of many aspects of social reality. In many ways this shortcoming is a legacy of the positivist methodologies so entrenched in the social sciences.

Along these lines this chapter has laboured to demonstrate that, far from being in decline, pastoralism may be securing its long-term survival through forceful responses to a dynamic natural and social environment. Over the centuries, African dryland pastoralism has developed into systems that are not stable and balanced but rather extremely diverse, dynamic and flexible. This dynamism finds expression in the active responses of African rural societies to the shifting opportunities and constraints of the physical and social environment, as well as the creative effort to harness new economic opportunities and generally remoulding their productive regimes, in both the short and long term. Secure pastoral systems are those able to link with economic activities occupying other niches, where alternative production regimes compensate for the loss of livestock. Although pastoralism has gone through noticeable vacillations, the basis of this dynamic relationship in most African drylands has remained remarkably stable over time. Pastoralism has thrived, declined and flourished again as periods of ecological disaster and/or civil strife have set in and then retreated (Anderson 1993). Flexibility and adaptability (a broad resource base with repeatedly shifting emphasis between its various components) have been central features in the resilience of African dryland pastoralism.

Pastoralism and farming in most African drylands can thus no longer be considered as total ways of life; instead we should see them as technical activities, whose role in the local economy has always been ascending or descending, both in absolute terms and relative to each other. In most cases, the movement between pastoralism and farming is a voluntary response to changing constraints and opportunities in the biophysical and socio-economic environments. For example, during drier periods most African dryland economies appeared to be predominantly agricultural, and in the wet phases looked more pastoral. Thus the movement between pastoralism and agriculture is a two-way process in the sense that it is not necessarily unidirectional or irreversible. Moreover, such changes in orientation of activities from more to less pastoral, and more to less agricultural, are often shifts of emphasis between patterns present in the local economy, rather than a radical transformation from one activity to another.

However, the position taken here should in no way be construed as a negation of the fact that pastoralism has always been experiencing massive transformation. On the contrary, the main feature of African dryland pastoralism in the beginning of the twenty-first century is rooted in the intensification of livestock concentration within a network controlled by economic agents who are for the most part from outside the local communities (commercial banks, livestock traders, bureaucrats). However, this in itself has not fundamentally transformed the internal organisation of the pastoral economy. What is happening is that new external technical factors, such as technological innovations, commercial credit facilities, intensification of veterinary care, and secured water supplies, are all combined to facilitate the imposition of a modern marketing operation on an essentially traditional pastoral production system.

Of course, it is impossible to grasp these dynamics through synchronic case studies whereby phenomena are dealt with at one point in time while totally ignoring previous historical developments. Instead, what is required is a diachronic approach to the historical development of phenomena whereby material from various periods is examined and analysed (Niemeijer 1996). A diachronic study of the history of African dryland pastoralism reveals that many of our prophesies about its future are invalid. African dryland communities are not sluggish and enervated; rather, they dynamically and innovatively respond to the caprices of their social and physical environments. One legitimate response in this context, perhaps, is to abandon pastoralism altogether. This is a trajectory only the concerned people have the right to make the decision about. Why should the people we label pastoralists remain pastoralists?

References

Anderson, D. M., 1988, 'Cultivating Pastoralists: Ecology and Economy among the Il Chamus of Baringo, 1840–1980', in D. H. Johnson and D. M. Anderson (eds.), *The Ecology of Survival: Case Studies from Northeast African History*, London: Lester Crook Academic Publishing, pp. 241–60.

—— 1989, 'Agriculture and Irrigation Technology at Lake Baringo in the Nineteenth Century', *Azania*, 24: 84–97.

—— 1993, 'Cow Power: Livestock and the Pastoralists in Africa', *African Affairs*, 92, 366:121–33.

Aronson, D. R., 1980, 'Must Nomads Settle? Some Notes toward Policy on the Future of Pastoralism', in P. C. Salzman (ed.), *When Nomads Settle:*

Processes of Sedentarization as Adaptation and Response, New York: Praeger Publishers, pp. 173–84.

—— 1984, 'Pastoralism in Contemporary Development Perspective', *Nomadic Peoples*, 16: 73–83.

Baker, R., 1977, 'Polarization: Stages in the Environmental Impact of Alien Ideas on a Semi-Pastoral Society', in P. O'Keefe and B. Wisner (eds.), *Land Use and Development*, London: International African Institute, pp. 152–70.

Barfield, T. J., 1993, *The Nomadic Alternative*, Englewood Cliffs, NJ: Prentice-Hall.

Barth, F., 1981, 1967, 'On the Study of Social Change', in *Process and Form in Social Life: Selected Essays of Frederik Barth*, Vol. 1, London: Routledge and Kegan Paul, pp.105–18.

Behnke, R. H., 1983, 'Production Rationales: the Commercialisation of Subsistence Pastoralism', in *Nomadic Peoples*, 14: 3–34.

Bennett, J. W., 1976, *The Ecological Transition: Cultural Anthropology and Human Adaptation*, New York: Pergamon Press.

—— 1988, 'The Political Economy and Economic Development of Migratory Pastoralist Societies in Eastern Africa', in D. W. Attwood, T. C. Bruneau and J. G. Galaty (eds.), *Power and Poverty: Development and Development Projects in the Third World*, Boulder, CO: Westview Press, pp. 31–60.

Carr, C. J., 1977, 'Pastoralism in Crisis: the Dasanetch and Their Ethiopian Lands', Research Paper No. 180, Department of Geography, University of Chicago.

Cupchik, G., 2001, 'Constructivist Realism: an Ontology that Encompasses Positivist and Constructivist Approaches to the Social Sciences', *FQS-Forum: Qualitative Social Research*, 2, 1.

Dyson-Hudson, N. and R. Dyson-Hudson, 1982, 'The Structure of East African Herds and the Future of East African Herders', *Development and Change*, 13: 213–38.

El-Tayeb, G. E. (ed.), 1985, 'Gedaref District Area Study', Khartoum: Institute of Environmental Studies.

Firth, R., 1964a, 'Comments on "Dynamic Theory" in Social Anthropology', in R. Firth, *Essays in Social Organisation and Values*, London: Athlone Press, pp. 7–29.

—— 1964b, 'Social Organisation and Social Change', in R. Firth, *Essays in Social Organisation and Values*, London: Athlone Press, pp. 30–58.

Gartrell, B., 1985, 'Searching for "the Roots of Famine": the Case of Karamoja', *Review of African Political Economy*, 33:102–9.

Godelier, M., 2000, 'Is Anthropology Still Worth the Trouble? A Response to Some Echoes from America', *Ethnos*, 65, 3: 301–16.

Haaland, G., 1972, 'Nomadisation as an Economic Career among the Sedentaries of the Sudan Savannah Belt', in I. Cunnison and W. James (eds.), *Essays in Sudan Ethnography*, London: C. Hurst, pp. 149–72.

Hogg, R., 1992, 'Should Pastoralism Continue as a Way of Life?' *Disasters*, 16: 131–37.

Holy, L., 1988, 'Cultivation as a Long-Term Strategy of Survival: the Berti of Darfur', in D. H. Johnson and D. M. Anderson (eds.), *The Ecology of Survival: Case Studies from Northeast African History*, London: Lester Crook Academic Publishing, pp. 135–54.

Johnson, D. L., 1969, 'The Nature of Nomadism: a Comparative Study of Pastoral Migrations in Southwestern Asia and North Africa', Research Paper No. 118, Department of Geography, University of Chicago.

Kavoori, P. S., 1996, 'Pastoralism in Expansion: the Transhuming Sheep Herders of Western Rajasthan', unpublished PhD dissertation, Institute of Social Studies, The Hague.

Khazanov, A. M., 1984, *Nomads and the Outside World*, Cambridge: Cambridge University Press.

Kottak, C. P., 1997, *Anthropology: the Exploration of Human Diversity*, New York: McGraw-Hill Companies Inc.

Leach, E., 1978,1970, *Lévi-Strauss*, London: Fontana.

Leach, M. and R. Mearns, 1996, 'Environmental Change and Policy: Challenging Received Wisdom in Africa', in M. Leach and R. Mearns (eds.), *The Lie of the Land: Challenging Received Wisdom on the African Environment*, London: James Currey Publishers, pp. 1–33.

Mace, R., 1993, 'Transition between Cultivation and Pastoralism in Sub-Saharan Africa', *Current Anthropology*, 34, 4: 363–82.

Morton, J., 1988, *The Decline of Lahawin Pastoralism*, Pastoral Development Network, paper 25c, London: Overseas Development Institute.

—— 1993, 'Pastoral Decline and Famine: the Beja Case', in J. Markakis (ed.), *Conflict and the Decline of Pastoralism in the Horn of Africa*, London: Macmillan, pp. 30–44.

Mustafa, B., 2001, 'Resource Competition and Conflict: Herder/Farmer or Pastoralism-Agriculture?' in M. A. M. Salih, T. Dietz and A. G. M. Ahmed (eds.), *Pastoralism in Africa: Conflict, Institutions and Government*, London: Pluto Press, pp. 134–44.

—— forthcoming, *Dar Hamar pastoralism: from 'Crisis in Survival' to 'Survival in Crisis'*. Addis Ababa: OSSREA.

Niemeijer, D., 1996, 'The Dynamics of African Agricultural History: Is It Time for a New Development Paradigm?' *Development and Change*, 27, 1: 87–110.

Pahl, R. E., 1966, 'The Rural–Urban Continuum', *Sociologia Ruralis*, 6, 4: 299–329.

Spaulding, J., 1979, 'Farmers, Herdsmen and the State in Rainlands Sinnar', *Journal of African History*, 20: 329–47.

Toulmin, C., 1983, *Herders and Farmers or Farmer-Herders and Herder-Farmers*, Pastoral Development Network, paper no. 15d, London: Overseas Development Institute.

9

An Invisible Religion?
Anthropology's Avoidance of Islam in Africa

Robert Launay

A prominent French anthropologist once confessed to me that his
mentors had warned him against studying Muslims in West
Africa. Muslims, he was told, were just not 'authentic' enough;
'authenticity', by that time, had euphemistically replaced 'primitive-
ness' without effacing what Johannes Fabian (1983) has called the
denial of coevalness. Such an omission is indeed a glaring one. There
are now over 200,000,000 Muslims in sub-Saharan Africa, a very
sizeable proportion of the entire population, especially (but hardly
exclusively) in West Africa. This Islamic presence is in no way a recent
phenomenon, but rather represents over a millennium of history.[1] As
it happened, the very period during which anthropologists began
systematic programmes of field research in Africa was a time of
unparalleled Islamic expansion. Anthropologists' failure to come to
terms with Islam in Africa (and, in large measure, with Christianity as
well) was hardly an accidental omission but rather, as my colleague
admitted, a very deliberate policy.

Arguably, there existed a tacit partition of African realities among
academics, with anthropologists appropriating the study of 'authentic'
Africans with genuinely 'traditional' religions while the study of
African Muslims, those whose pristine authenticity had apparently
been violated, was left to historians if not to 'Orientalists'.

Paradoxically, the earliest French anthropologists were not nearly
so reluctant to acknowledge the existence and importance of Muslims
and of Islam. The first self-consciously ethnographic studies of
African cultures (as distinct from descriptive passages in explorers'
narratives) were conducted by a cadre of scholar-administrators in the

early twentieth century.[2] As administrators, they were concerned with acquiring first-hand practical knowledge about the peoples over whom they were attempting to rule, including Muslims. Disciplinary boundaries were in any case still relatively fluid, and the contributions of these scholars bridged linguistics, history and geography as well as ethnography. Admittedly, the quality of the work was extremely variable, and many of the administrators were dilettantes at best; others, most notably Maurice Delafosse, cannot be so easily dismissed.[3] Delafosse began his African career in southern Côte d'Ivoire in the last decade of the nineteenth century, among the Agni and the Baule, simultaneously attempting to suppress a Baule revolt while publishing on the language, history and social organisation of the region.[4] After his transfer to the less restive north of the colony, he published the first (and unquestionably the best) colonial monograph on the Senufo in a journal edited by the noted anthropologist Arnold Van Gennep.[5] Although these early ethnographic works contain relatively few references to Islam and to Muslims, Delafosse was in fact thoroughly trained in Arabic, studying the language at the École des Langues Orientales under Octave Houdas, whose daughter he married. Later, he collaborated with Houdas on the translation of the *Tarikh el-Fattach*, the Timbuktu cleric Mahmud Kati's seventeenth-century chronicle of the Songhai empire. This first-hand knowledge of Islamic historical sources was a critical element of Delafosse's magnum opus, *Haut-Sénégal-Niger* (1912), a three-volume survey of the geography, history and anthropology of what is now Mali. Nor was Delafosse the only administrator/anthropologist to concern himself with Muslim peoples. Charles Monteil, for example, published a detailed study of the famous Muslim trading city of Djenne in 1903, before publishing ethnographic monographs about the Khassonke and the Bambara.

However, the French administration was not prepared to have its Muslim policy dictated by the ethnographic preoccupations of district administrators. Prior experiences in Algeria, where Islam had very definitely served to mobilise resistance to colonial rule, left the French perennially suspicious of, if not always antipathetic to, Islam.[6] The administration kept virtually all Muslim clerics under surveillance, keeping files which were synthesised by Delafosse's contemporary, Paul Marty, in a series of detailed studies on Islam in different French West African colonies. These studies among others led to the formulation of the idea that there existed an *Islam noir*, a specifically

Africanised variety of Islam, a dilution of the 'pure' (and more dangerous) religion with traditional African beliefs and practices. However comforting this illusion may have been for French administrators who felt that they no longer had to fret about the Islamic peril, it had disastrous consequences for the anthropological study of Islam in French colonial Africa. Once 'African Islam' could be reduced to its component parts – Arab Islam and African 'fetishism' – then the study of Islam could properly be left to Orientalists, leaving to anthropologists the task of decoding more 'authentically' African beliefs and practices.

In any case, the kind of anthropology practised by Delafosse and his cohort was doomed in the long run, a victim of attacks from all sides. Colonial authorities were increasingly impatient with district administrators who spent too much time pursuing academic inquiries rather than implementing administrative policy. At the same time, the growing professionalisation of academia in the context of universities increasingly relegated scholar-administrators to the status of dilettantes whose first-hand knowledge of the terrain could not quite make up for inadequate theoretical training. The Dakar-Djibouti Mission (1931–3) under the leadership of Marcel Griaule marked the eclipse of the era of scholar-administrators and the triumph of academic anthropology under the aegis of Griaule himself.

The Dakar-Djibouti Mission was Griaule's first encounter with the Dogon, who were to become the subject of his life's work.[7] Griaule's approach was characterised by the quest for esoteric initiatory knowledge. In his *Conversations with Ogotomelli* (1970 [1948]) he describes a series of 33 sessions during which a Dogon elder gradually unfolded a vast mytho-cosmological system encompassing the key features of their esoteric knowledge. Griaule's students, notably Germaine Dieterlen and Dominique Zahan, set themselves to discovering and describing comparable systems among the neighbouring Bambara. It must be stressed that this was a profoundly humanistic project, an attempt to demonstrate that African systems of thought were by no means primitive and illogical, but on the contrary highly systematic, elaborate and sophisticated. But for this very reason, it was essential to the project to depict these systems as authentically African, uncontaminated by either European or Islamic influences. As Amselle (1998: Chapter 7) has aptly pointed out, such a presentation erases the impact of centuries of interaction between African Muslims and their non-Islamic neighbours, to the extent that it is extremely difficult (and, more important, probably quite pointless) to attempt to disengage Islamic from pre-Islamic features of West African cosmologies. For example, one of Griaule's sessions with Ogotomelli details Dogon ideas about the constellations of the zodiac. However, the zodiac is by no means a self-evident intellectual construct; rather, it is a Mesopotamian invention which was clearly diffused to West Africa along Muslim trade routes.[8] What is more, Griaule's system not only ignored the deeper interaction between Dogon and Islamic thought, but also the more recent history of the Dogon. In fact, the Dogon were allies of the *jihad* leader al-Hajj Umar in his campaign against another Islamic state, the Fulbe empire of Macina. While the Umarian state made few deliberate attempts to convert the Dogon, Islam (and Christianity as well) were making significant inroads among the 'pristine' Dogon by the time Griaule was conducting his field research.

Ultimately, the Griaulist project portrayed African cosmologies as pristine works of art, to be contemplated and admired by European audiences. It was also profoundly idealist. To the extent that the physical realities of everyday life entered into Griaule's account, it was as reflections of an underlying mythical system. Weaving, black-smithing and even farming were depicted as deeply symbolic forms of activities, paralleling aspects of the primeval act of creation.

Contemporary British approaches to anthropology in Africa were, not surprisingly, more down to earth. Structural-functionalism was concerned with examining the properties of societies as quasi-organic functioning wholes, whose unwritten rules were effectively maintained by the ebb and flow of the everyday actions of groups and individuals. From such a perspective, 'tribes without rulers'[9] constituted a particularly important theoretical challenge, an occasion to demonstrate how social order could be maintained in the absence of central authority. Accordingly, British anthropologists tended to focus on small-scale societies and the central role of the application of kinship norms. Ancestor cults best exemplified the operation of the system in the religious domain. Such small-scale societies were often in close (though not always amicable) contact with Muslims; the Nuer and the Tallensi both come to mind in this regard, but they were not to any extent Islamised. This is not to say that their religious systems, like that of the Dogon, may not have been influenced in fundamental ways by Islamic concepts and practices. However, unlike the French anthropologists who were concerned with the authentic

Africanity of the religions they studied, their British colleagues focused on the way in which religious systems operated and tended to bracket questions of origin. In any case, even when British anthropologists undertook the analysis of African state systems, most of the societies they described were located in southern Africa, remote from Islamic influences: Tswana (Schapera), Zulu and Lozi (Gluckman), Swazi (Kuper), Bemba (Richards). In West Africa, the work of Meyer Fortes among the Ashanti was almost exclusively confined to the domain of kinship. But even M. G. Smith's study of *Government in Zazzau* (1960) – an Islamic emirate – pays relatively scant attention to Islam (listed in the index as 'Muhammadan religion'!).

This is not to say that all structural-functionalists were ignorant of, much less oblivious of Islam. Indeed, Evans-Pritchard's *The Sanusi of Cyrenaica* (1949) is perhaps the first anthropological monograph to concern itself centrally, not only with Muslims but with Islam as a religion. Admittedly, the title itself hardly betrays this concern to anyone previously unfamiliar with the Sanusiyya. The uninformed might easily be beguiled into imagining that the Sanusi of Cyrenaica are just another 'tribe' like the Nuer of southern Sudan. Instead, as Evans-Pritchard admittedly points out in the first sentence of the book, the Sanusiyya is a Sufi brotherhood, an explicitly religious Islamic organisation. Even so, Evans-Pritchard's primary analytical focus was more social-structural, and in particular political, than religious. First, he sought to demonstrate how the Sanusi had managed to establish a trans-Saharan network of lodges strategically situated along lucrative trade routes in the interstices of tribal Bedouin society, whereby religious authorities attracted the loyalty of the desert nomads by mediating tribal conflicts. Second, he showed how these loyalties were effectively mobilised by the Sanusi in order to mount an extremely effective, if ultimately unsuccessful, resistance to the Italian occupation of Libya. In this way, his work on the Sanusi, like his study of the Nuer, examined the ways in which social order might be maintained in the absence of centralised governmental authority. Curiously enough, given Evans-Pritchard's personal religious convictions and sensibilities, as evidenced in his monograph on *Nuer Religion* (1956), by and large Islam was treated as epiphenomenal in his Sanusi ethnography.

The work of S. F. Nadel in the Kingdom of Nupe constituted another outstanding exception to the structural-functionalists' avoidance of Islam. After all, Nupe's rulers had converted to Islam even before the kingdom succumbed to the Sokoto *jihad* in the early nineteenth century. Indeed, Nadel's (1954) monograph *Nupe Religion* included an entire chapter on 'Islam in Nupe'. But this is also the last chapter (except for the conclusion), the appendix to a fuller discussion of 'traditional' religious beliefs and practices onto which Islam, it would seem, had been grafted to produce a syncretic mix.

For obvious reasons, American anthropologists began to study African cultures much later than their French and British colleagues; simply put, the United States had no African colonies. On the other hand, the theoretical focus on cultural diffusion which, thanks to Franz Boas, had infused American anthropology might have seemed *a priori* more amenable to the study of Islam in Africa than the French quest for an authentically African cosmological system or the British emphasis on the systematic functioning of relatively small-scale and (apparently) self-contained societies. Indeed, it was this very issue of cultural diffusion which attracted Boas's student Melville Herskovits, the pioneer of American anthropological interest in Africa. For Herskovits, however, the diffusion of African culture to the New World constituted the raison d'être for his African research, notably his studies of the kingdom of Dahomey. The diffusion of Islamic ideas to Africa was out of his purview. His student, Joseph Greenberg, wrote an early monograph on Bori spirit cults among the Hausa entitled *The Influence of Islam on a Sudanese Religion* (1946). However, as the title suggests, Islam and 'African religion' are implicitly depicted as independently constituted entities; Islam is presented as an external influence, not as a constituent component of African religions *per se*.

All in all, French academic anthropology during the colonial period, especially as practised by Griaule and his students, in its quest for authentic and coherent African systems of thought, was least open to the study of Islam and its impact in Africa. At best, Islamic ideas were reconfigured in African terms to produce an *Islam noir*, a 'black Islam', which was ostensibly as profoundly African as it was superficially Islamic. At worst, Islam was frankly considered as a menace, a threat to the integrity of the wonderful cosmologies which, in their eyes, constituted works of art. However different the projects of American cultural and British social anthropologies were, neither was conceptually averse to taking Islam into account. Even so, and as we have seen with some notable exceptions, Islam tended to be peripheral to their understanding of African cultures and societies.

Decolonisation had profound effects on the nature of anthropological understandings of Africa, whether British, French, American or, at long last, African. The fact that anthropologists began to show serious interest in Muslim societies, if not in Islam, must certainly count as one of the most unanticipated consequences. In the first place, decolonisation made it blatantly apparent that African societies, no matter how small-scale, were in no way self-contained. Of course, reading their work carefully, one realises that an earlier generation of Africanist anthropologists had never been unaware of the fact; the depiction of societies in equilibrium was arguably a heuristic device rather than a reflection of deeply held convictions. Be this as it may, the political ferment leading up to and following decolonisation rendered such heuristic fictions increasingly unconvincing, not to mention, as means of understanding present circumstances, irrelevant.

Perhaps because French colonial anthropology had been the most radically idealist, the most divorced from the day-to-day realities of African life, the pendulum was to swing most radically in France, where for a while Marxist materialism prevailed as a radical antidote to the errors of the past, political as well as intellectual. It may seem paradoxical that Marxist anthropologists might be attracted to the study of Muslim societies; arguably, from a Marxist perspective, religion would appear to be at best superstructural, at worst a form of false consciousness. (Some Marxist anthropologists resisted – at times tortuously – the temptation to succumb to such a mechanistic analysis of religion.) In fact, it was precisely their renewed attention to the economic 'infrastructure' of African societies that obliged French Marxist Africanists to engage with the study of Muslims. In fact, throughout the West African Sahelian and Sudanic zones, long-distance commerce had been firmly ensconced in the hands of Islamic trading networks. For example, Jean-Loup Amselle (1977) studied the Kooroko, a group who had originally been hereditary blacksmiths in the Wassulu region of Mali but who had managed in the course of the twentieth century to achieve dominant roles in the kola trade between Bamako and Bouake, in Côte d'Ivoire. Amselle devotes a chapter of his monograph to 'Religious Ideology', in which he discusses the underlying reasons why Kooroko have been attracted to an Islamic reform movement which was (misleadingly) labelled 'Wahhabi' by the French. Admittedly, the very terminology of 'religious ideology' suggests that Amsell's concern was not to analyse

Islam on its own terms. However, the argument was not nearly as mechanistic as this may seem, and pointed to important ways in which the anthropological study of Islam in Africa might develop. In the first place, it is significant to note that Amselle chose to study a group whose 'modern' identity was entirely distinct from its traditional status, in economic and social as well as religious terms. Their traditional and hereditary occupation as smiths conditioned the nature of their interrelationship with neighbouring groups, whereas their entry into the ranks of the merchant élite necessitated a thoroughgoing transformation of social relationships with outsiders. Such a transformation, Amselle suggested, involved conversion to Islam in the first place (essential for anyone entering into that sector of the economy), but also a choice between competing Islamic trends. The intrinsic foreignness or Africanity of such Islamic trends was simply not an issue, nor was Islam depicted as a unitary, much less unified, body of doctrine.

Such theoretical and empirical interest in African merchant communities was not necessarily restricted to anthropologists who were either French or Marxist. The theoretical orientations of Anglo-Saxon anthropologists during the colonial period had in no way excluded a concern with economic relations. Admittedly, the depiction of societies or cultures as relatively self-contained tended to draw attention away from groups such as merchants, whose livelihoods depended precisely on bridging disparate social or cultural entities. Even so, when these anthropologists began to pay serious attention to Muslim merchants, this represented a readjustment of focus rather than, as in France, a radical change of approach. For example, Abner Cohen (1969) described the community of Hausa migrants in Ibadan, detailing the practices by which they maintained their monopolies over the long-distance trades in cattle and in kola. Cohen was particularly interested in the maintenance of ethnic boundaries, in the ways in which Hausa immigrants demarcated themselves from the Yoruba majority in the town as a means of maintaining their ethnic monopoly over certain sectors of the economy. As a matter of fact, the Yoruba community included large numbers of Muslims as well as Christians, and so Islam in itself did not distinguish one ethnic community from the other. As a result, Cohen argued, Hausa in Ibadan affiliated themselves with the Tijaniyya, a particular Sufi brotherhood, in this way perpetuating the boundary between their community and Yoruba Muslims. Cohen's argument, though not framed in Marxist terms, offered a similar kind of argument: economic relations (in this case the preservation of a strategic trade monopoly) dictated the preservation of a specific ethnic boundary, which was in turn reflected by Sufi brotherhood affiliations. One way or the other, religion in general and Islam in particular were in large measure depicted as epiphenomenal.

My first monograph on the Dyula of Côte d'Ivoire (Launay 1982) was virtually the inverse of the scenario that Amselle had detailed for the Kooroko. I studied a population that had enjoyed a regional trade monopoly in the nineteenth century, which it had lost in the course of the twentieth, and indeed which (for the most part at least) rejected the 'Wahhabi' ideology of reform as adamantly as the Kooroko espoused it. Like Cohen, I was concerned with the complex (though not straightforwardly epiphenomenal) relationship between Islamic practice and ethnic identity.

Not all of this mini-surge of anthropological interest in Islam in Africa focused exclusively on merchant communities. Jean Copans (1980), notably, studied the role of the Murid brotherhood in the organisation of peanut production in Senegal. Jack Goody's interest in Islam was not as intimately related to the study of a particular society as it was to the broader understanding of West Africa as a region and indeed of its place within broader global systems. Very broadly, he proposed a model of West African Sudanic state systems in terms of 'estates': an aristocratic warrior cavalry; a Muslim estate of merchants and clerics; commoners; and slaves.[10] The characterisation of hierarchy in terms of 'estates' rather than 'classes' was deliberate. For Goody, in pre-colonial sub-Saharan Africa, the prevalence of horticulture as opposed to plod agriculture precluded the development of class differences based on the ownership of means of production. Conversely, the nature of state systems depended more integrally on means of destruction – horses in the grasslands as opposed to guns in the forest zones where, because of tsetse, horses could not survive. At the same time, Goody's interest in literacy and writing systems led him to focus on the impact of Islamic writing on neighbouring, non-Muslim societies (Goody 1968), simultaneously challenging the notions that so-called traditional African religions were impervious to outside influences as well as the suggestion that the use of Arabic writing for 'magical' purposes was in any way an Africanisation of Islam, a characteristic of *Islam noir* rather than of Islam throughout the Muslim world.

Admittedly, all of these studies focused on 'Muslim societies' (or at least societies with important Muslim minorities) rather than on 'Islam' per se. But it was difficult to engage in the ethnographic description and analysis of these Muslim societies without paying substantial attention to religious issues, especially when – as was very often the case – these issues were controversial and absorbed the attention of the people in question. Most important, they represented a clear theoretical departure (more explicitly in the case of French, rather than Anglo-Saxon, ethnographies) from their immediate colonial predecessors. The willingness to engage with Islam was symptomatic of more general (and no doubt more important) shifts. First, they challenged the salience of the quest for African 'authenticity'. The realm of religion and cosmology was the prima facie location of any such 'authenticity'; the domains of kinship, political organisation, or economics were intrinsically more amenable to sociological inquiry and as such less culturally specific. Second, they expanded the scope of inquiry from relatively small-scaled and seemingly self-contained social units to focus instead on wider regional fields of interaction. Obviously, Muslim societies in Africa could not by their very nature be self-contained; they were part of the Muslim world, one which extended beyond continental, much less regional borders. Last and, I would argue, most importantly, they focused close theoretical attention on historical processes. They rejected the heuristic utility of apparently timeless synchronic analysis. On the contrary, the very questions which focused their attention revolved around the analysis of concrete historical changes in the societies which they studied. Obviously, none of these developments was in any way specific to the anthropology of Muslim societies in Africa, but it is fair to say that those studied not only reflected but indeed epitomised general changes in the discipline as a whole.

Paradoxically, the search for 'authenticity' so central to colonial anthropology was occasionally echoed by certain European-trained African scholars who employed such an ideology in a different political and social context. For example, Sinali Coulibaly's generally excellent study of the Senufo peasantry of northern Côte d'Ivoire uses colonial ethnographic sources to draw a sharp contrast between the Senufo and their Muslim neighbours, 'les Dioula, antithèse du Sénoufo (the Dyula, antithesis of the Senufo)' (Coulibaly 1978: 54). By drawing such a sharp contrast between 'traditional' peasants and Muslim traders, Coulibaly was not so much advocating ethnic exclusiveness but instead reacting to the Islamisation of much of the Senufo population, a blurring of the very distinctions at the heart of his argument. In a very different vein, recent political rhetoric in a divided Côte d'Ivoire is evidence of the persistence of colonial anthropological discourses of 'authenticity' and their use as ideologies of ethnic exclusion.

In any case, a full-blown anthropology of Islam began to emerge outside of Africanist circles. Its inception was heralded by Clifford Geertz's *Islam Observed* (1968), whose title aggressively called attention to the fact that Islam was its focus of study, as opposed to earlier works such as Evans-Pritchard's study of the Sanusi or, for that matter, Geertz's previous work on Java, whose titles only implied their Islamic emphases to cognoscenti. Until then, anthropologists had (if only tacitly) left the study of Islam as a religion to 'Orientalist' experts.[11] I certainly cannot assert that anthropologists in general, much less Geertz in particular, have entirely freed themselves of the epistemological failings of 'Orientalism'. Even so, Geertz's willingness to assert that anthropology had something distinctive to add to the study of Islam as a religion was, at the time, a daring move. His tactic was to contrast Islam in Morocco and in Indonesia which 'both incline toward Mecca but ... bow in opposite directions (*ibid.*: 4)'. This is not the place to evaluate Geertz's contribution in the light of his numerous critics. However debatable his conclusions, he very definitely set an agenda for the anthropological study of Islam: the analysis of variation in Islamic belief and practice over space and time as well as within Muslim communities, especially given the tremendous ideological emphasis within Islam on its quintessential oneness. Not surprisingly, in the wake of Geertz's work, Morocco and Indonesia became the privileged sites for anthropologists (most especially from the United States) interested in Islam.

Africanist anthropologists were relatively slow to respond to the call. The very first contribution was a strikingly original if rather atypical book, El Zein's (1974) study of Islam in Lamu, Kenya. Labelling itself a structural analysis, the book makes more specific reference to Claude Lévi-Strauss than to Geertz, while its Malinowskian emphasis on myth as sociological charter also calls to mind Edmund Leach's approach. El Zein's analysis is centered on a process squarely situated in the history of Lamu, the supplanting of the traditional Swahili élite, the Wangwana, by sharifs from

Hadramaut (modern Yemen) in the early twentieth century. He contrasts Wangwana and Hadrami interpretations of the myths of creation as well as the ways in which mythical constructs are anchored in ritual performances in Wangwana as opposed to Hadrami mosques. The kind of structuralist analysis which El Zein employs has admittedly tended to fall out of fashion. This in no way detracts from the importance of his focus on differences in discourse (though not necessarily in doctrine!) and practice (especially ritual) between different segments of a single Islamic community in Africa, analysed diachronically and not simply synchronically. Unfortunately, El Zein's study remained unique for at least a decade, at least as far as sub-Saharan Africa is concerned.[12] More recently, anthropologists have begun to focus again on Islamic diversity in historical and political-economic perspective within the confines of local communities, for example the town of Korhogo in Côte d'Ivoire (Launay 1992) or Nioro du Sahel in Mali (Soares, in press).

The anthropology of Islam has also led to a systematic re-evaluation of the boundary between Islam and 'traditional' religion in Africa. In particular, cults of spirit possession – once considered the hallmark of pre-Islamic religious survivals in Muslim societies and of the essential syncretism of 'African Islam' – have now been placed squarely within their Islamic context. In particular, the zar cults of Sudan and Somalia have been the focus of several detailed studies which place them securely within the orbit of Islamic discourse and practice, even if certain Muslims dismiss them as un-Islamic.[13] Adopting a somewhat different approach, Lambeck (1993) includes spirit possession within a wider umbrella of different forms of Islamic knowledge in Mayotte, alongside divination and Koranic instruction. (Studies of spirit possession in West African Muslim societies have, alas, not always demonstrated the same level of sophistication, and still tend to treat the phenomenon as non- if not anti-Islamic.) In a very different vein, Shaw's remarkable study (2002) of ritual ideology and practice among the Temne of Sierra Leone, among Muslims and non-Muslims alike, shows how profoundly religious beliefs and practices, especially divination, were moulded by centuries of the slave trade. Specifically, she examines the historical circumstances in which Islamic systems of divination have been incorporated into Temne religious preoccupations with safety and closure as a response to predatory incursions and political instability.

All in all, the paradigm shift – from the colonial focus on 'authentically' African small-scale (only apparently!), self-contained societies frozen in time to post-colonial emphases on broader inter-related units, adapting to shifts in regional, national and global political economies in historical time before, during and after the colonial period – has obviously changed the ways in which anthro-pologists have taken Islam into account. Instead of being seen as an external, if not disruptive, factor in African societies, it has finally been acknowledged as a complex, differentiated and historically changing, but also integral, aspect of African realities. However, it remains true that the anthropology of Islam in Africa is largely in the hands of outsiders, scholars who are neither African nor Muslim. There are, fortunately, outstanding exceptions: Kagabo's (1988) study of Muslim minorities in Rwanda, and Ibrahim's (1994) depiction of the tension between folk performance and *shari'ah*-mindedness among the Rubatab of Sudan.

I suspect that this relative paucity of African voices is due to the fact that anthropology as a discipline was so slow to engage with Islam (or, for that matter, with Christianity), especially in Africa. The study of Islam in Africa was, for a long time, largely the preserve of historians. Consequently, a whole generation of Muslim African academics who received their training after the end of colonial rule gravitated, as a matter of course, to the discipline that had engaged long and constructively with Islam in Africa rather than to a discipline that, for so long, had chosen to ignore the importance of the Islamic presence. There is a distinguished and rapidly growing cadre of African Muslim historians – Muhammad Sani Umar, Ousmane Kane, Abdel Wedoud ould Cheikh, Ibrahima Sall, Cheikh Babou Anta M'Backe, Bintou Sanankoua to name only a few. Given the scarce resources available to academics in Africa, it is hardly surprising that historians have continued to dominate the study of Islam as an area of specialisation. One can only hope that, in time, a similarly Africanised anthropology of Islam will emerge.

Notes

1 Levtzion and Pouwels (2000) provide an excellent overview of the sweep of the history of Islam in Africa.
2 For a detailed historical study of this cadre, see Sibeud 2002.
3 The collected papers in Amselle and Sibeud 1998 provide a detailed assessment of Delafosse's career.

4. Weiskel 1980 (especially pp. 112–22) gives a thorough and critical account of Delafosse's conduct as an administrator, while noting that 'Delaffosse's publications on the Baule provide the foundation for any serious inquiry into Baule pre-colonial history and social organisation' (p. 257).

5 See Launay 1998 on Delafosse's Senufo ethnography.

6 See Harrison 1988 on French colonial attitudes towards Islam in West Africa.

7 For recent and radically different evaluations of Griaule's contributions, see Clifford 1983, Van Beek 1991.

8 I am indebted to Jack Goody for this point.

9 The title of a collection of essays (Middleton and Tait 1964).

10 See, for example, his description of 'The Over-Kingdom of Gonja' (Goody 1967).

11 Indeed, Edward Said (1978: 326) explicitly cited Geertz's work in Orientalism as an example of scholarly work on Islam that had managed to escape the intellectual hegemony of the Orientalist tradition.

12 At the same time, the anthropological study of Islam in Morocco and in Egypt began to flourish; see, for example, Gilsenan 1973, Eickelman 1976.

13 Boddy 1989; Lewis, el-Safi and Hurreiz 1991; Makris 2000.

References

Amselle, J., 1977, Les Négoçiants de la Savane, Paris: Editions Anthropos.

—— 1998, Mestizo Logics: Anthropology of Identity in Africa and Elsewhere, translated by Claudia Royal, Stanford, CA: Stanford University Press.

Amselle, J. and E. Sibeud (eds.), 1998, Maurice Delafosse, entre Orientalisme et Ethnographie: l'Itinéraire d'un Africaniste (1870-1926), Paris: Maisonneuve and Larose.

Boddy, J., 1989, Wombs and Alien Spirits: Women, Men, and the Zar Cult in Northern Sudan, Madison, WI: University of Wisconsin Press.

Clifford, J., 1992, 'Power and Dialogue in Ethnography: Marcel Griaule's Initiation', in G. Stocking (ed.), Observers Observed: Essays on Ethnographic Fieldwork, Madison, WI: University of Wisconsin Press, pp. 121–56.

Cohen, A., 1969, Custom and Politics in Urban Africa, London: Routledge and Kegan Paul.

Copans, J., 1980, Les Marabouts de l'Arachide: La Confrérie Mouride et les Paysans du Sénégal, Paris: Le Sycomore.

Coulibaly, S., 1978, Le Paysan Sénoufo, Abidjan and Dakar: Nouvelles Editions Africaines.

Delafosse, M., 1912, Haut-Sénégal-Niger (Soudan Français). I. Le pays, les Peuples, les Langues. II. L'Histoire. III. Les Civilisations, Paris: Larose.

Eickelman, D., 1976, Moroccan Islam, Austin, TX: University of Texas Press.

El Zein, A. H. M., 1974, The Sacred Meadows, Evanston, IL: Northwestern University Press.

Evans-Pritchard, E. E., 1949, The Sanusi of Cyrenaica, London: Oxford University Press.

—— 1956, Nuer Religion, London: Oxford University Press.

Fabian, J., 1983, Time and the Other: How Anthropology Makes Its Object, New York: Columbia University Press.

Geertz, C., 1968, Islam Observed, New Haven, CT: Yale University Press.

Gilsenan, M., 1973, Saint and Sufi in Modern Egypt, Oxford: Clarendon Press.

Goody, J. R., 1967, 'The Over-Kingdom of Gonja', in D. Forde and P. M. Kaberry (eds.), West African Kingdoms in the Nineteenth Century, London: Oxford University Press, pp. 179–205.

—— 1968, 'Restricted Literacy in Northern Ghana', in J. R. Goody (ed.), Literacy in Traditional Societies, Cambridge: Cambridge University Press, pp. 199–264.

Greenberg, J., 1946, The Influence of Islam on a Sudanese Religion, New York: J. J. Augustin.

Griaule, M., 1970, Conversations with Ogotomelli: an Introduction to Dogon Religious Ideas [first published in French in 1948], London and New York: Oxford University Press for International African Institute.

Harrison, C., 1988, France and Islam in West Africa, 1860–1960, Cambridge: Cambridge University Press.

Ibrahim, A. A., 1994, Assaulting with Words, Evanston, IL: Northwestern University Press.

Kagabo, J. H., 1988, L'Islam et les "Swahili" au Rwanda, Paris: Editions de l'École des Hautes Études en Sciences Sociales.

Lambeck, M., 1993, Knowledge and Practice in Mayotte, Toronto: University of Toronto Press.

Launay, R., 1982, Traders without Trade: Responses to Change in Two Dyula Communities, Cambridge: Cambridge University Press.

—— 1992, Beyond the Stream: Islam and Society in a West African Town, Berkeley and Los Angeles: University of California Press.

—— 1998, 'A Question of Character: Delafosse among the Senufo', in J. Amselle and E. Sibeud (eds.), Maurice Delafosse, Entre Orientalisme et Ethnographie: l'itinéraire d'un Africainiste (1870-1926), Paris: Maisonneuve et Larose, pp. 39–48.

Levtzion, N. and R. A. Pouwels, (eds.), 2000, The History of Islam in Africa, Athens, OH: Ohio University Press.

Lewis, I. M., A. el-Safi and S. Hurreiz (eds.), 1991, Women's Medecine: the Zar-Bori Cult in Africa and Beyond, Edinburgh: Edinburgh University Press.

Middleton, J. and D. Tait (eds.), 1964, Tribes without Rulers: Studies in African Segmentary Systems, London: Routledge and Kegan Paul.

Nadel, S. F., 1954, Nupe Religion, London: Routledge and Kegan Paul.

Said, E., 1978, Orientalism, New York: Pantheon Books.

Shaw, R., 2002, Memories of the Slave Trade: Ritual and the Historical Imagination in Sierra Leone, Chicago: University of Chicago Press.

Sibeud, E., 2002, Une Science Impériale pour l'Afrique? La Construction des Saviors Africanistes en France 1878–1930, Paris: Editions de l'École des Hautes Études en Sciences Sociales.

Smith, M. G., 1960, Government in Zazzau, 1800–1850, London: Oxford University Press.

Soares, B. F., in press, Islam and the Prayer Economy: History and Authority in a Malian Town, Edinburgh: International African Institute.

Van Beek, W. E. A., 1991, 'Dogon Restudied: a Field Evaluation of the Work of Marcel Griaule', Current Anthropology, 32, 2: 13–67.

Weiskel, T. C., 1980, French Colonial Rule and the Baule Peoples, Oxford: Clarendon Press.

PART III

The Future of Anthropology in Africa:
Application and Engagement

10
Anthropology in Post-colonial Africa
The Nigerian Case

P.-J. Ezeh

Azikiwe and anthropology

Nigeria's first post-colonial leader was a trained anthropologist. Dr Nnamdi Azikiwe studied for a Master's in the discipline in the US, and remained a keen promoter of the discipline within Nigeria's universities. Known to many simply as Zik, he became the first African Governor-General of Nigeria in 1960 and then went on to become the new nation-state's ceremonial President three years after independence from Britain in 1960. He held the post until 1966 when the government came to an abrupt end following a putsch.

While in America he studied for a Master's degree in Anthropology at the University of Pennsylvania. By chance Bronislaw Malinowski listened to a seminar paper he gave on the origin of the state from an anthropological perspective. Apparently Malinowski spoke approvingly of his presentation, hoping that Azikiwe would come and study with him in London. After returning to England, Malinowski helped him to become a Fellow of the Royal Anthropological Institute (Azikiwe 1970: 187). At another such seminar a member of Azikiwe's audience was so moved by his paper on the oral literature of his Onitsha Igbo people of south-eastern Nigeria that she sent him a cheque to assist in his research. His Master's thesis was entitled 'Mythology in Onitsha Society' (Azikiwe 1970: 156).

Azikiwe's greatest gift to anthropology in Nigeria was the founding of the country's first autonomous university – the University of Nigeria, Nsukka – in 1960. The discipline was included in the curriculum from the start. Many thus also see him as Nigeria's first anthropologist, even though he did not pursue a career in the discipline. In what follows, I discuss the development of anthropology in Nigeria's universities since that point, and the challenges it faces today.

Anthropology and Nigerian universities

The first Nigerian to get a PhD in Anthropology, awarded by the University of London in 1939, was Nathaniel Fadipe. The distinctive styles of scholarship of Azikiwe and Fadipe set a precedent for two broad disciplinary traditions of scholarship. Either the researcher studied their own ethnic group or they identified a developmental problem in the nation-state as a whole, attempting a supra-ethnic analysis. This second strategy was favoured by, amongst others, Bassey Andah, M. O. Awogbade and Inno Modo (Otite 1999). Besides these two basic thrusts, descriptive texts introducing various aspects of the subject to new students have also been written by, among others, Oke (1984) and Onwuejeogwu (1975).

In the government-funded universities, the teaching of anthropological subjects is duplicated in various faculties under different names. The University of Nigeria, Nsukka was not the first to offer university-level education on Nigerian soil. The University of Ibadan had done so since 1948, remaining a college of the University of London until independence in 1960. I will discuss the histories of each institution separately.

The current state of anthropology in Nigeria cannot be fully understood without acknowledging the process by which the discipline came to occupy a central position in the University of Ibadan. At Ibadan there is now a Department of Anthropology and Archaeology, and a department that teaches the linguistics of Nigeria's largely unwritten languages. There is also an Institute of African Studies, with programmes that have anthropological content.

The department that now combines Anthropology and Archaeology in its name was originally founded as a Department of Archaeology in the late 1960s. Its first head was the eminent British field archaeologist Thurstan Shaw. As noted by Shaw *et al.* (2001), the initial inclusion of anthropology was discouraged on grounds of anthropology's poor public image at the time.

A decade afterwards, Bassey Andah, a Nigerian and also an archaeologist by disciplinary specialisation, entered the arena with reformist zeal. He pointed to the futility of neglecting anthropology in a pluralistic nation-state like Nigeria. Andah's justification of a reorganisation to include anthropology was to make 'courses more practical in outlook and more relevant to the developmental needs and aspirations of contemporary Nigeria and other African societies' (1997: 21). As a result, a fully-fledged degree course in anthropology came to be offered at Ibadan.

At the University of Nigeria, Nsukka, the Department of Sociology and Anthropology was established in the earliest days of that first autonomous indigenous university's existence. In the first 15 years after independence, the departmental headship was almost exclusively in the hands of foreign members of staff, save for a few months when the radical Cambridge-trained Nigerian anthropologist, Ikenna Nzimiro, stood in as an acting head. Besides Nzimiro (1970–1), the list includes Mozel Hill (1960–3), Janet Hartle (1963–7) and Jean Comhaire (1971–5). Professor Nzimiro, who was one of Azikiwe's younger colleagues in the anti-colonial campaigns, ended up replacing Comhaire, who was the last non-Nigerian to head the department. From then until now, nine of the fourteen heads of this bi-disciplinary department have been anthropologists.

Apart from the Department of Sociology and Anthropology, and inputs from the Department of Archaeology, University of Nigeria, Nsukka also has a separate department that teaches the linguistics of Nigerian indigenous languages. My own voyage into mainstream anthropology began there.

Besides formally training students in anthropology, individual anthropologists also get invited to play important national roles, allowing them to give the discipline a public face. Professor Azuka Dike, a head of department at two different periods, was the Chairman of the National Commission on Museums and Monuments, while Professor Ikenna Nzimiro was an adviser to President Ibrahim Babangida in the 1980s, despite the criticism that such a relationship with the head of a junta drew down on him.

Nonetheless, the future of anthropology in post-colonial Nigeria is not secure. Some of the best-known African names in the field come from these parts: Victor Uchendu, Philip Nsugbe, Ikenna Nzimiro, Azuka Dike, Angulu Onwuejeogwu, Ifi Amadiume, Felicia Ekejiuba, M.O. Awogbade, Onigu Otite, Daniel Offiong and Bassey Andah, to name but a few. But any survivors of the pioneering generations are now retiring, and younger scholars seem reluctant to replace them. Whilst the intellectual utility of anthropology seems not to be in doubt, since the 1980s not many in Nigeria have hurried to take it up as a career.

When I began my PhD in 1998 at the University of Nigeria, I was only the third Nigerian to do so in its forty years of existence, and the first candidate to undertake participant observation outside his own ethno-linguistic group. The department's first PhD in the field, P. C. Dike, is currently the Director of Nigeria's National Gallery of Arts. The second is Innocent Modo, now Professor of Anthropology at the University of Uyo, further south. Instead, the department has hosted many international students – from Britain, America, Holland, Norway and Japan, to name but a few countries – doing research in neighbouring communities. Happily, one other Nigerian PhD candidate has just joined.

The problem appears to lie not with anthropology itself but with an intellectual *zeitgeist* that favours such market-oriented older professions as law, medicine, pharmacy, engineering, education and the like. The fields of business education and even computer technology are beginning to flourish, too. The litmus test of what is worth pursuing seems to be any training that will guarantee quick access to a job. With a struggling economy that cannot support a growing number of university graduates, students and their parents alike are seeking a degree that is 'marketable'.

There are several ways to challenge the apparent decline of interest of students in anthropology. One is to boost the profile of the subject. This can be done by bringing out its relevance to the challenges of the present time. We can show how anthropology offers a perspective on social issues at local, national and continental levels. We also need to find a way of teaching that communicates such relevance to students. This calls for a collective effort among Nigerian anthropologists not only to continue marketing the discipline in their respective institutions and communities, but also to share expertise and experiences that will lead to a curriculum responsive to this utilitarian approach to tertiary education. This can all be done without compromising its disciplinary identity and rigour.

It is not that students do not find the topic stimulating. My own experience has shown that students become interested in anthropology through taking courses as elective options. My core teaching area, anthropological linguistics, draws one of the largest populations for any one course hosted by a department in the school: 246 students in 2003. And those came from five departments. Introduction to Anthropology has an even larger population of students, coming from many more disciplines.

Anthropology is not alone in facing a decline in student enrolment. Archaeology, history, geography, mathematics, physics, zoology and botany all have problems. What makes anthropology stand out, perhaps, is its potential role in helping African countries in their present transition to a post-traditional pluralistic society. Making the discipline relevant to the labour market does not entail sacrificing its intellectual commitments.

It would not be a bad idea for departments that teach anthropology to take a leaf from the book of the Department of Archaeology at Nsukka. Degree programmes there reflect utilitarian concerns. The Chair, Professor Alex Okpoko, introduced a special pre-degree diploma programme on Cultural Resources Management and Tourism. It was first run in 2002/3 with a student population of 120. At 289 students, the intake for the following year was more than twice the size of the first year and still heavily over-subscribed (only half of those who applied got places). The promise of the programme is such that there are now plans to extend it to degree level. Its aim is to train the growing workforce that is needed in this sector of the Nigerian economy. Yet it remains to be seen how this increased enrolment will be translated into more majors in anthropology, and so to more graduate training in the discipline – necessary to avoid its redefinition as a service to other disciplines through elective courses.

Curriculum planners at universities are aware of the importance of such a strategy, but the rhetoric usually outweighs practical design. For example, Oloruntimehin (1999: 128), employing the term sociology to include social anthropology, counted 'manpower development' as among the accomplishments of the twin disciplines in the forty years they had been taught in Nigerian universities. The Department of Sociology and Anthropology at the University of Nigeria, Nsukka makes a similar claim in the brochure with which it advertises for students. 'Students planning careers in various fields find the sociological and anthropological understanding complementary and enriching', it states (University of Nigeria 2001: 626), and goes on to enumerate twenty such careers. Unfortunately the departmental teaching and course outlines still tend to be dominated by theoretical anthropology. The difference is stark when compared with the innovations at the Department of Archaeology.

Conclusion

Dr Nnamdi Azikiwe did not continue his academic career in the discipline or ever write a fully-fledged ethnography, as Jomo Kenyatta did. Instead he became first a politician and then a political journalist and writer. After being forced out of the Presidency he returned to his chieftaincy in his home town, Onitsha. This is a community on the south-eastern bank of the River Niger, famous for its commerce and ancient monarchy. He found himself mediating a crisis in the regulation of the town's market. He saw the origin of the crisis in the fact that officials in an ethnically pluralist state sought to bypass the Onitsha traditional social structure. The monograph he produced on the troubles reads like a study in applied anthropology. It opens with the words 'this is ...the tragic story of a clash of cultures with avoidable repercussions' (Azikiwe undated: 1). His demonstration of how anthropology can contribute to public debates sets the standard for today's professional anthropologists.

There is clearly a future for anthropology in Nigeria, despite the challenges it continues to face. Nigerians are rediscovering the subject and using it in various ways. Out of the 46 officially recognised universities in the country, 35 are teaching anthropology in some form, usually in combination with sociology. Like a good man who has suffered a serious libel, its social standing is bound to soar again once its character is restored. Nigerians in other walks of life, not least scholars in different disciplines, recognise that anthropology is irreplaceable in dealing with, or even making sense of, many of the problems of contemporary multi-ethnic social organisation.

As others in this volume have shown, there was a continent-wide reluctance to identify with anthropology during the 1960s and 1970s. To some extent, that was true also in Nigeria, and traces of such ambivalence may still be found. But ever since Azikiwe and Fadipe, there have been committed Nigerian anthropologists of international standing who continue to identify with the discipline and are proud to wear its badge.

References

Anafulu, J. C., 1981, *The Ibo-speaking Peoples of Southern Nigeria: a Selected Annotated List of Writings 1627–1970*, Munchen: Kraus International Publications.

Andah, B., 1997, 'The Ibadan Experience to Date', in C. D. Ardouin (ed.), *Museums and Archaeology in West Africa*, Washington: Smithsonian Institution, pp. 12–23.

Azikiwe, N., 1970, *My Odyssey: an Autobiography*, Ibadan: Spectrum Books Limited.

—— undated, *Onitsha Market Crisis: an Example of Monocracy*, Nsukka: Zik Enterprises Limited.

Esedebe, P. *et al.*, 1986, 'Early History of the University: 1960–1966', in E. Obiechina, C. Ike and J. A. Umeh (eds.), *University of Nigeria 1960–1985: an Experiment in Higher Education*, Nsukka: University of Nigeria Press, pp.12–26.

Ezeh, P. J., 2003, 'African Anthropology', *Anthropology Today*, 19, 1: 24.

Henderson, R., 1972, *The King in Every Man*, New Haven: Yale University Press.

Kenyatta, J., 1938 (reprinted 1978), *Facing Mount Kenya*, Nairobi: Kenway Publications.

Ncukwe, P. I., 1996, Fulani, New York: Rosen Publishing Group.

Oke, F. A., 1984, *An Introduction to Social Anthropology*, London: Macmillan.

Oloruntimehin, O., 1999, 'Forty Years of Sociology in Nigeria', *Annals of the Social Science Academy of Nigeria*, 11: 121–34.

Onwuejeogwu, M. A., 1975 (reprinted 1992), *The Social Anthropology of Africa*, London: Heinemann.

Otite, O., 1999, 'Social Anthropology in Nigeria: a Bibliographic Survey', *Annals of the Social Science Academy of Nigeria*, 11: 105–20.

Shaw, T., P. Ucko and K. MacDonald, 2001, 'A Tribute to the Life and Work of Professor Bassey Wai Andah', *World Archaeological Bulletin* (http://www.wac.uct.ac.za/bulletin/wab11/andah.html), 12 June 2003.

University of Nigeria, 2001, *University of Nigeria 1999–2001 Calendar*, Nsukka: University of Nigeria.

11
Reflections on the Challenges of Teaching Anthropology to American Students in Post-colonial Kenya

Mwenda Ntarangwi

This chapter explores the challenges of teaching anthropology to American students participating in a 'study abroad' programme in Kenya. It is an attempt to interrogate the relationship between the content of my teaching and the social and cultural realities of various communities in Kenya unfamiliar to me within a context in which my position as a local person creates, in my students, the expectation that I know everything about local cultures, even those different from mine. This chapter is also an inquiry into how teaching one's culture to students of a different culture involves both the position of subjectivity and the distance of objectivity. In this way, I, as the teacher teaching students about my community/country, play the role of the knower teaching something unknown to students and yet known to me in a limited way because of my inability to know all that my students are interested in about my community/country. It thus denotes a process where learning is continuous for both my students and myself.

Recent anthropological narratives tell of the challenges of conducting research on familiar territories, especially within one's own communities (see Ntarangwi 2003 for a discussion of ethnography in familiar territories, and Onyango-Ouma, this volume). In many cases it is assumed that there is something about objectivity that may be compromised when one conducts research on one's own community; that the insider/outsider divide is blurred, and that one may turn to propaganda rather than realism in dealing with issues pertaining to one's culture. Granted that there are various ways of negotiating and managing these challenges, there is yet another challenge that faces the locally situated anthropologist – that of teaching about their own communities. To do so requires familiarity with the anthropological details of one's community and the ability, overcoming personal biases and 'patriotism', to objectively present that community's ethnographic realities to an audience with little or no information about it.

I also reflect on my personal experiences as an anthropologist trained in America and my subsequent role as a teacher of American students studying abroad in post-colonial Kenya, my native country; their programme included critical as well as experiential study of the Meru, my own cultural group. Anthropology as a discipline has been critical in showing that a person's experience, be it through academic training or cultural location, is a site for ideological formation and the mobilisation of affects that influence one's subject position (Bruner 1986; Clifford and Marcus 1986; Marcus and Fischer 1986). This subject position shapes the views, values and ideas that are considered important and critical when shared with students and others over whom I may have some responsibility. The things I teach and know about my culture, other cultures, and anthropology itself, are all products of my locations, contexts and perceptions of place and time; and also of the interlocution between what I know and what I want to say about those cultures to the attendant audience. I am thus taking a reflective stance in the sense that I occupy the dual categories of teacher and cultural broker, especially since this is a field course that enables students to make trips to various communities in East Africa besides my own. This teaching process has been an experience traversing both temporal and geographical spaces – among them my own encounter with training in anthropology in a racially sensitive American academic culture; the often colonial and racist past associated with the discipline of anthropology; and my ever-present desire to project a picture of Kenya as a country and a people with a self-determination to withstand the overwhelming threat of globalisation and Westernisation.

Anthropology, the past and reflexivity

Anthropology as a discipline has had a well-documented past; the narrative discloses its beginnings, its theoretical assumptions, and its relations to other socio-economic, political and cultural realities of its time. Indeed, as Sally Falk Moore shows in *Anthropology and Africa*, the discipline has been mostly associated with the study of 'others' or 'the other'. I remember in the 1990s, while in graduate school in America, encountering these and other critical sentiments about anthropology from Africanists and African students in such departments as sociology and cultural studies who could not see beyond anthropology's past relations with colonialism. For an African, they would say, to study anthropology is to participate in the discipline that not only enabled colonialism to take root in Africa and other continents, but also denied its practitioners the opportunity to study themselves. Such critics seemed unaware that anthropology was born out of an intellectual movement, influenced by both social Darwinism and the Enlightenment, that left its mark on other academic disciplines as well. That anthropology was directed towards studying 'primitive' peoples was part of what Immanuel Wallerstein (1999) calls the 'disciplinarisation' of the social sciences that between 1850 and 1945 led to a division of labour, with sociologists, economists and political scientists studying developed societies while anthropologists studied small non-Western societies. All social sciences were meant to assist in the understanding of the changing socio-cultural world humans inhabit. Unlike other disciplines, anthropology found itself to be the most adapted to a multi-disciplinary approach that emphasised fieldwork as its distinct mark of identity. It is this multidisciplinary approach in anthropology that was attractive to me, especially after feeling stifled in language and linguistics training while at Kenyatta University in Kenya.

I was also attracted to anthropology because of its ability to be reflexive – willing to look at itself, acknowledge its flaws and seek to mend them in subsequent studies. I was drawn to some of the writings by younger anthropologists who had revisited the research sites, reread some classic ethnographies and showed how specific knowledge contained in them was informed by the prevailing theoretical and social thinking of the time. This is an aspect of anthropology I felt was not acknowledged in the critiques I heard from fellow students at Illinois. It seemed to me that they neither knew nor cared much about anthropology's reflexivity, displayed in the works of authors such as Marcus and Fischer (1986), Rabinow (1977), Clifford (1986), Freeman (1983), Ruby (1982), Clifford and Marcus (1986), and Bell, Caplan and Karim (1993); nor did they seem to be aware of studies of self and one's community (Jackson 1987; Mannheim 1979) and numerous other works that constantly help anthropologists critique themselves. I was glad that anthropology had indeed been engaged in a reflexivity project over the past few decades, one that may not have changed the tools of our work but had certainly changed our attitude to the field and the people in that field (Amselle 2002). In anthropology I see a discipline that is critical in navigating the complexities of cultures as they are caught up in and/or encounter major global shifts and pressures, as well as a reflexive anthropology that is not only conscious of its own controversial past but also helps me to review my positionality as I go about my work.

By reflexivity here I refer to the relationship of identity between subject and object, the inclusion of the actor (anthropologist, researcher, observer) in the account of the act and/or its outcomes. In this sense reflexivity shows that all knowledge is 'subjective' and that anthropological accounts of other communities and cultures are indeed constructed with the actor's own subjectivity playing a key role in the final account. Since we as anthropologists are in the business of knowledge creation and construction, we have to look at our subjectivity critically in the process of shaping that knowledge. All knowing is subjective, and the 'objective world' is what knowers claim to know about. Reflexivity in knowledge making involves bringing the subject, the 'doer' of the knowledge-making activity, back into the account of knowledge (Hufford 1995: 57). As Edward M. Bruner puts it in his Introduction to *The Anthropology of Experience*, in inquiring into knowledge 'we take expressions as objects of study and we become 'conscious of our self-consciousness of these objects. We become aware of our awareness; we reflect on our reflections. Anthropologists of experience take others' experiences, as well as their own, as an object. Our activity is inherently reflexive' (1986: 23). Here the metaphors of the mirror and of the reflexive sentence combine, showing us ourselves in our images and our sentences.

To study the 'other' may be seen as a clear indication of anthropology's colonial and post-colonial underpinnings, but it is also a reflection of the assumptions of scientific validity that surrounds academic disciplines in the West and Westernised post-colonial locales. Thus there has existed a long-standing assumption that anthropology, like many other disciplines in the West, conducts its business of studying people and their ways of life in an objective and hence empiricist manner (cf. Ingold 1996). We could draw an analogy between anthropological work and other sciences by seeing the fieldwork site as the deliberate construction of a bounded space/territory, a kind of laboratory, where the study object is observed in a controlled set-up (by the mere assumption of a cultural exclusivity) and the results are recorded in order to inform the larger human community. It is, indeed, only in the 1990s that many anthropologists openly accepted memoirs and reflexive accounts of their projects/ethnographies as 'real' anthropological work. For a study to be considered objective, a certain degree of separation is required between the anthropologist and the subject, whether a person, community or society is being studied: it is this distance that allows one to be an empiricist. This may explain why, when some anthropologists conduct their research and studies in familiar territories such as their own communities and at home, they are identified not generally as anthropologists but specifically as 'native' anthropologists, as if they are using a different set of analytical tools to those carried by other anthropologists.

Nevertheless, 'native ethnography', denoting fieldwork conducted by researchers belonging to the society they study, has become a familiar inclusion in the ethnographic repertoire in the social sciences (see, for example, D'Amico-Samuels 1991; Ginsburg and Tsing 1990; Kim 1995; Limon 1991; Narayan 1993; and Onyango-Ouma, this volume, among many others). This category itself is a welcome addition to the ever-changing content of ethnographies and other social science projects; it reflects social and cultural realities that have seen many of the members of communities that were the focus of social science research in its formative years now training as social scientists themselves and often using their own societies as their subject matter. In a sense, these 'native ethnographers' are seen to 'belong' to societies that they study, something that every anthro-pologist, for instance, attempts to achieve through what Malinowski long ago called the 'native's point of view' (1922: 25), or, as Mead put it, 'the inclusion of the observer within the observed scene' (1977: 6).

To a large degree when we complete fieldwork and embark upon writing our ethnographies, many of us may attempt to present accounts of our experiences in ways that illuminate both the 'insider' and 'outsider' perspectives. We want to write about our experiences objectively so as to communicate useful information to our readers while also emphasising the fact that we got all that information from being part of the culture and community we studied. Indeed, most ethnographies take pride in the anthropologist's acceptance into the local community that consequently permits a privileged access to the local nuances and practices that form the bulk of ethnographies. This 'insider' position of the anthropologist that has subsequently brought forth the notion of 'native' ethnography has both its strengths and weaknesses. On the one hand, there is the ability of the 'native' ethnographer to enter the field from a privileged position that enables access to emotional and other intimate perspectives of the local culture (Ohnuki-Tierney 1984). On the other hand, this positioning of 'native' ethnographers within known social categories may hamper their ability to transform their observations into socio-scientific knowledge of how culture is constituted (Mascarenhas-Keyes 1987). Projects emanating from these two trajectories are anthropological and are informed by a particular set of ideas that propelled the discipline in its formative years. One tries to find the best fit between those ideas and the specific field or topic being confronted, while acknowledging the challenges that each option of participation entails. It is in the ability to overcome such challenges by bridging the process of 'knowing' with that of 'understanding' culture (ibid.: 175) that 'native' ethnographers are able to present rich accounts of their own cultures. Thus, 'nativity' as a concept has been used in anthropology to differentiate between the anthropologist (who often is the outsider) and the subject material of the anthropological project – the local people are often referred to as 'natives'. This differentiation takes on a different meaning when placed in the context of authoritative academic learning, especially when the same 'native' is the 'authority' (or teacher) in the culture concerned.

Nativity and authority: a Kenyan teaching anthropology to Americans in Kenya

Anthropology as a discipline may embody certain critical entities that form part of its identity (for more examples see, for instance, Mascarenhas-Keyes, 1987; Narayan, 1993; and Ohuki-Tierney, 1984). It is assumed that anthropology enables one to have an in-depth understanding of a culture through extended contact with the community, preferably in the community's own language and in their local contexts (McLancy 2002). This is achievable through fieldwork that is later documented in an ethnography. While in the field the anthropologist keeps notes, preferably in a journal or field notebook, takes pictures, and keeps mental notes for future reference. Anthropologists highlight the uniqueness and diversity of human cultures, their underlying basis of operation and of being different, in a holistic and comparative way. My own contribution to that expectation as an anthropologist can be expressed through my experiences working with the St Lawrence University Kenya Semester Programme in Kenya between 1998 and 2003. Besides administrative duties I also taught a field-based anthropology course entitled 'Culture, Ecology and Development in East Africa'; this was taken by all students enrolled in the programme, irrespective of their individual academic majors and/or interests.

St Lawrence University Kenya Semester Programme (KSP), based in Nairobi, is a 'study abroad' programme offered by the St Lawrence University in Canton, New York. Like many other American 'study abroad' programmes, it is a product of a vibrant cultural initiative stemming from Peace Corps volunteers who were able to see beyond their national borders and craved educational experiences in faraway places. The programme started informally in 1972 when a group of St Lawrence University students decided to use their long winter break (between Christmas holidays and the last week of January) travelling to Kenya. This visit proved to be very useful, setting off a keen interest not only in visiting Kenya but also in structuring such a visit as an academic trip. The programme then started officially in 1974, mostly operating from and around the capital city, Nairobi, and continually expanding to include a curriculum that covered various parts of Kenya and Northern Tanzania in 2003. The programme currently operates from a five-acre property in Karen Nairobi, owned and run by St Lawrence University, where students, administrators and other staff members reside. For a long time two of the senior administrators (director and associate director) doubled as instructors for the field course, but beginning in 2004 the academic director took sole responsibility for the academic arm of the programme. The curriculum also includes up to four other elective courses taught by instructors drawn from public universities based in Nairobi. Here is a short summary of the programme that can be found on the St Lawrence University website:

> St Lawrence University's semester-long study programme in Kenya has for twenty-eight years offered a remarkable, multifaceted, intensively cross-cultural opportunity that intertwines classroom instruction and field learning. The programme's home base is in Nairobi, the capital, but students spend many weeks on various field components, including

homestays in a rural agricultural community and in a Samburu pastoralist community, on a field trip to Tanzania which includes interaction with the Maasai and with the Hadza (a hunter-gatherer community), and in the Swahili island community of Lamu. Students also have a three-week homestay with a family in urban Nairobi. Through direct interaction with several of the many ethnic groups who make up Kenya and with Kenyans from many different walks of life, students learn to appreciate the diversity and the creativity of Kenyans as well as the complexity of the challenges they face. The programme serves majors from many different disciplines. Some of the issues considered during the semester are: the balance between conservation, biodiversity and ecological change; conflicts between sustainable development and democratisation; cultural development, Westernisation and the maintenance of indigenous traditions; economic growth and equity.[1]

The focus of the curriculum, while remaining the same in its basic structure (learning through experience), keeps changing in line with the philosophy of the leadership of the programme as guided by the office of International and Intercultural Education and members of the African Studies Board at the main university in New York.

The courses that students take while in Kenya transfer to their various schools and count towards their academic credits. The anthropology course I taught was divided up into six different but related components that entailed both critical and experiential learning. Students were first assigned readings relevant to a community or field site to be visited, and quizzed on those readings; they then visited and lived in that community; finally, upon returning to base in Nairobi, they wrote a research paper articulating issues of their field site experience. Below is a summary of the six different components.

Rural agricultural homestays

This first component included a week living in a rural agricultural setting where students had their first in-depth interaction with a Kenyan community. To help them prepare for this experience academically, students were issued with a set of readings that sought to address some critical issues of the course but specifically focused on that field component. Thus in this case students' readings also incorporated some readings on cross-cultural encounters in general. The readings I used in the course can be divided into three main categories. The first one introduced students to some of the ways in which scholars and writers have written about their encounter with other cultures and with Africa at different levels in different contexts. The second specifically looked at the problems and conditions that face contemporary Africa from the point of view of different scholars. And the last category focused specifically on the life and cultural practices of people in the community where students would spend time in homestays. There were various issues that students encountered and engaged with during their homestays. Among those I asked students to focus on were:

1 What do you know about Africa from reading some of the assigned articles, and how has your image of Africa been shaped or influenced by that?

2 How does Christianity play itself out in the daily activities and experiences of your homestay family?

3 What issues of development do members of your family articulate and how can they best be addressed in view of their current socio-economic status?

4 How do gender roles play themselves out in and outside your rural home?

As an academic activity, the field experience also entailed the following assignments that were repeated, albeit with specific alterations to reflect each field component:

1 Each student was to keep a field journal or field notes.

2 Each student was to attend an orientation meeting before each field component.

3 Each student was to take an in-class reading to cover assigned texts.

4 Students were to form topic-based research groups (usually involving four researchers) while in the field and in making presentations at the end of each component.

5 Each student was to write a research paper of 6–10 pages tying in assigned readings, field observations and experience, and analysis.

Wildlife, conservation and economic change

This second component, which lasted two weeks, was to provide students with a comparative perspective on environment, development and wildlife conservation in northern Tanzania. Tanzania, Kenya's neighbour and also a British colony, took a very different post-colonial path between the 1960s and mid-1990s. The political ideology of *Ujamaa* designed by Julius Nyerere sought to de-emphasise the competition and accumulation of wealth favoured by Kenya's capitalist identity, and to promote sharing, self-reliance and national unity, especially through the national language, Kiswahili. Field experiences while in Tanzania included visits and discussions with a hunting and gathering community of the Hadzabe in Yaeda Valley (made famous in anthropology through the work of James Woodburn), the Maasai of the Ngorongoro Conservation Area, and the Waarusha community living along the slopes of Mount Meru near Arusha. In addition to lectures and discussions on topics including evolution and pre-history, geology, conservation, ecotourism, wildlife behaviour and ecology, land management and development, students were provided with an unparalleled opportunity to view wildlife in several of Africa's richest ecosystems. Some of the issues raised in this component included:

1 What is unique about the culture and traditions of the Waarusha of Mount Meru compared to other agricultural communities you have encountered?

2 What are the reasons behind the establishment of Lake Manyara National Park and what controversies might this have caused?

3 If you were a Peace Corps volunteer asked to help set up a cultural tourism programme for Yaeda Valley, what would you do?

4 How do the many different species of herbivores observed in the Ngorongoro crater manage to live together with minimal competition?

Urban life in Nairobi

The third component related to the urban homestays in Nairobi, in which students were introduced to issues relating to the city and its environs. Students usually collected most of their information on Nairobi from the readings provided, from discussions with their homestay hosts, and from their own experiences in the city. Students were often asked to draw comparisons between the cultural activities and experiences that they observed between Kenyans in Nairobi (a cosmopolitan city) and those in rural areas where some of the Nairobi residents have very strong filial and cultural roots. Here are examples of some of the topics that students used in trying to understand various issues related to Nairobi:

1 Explore the impact of migration in Nairobi as presented in your readings.

2 What tensions exist between the development and expansion of the city and the environmental concerns of the Nairobi National Park?

3 Identify some major management problems and challenges facing the city of Nairobi.

4 Identify problems related to sanitation, drainage, and refuse collection in Nairobi city.

5 What are the health implications of the informal settlements (popular settlements)?

Pastoralism and social change

The fourth component took students to Northern Kenya for two weeks, where they learned through interaction with the pastoralist community of the Samburu. The students were able to learn from the Samburu their pastoral lifestyles, the challenges of development, cultural change and adaptability, their social structure and political organisation, and ecology. Each student had an opportunity to live with a Samburu family, sharing their daily activities and chores. Here are examples of some topics that students focused on while engaging with this component:

1 What is required to maintain a culture of pastoral land use over several generations?

2 What are the consequences of the overuse of plant resources as the pastoral population grows faster than livestock increases? What are the resultant ecological and cultural consequences?

3 How can the Samburu balance their needs for food with the need to protect the resources on which their livestock depend, and also maintain the integrity of their ecosystem?

4 What are the effects of Western education on pastoral lifestyles?

How is traditional knowledge used against the backdrop of a 'modernising' Kenyan state?

5 What cultural and social roles are assigned to different genders among the Samburu and why?

Islam and social change

The fifth component was based on my own anthropological research among the Swahili of Lamu. It lasted a week and contrasted students' experiences with rural, traditional and ethnically distinct communities with those of a Muslim urban-dwelling Swahili community. Many students had never lived or interacted with a Muslim community and this component enabled them to do so. The component was often interrupted by world events that constructed Muslim locales in Kenya as dangerous for Americans. The following topics introduced students to the complexity of Swahili culture and its various manifestations:

1 What aspects of Swahili identity may be changing in the context of Kenya as a nation-state?

2 How is religion reflected in the daily activities, aspirations and interactions of the Lamu residents?

3 How does tourism affect the lives of Lamu residents both positively and negatively?

4 What is 'development' in the context of Lamu? Is it necessary? What would be the appropriate steps to be taken towards such 'development'?

Independent study

The final component lasted up to three and a half weeks, in which students were placed individually in independent study contexts to learn from local people and institutions. Here each student pursued some particular skill, topic or service that captured a personal interest or projected career. Students were assisted to find individual placements with organisations, communities or individuals where they would work. As in all other components, students would write research papers.

By the end of the fourteen weeks that the students spent in East Africa, they had lived and interacted with different communities and tried to understand the communities' cultures while reflecting upon their own. To enable that cherished 'nativising' project in anthropology, all students were required to study Kiswahili and use it as much as possible during interactions with local people. A further emblem of anthropological tradition was a field journal that each student kept throughout his/her stay in the programme. These journals were collected after each field component so as to make sure that students made regular entries and that these entries enabled students to engage intellectually with their field experiences.

A field-based course in anthropology is a very important part of training young people in many life skills. Indeed, my own experiences working with these students indicated that their research and internship interests while in Kenya, and later when some of them went on to graduate education programmes, were motivated primarily by practice. They wanted to be able to apply their knowledge to solving problems in their communities or elsewhere. Such students used and continue to use anthropological theory to help them understand or address problems derived from their practice, especially because by being in another culture they were able to stand back and critique their own cultures and practices (Jacob 2001).

In teaching anthropology in Kenya to American students, I was faced with a major challenge – that of enabling the students to engage the practicality of knowledge learned in a different context and apply it to their own worlds. In this process of being a teacher and one who had grown up in Kenya, I embodied a sense of legitimacy – that of a locally situated person who had local knowledge as well as an academic degree to legitimise that knowledge. By being so positioned I was expected to know everything about the local, otherwise I would be regarded as a dislocated native. Rarely would my students consider me a stranger to the cultural practices of a number of other ethnic groups that we visited and interacted with in my own country, and even in Tanzania. There were many instances when students would counter my response that I did not know why group X was doing that, with 'but you are African, you should know that'. This, I presume, said more about my students' perception of Africa that it said about my position as their teacher.

To be an African means being an embodiment of African social, political and cultural realities. When my students encountered new places, people and phenomena, they turned to me for explanations and information. Their idea of Africa owed much to discourses in students' local communities, through popular media such as television and newspapers or professional magazines, and through movies and other media where Africa is constructed in very specific ways. To such students Africa was a monolithic continent stuck in a timeless mode where things remain the same for years and years on end. Thus it was not unusual that after a week of just being in Nairobi, my students were quick to talk about how they love Africa, how everything in Africa is so different, and how they cannot believe they were actually in Africa. Having imbibed the Western media's depiction of Africa as that remote part of the world characterised by civil strife, disease, abject poverty and starvation, my students were astonished at the abundance of food in some rural areas they visited. This is not to negate the presence of starvation in some parts of Africa, but rather to show that the image of Africa as one place with one African language, where every other community had elephants trumpeting in their backyards, or else deserts stretching as far as the eye could reach, tended to recede from their minds as they encountered scenes that they may not have associated with Africa.

The students were not unique in this conception and construction of Africa. The depiction of Africa as an immobilised, timeless place where things have remained the same since they came to being is also depicted in much of the tourist discourse (Kaspin 1997). In their quest to maintain or increase the flow of foreign tourists into Kenya, many Kenyan and international tour operators are fond of using images of Africa as abounding in timeless cultural practices, with the Maasai – who have come to signify the quintessential African culture – often depicted as epitomising this timeless state. Indeed, the irony is that this depiction of cultures such as the Maasai has led to the decontextualisation of their existence: often they are depicted without that which defines their uniqueness as a culture – their cattle (Sabania 2002). This is common in safari brochures that tend to exoticise Maasai 'otherness' in a nativistic way quite similar to the colonial discourse that located difference in a primeval past of cultural authenticity. Cultural difference is thus essentialised for commercial purposes in ways that ignore the historical and cultural dimensions of constructing difference. In this way it is assumed that there is actually an 'authentic' Maasai culture that is unspoiled, autonomous, self-contained and self-directed. Further, that there is this place called

Africa where everything is the same and where once you have encountered one part of it you have encountered the entire continent.[2] What is most intriguing about these cultural constructions of the Maasai, for instance, is that some of the Maasai people themselves take up these constructions and present them as their own cultural reality and identity.[3] The exotic story told about the other becomes the story told by the other about self. The other and the self merge to become one in this timeless warp of cultural consumption. This is the complexity that many of my students had to encounter as well, and only those keen on going beyond the surface would discern the often entangled worlds of performed and lived cultures.

Understanding the construction of these images of Africa and its people in the minds of many from the West, and in post-colonial subjects, is important, because my students are drawn to Kenya by the promise of difference that Kenya can and does offer. Many of them may not have expressed the idea of the exotic in their applications to be part of a semester of learning abroad, but when asked why they chose Kenya, many were quick to mention the lure of the exotic, the animals, the different cultures, and the ability to get away from their familiar territories.[4] Given that anthropology as a discipline is predicated upon the same promise of difference or 'otherness', we may begin to understand the challenges I was faced with as an anthropologist teaching these students in Kenya about many of these 'other' cultures.[5] Many of the students may have joined the programme under the spell of exotic images of Africa that were being mobilised by some local people either to lay claim to a cultural distinctiveness that would allow for an essentialist sense of identity in a globalising world (Strathern 1995) or to create an attractive package to entice a foreign tourist. While I was aware of these competing agencies of cultural packaging of Africa, I was keen to challenge students to critique their own assumptions in order to see a more complex and constantly changing continent. For me their understanding of Africa's complexity was more than an academic objective. As an African I had a vested interest in the image of Africa. I detested the simplistic image of Africa depicted by some Westerners I had met, listened to, or read, and by those Westernised Africans who not only collaborate in propagating that simplified Africa but often see themselves as qualified agents of change in bringing it to market. I thus brought to this course a subjective bent that was bound to influence my teaching and interaction with my students in Kenya.

I was also faced with a paradox, that of being a teacher as well as an ethnographer. I taught American students about East African cultures, yet I continued to conduct some of my own research in some of the same areas I visited with my students.[6] As I visited the same communities with my students I started forming research questions on the broader theme of cross-cultural encounters and any subsequent socio-cultural changes that may occur through this encounter. The more interested I got in the communities, the more I became attached to them (the same attachment I have often noticed in other anthropologists towards communities they have lived with and continually studied and written about). For me this attachment went beyond an academic relationship; it brought me closer to people who, although often culturally different, were closer to me through sharing the same nation-state and similar underlying cultural principles and practices. They were thus 'my' people, and in them I saw myself. This relationship and the complexity it brought to my teaching will be made apparent shortly.

So, while teaching on the Kenya Programme for St Lawrence University, I was a teacher-researcher; while teaching my students about various cultures of East Africa, I was also engaged in research on those same local cultures, alongside the students that I was teaching.[7] Despite the complexity resulting from this dualistic encounter with the field – as teacher and researcher – I was also concerned about the well-being of the communities we visited and from whom we learned. The budget for academic encounter in our four main field programmes, which lasted a total of two weeks each, included remuneration for the communities we visited. These communities would host us and share their lived experiences through organised learning activities. Our hosts were paid for their time and expertise. Two programmes out of the four were subcontracted to private companies run and owned by Americans. As a Kenyan I was interested in seeing that those community members who were actively involved in enriching the academic experience of our students were appropriately compensated.

My own growing up had sensitised me to the principles of social justice and the possibilities of exploitation in unequal power situations. Being a member of a generation whose parents hardly went to college I was aware of the exploitation that was enhanced by a knowledge imbalance, where those who had access to information through their formal training (Western education) tended to use it to exploit those who had not received similar training. And herein lay the other dilemma – in order for us to be able to present different traditional cultures to our students, we had selected those communities where Westernisation had had the least impact. These were the same communities that were vulnerable to being exploited by those of us who were formally trained and thus often negotiated on their behalf. These concerns might appear programmatic to researchers, who could see them as within the domain of day-to-day practice rather than research. This might make the teacher in me feel that the field knowledge I possess is less elevated than the academic researcher's more theoretical knowledge (Kincheloe 2003). I felt compelled to play two roles – try to make my students understand that their learning did entail a commitment to certain subjective issues such as equity and social justice for the communities involved, while remaining objectively distant as a researcher interested in understanding the workings of the cultures and communities with whom we worked. Thus if I as a teacher am to encounter a researcher whose work with a community ends up with findings that enable an understanding of the problem but with no attempt to solve it, I may regard such research as less than adequate (Hammond and Spindler 2001). Teachers may easily discount researchers as people with their heads in the clouds who never address the 'nitty-gritty' problems of making reforms work; researchers, for their part, may judge teachers as people with their hearts in the subject being taught, who therefore lose the objective distance necessary for a good account. Yet by taking on both identities of a teacher and researcher who is also Kenyan and thus part of the local, I had to play both roles simultaneously. Here is an example: when I took students to field components I knew that for students to be able to stay and learn from the local people for two weeks, St Lawrence University had paid considerably large sums of money. Since much of the learning took place through student interaction with the local community members, it seemed only fair that the monies set aside for that learning be shared out among the members of the community involved. As a researcher I became aware that the local community members in some of our field components were poorly compensated for their work with their students, and that because they had not entered into any formal contracts with St Lawrence University they could not articulate those sentiments to the contracting company for fear of losing their roles as local teachers.

The teacher in me wanted to take action. I was caught in a bind where, despite the reality of poor compensation, my capacity as a researcher might not have encouraged me to consider it my duty to figure out how to change the situation for the benefit of the local teachers. As a teacher, however, I wanted to say that such information was of little use unless something could be done about it. These two identities – of a teacher and a researcher – created an incredible tension within me and I continue to negotiate it in my role as teacher and anthropologist, unable to let one prevail over the other, as an ideal world would demand.[8]

The 'othering' of the 'other'

While being subjected to the practice–theory dialectic of being a teacher-researcher highlighted the specific ways in which my personal beliefs and teaching practices intersected (Gibson 1998), the reality of my being Kenyan often became a prism through which my students sought to understand their experience in Kenya. It was thus quite a challenge to my teaching responsibility when one of my students, while spending time with an urban host family in Nairobi, was told by her hosts that the Samburu of northern Kenya are backward and in need of development. Such a perception is reflective of the socio-cultural realities often embodied by post-colonial subjects in Kenya today following their Western education and acquisition of Western values and aspirations. Yet my students were keen to know how to reconcile their own perceptions of exotic cultures with these ones projected by members of the exotic country they were learning in and about. It is the intersection of those constructions of 'otherness', the need to invite students to a broader engagement with other cultures, and the realities of anthropology's colonial past that made and continue to make my work as an anthropologist from a post-colonial nation an exercise in critical analysis and reflexivity. I, for instance, got very uncomfortable on encountering a Kenyan who was dismissive about other Kenyans. I could not (and still cannot) accept the fact that there are Kenyans who consider their fellow citizens backward and in need of 'development'.[9]

My lack of acceptance of such a reality is due to the fact that I want my fellow Kenyans to be able to critique the concept of development in a way that enables them to respect all lifestyles led by other Kenyans, without being prejudiced.[10] In a way I want my fellow

Kenyans to make positive representations of their own people to foreigners. It is a case of not wanting to wash dirty linen in public. Yet anthropology does teach us that socialisation is critical in shaping our values and worldviews. Thus if a Kenyan has grown up in a context where development means Westernisation, those that are not 'Westernised' will not be regarded as 'developed'. In the presence of my American students I wanted to apologise on behalf of fellow Kenyans for the negative representation of their fellow country people to foreign students.

On another level I found myself in another dilemma, one in which I am constantly observing my students in order to understand the basis of their behaviour. From this observation I was able to make my own students useful sources of research information that could be turned into academic writing. Thus I actually studied my own students, just as they were studying me as an individual and collectively as a part of the larger Kenyan society. One of my challenges was how to make my students aware of my research about them without alienating them from me as their teacher. Was I only to inform them of my project, or should I have involved them actively by way of not only informing them but also seeking their consent as human subjects? Was it acceptable for me to 'other' my students and make them my subjects of anthropological inquiry? My work on educational tourism (Ntarangwi 2000), empirically based mainly on my experience with my students on field components, did elicit various reactions from students. There were those who were angered by the issues raised in it, especially as the students felt that I should have clearly differentiated students from tourists. There were others who found the issues raised in the work quite useful as a reflexive exercise that allowed them to understand themselves and their colleagues, and asked if I would do more such writing. With such disparate responses, I was often reluctant to share my work with students lest it became a locus of intellectual disagreement that might end up injuring my personal relationship with them, which I found critical in enabling me to become a useful cultural broker for their experience in Kenya. Yet since writing about such experiences entailed an acknowledgement of the role played by students in the interactions I had with them – a role that was critical to my analysis – I felt compelled by my conscience and my duty as a teacher to involve my students, albeit at different levels, in the process of generating such analysis. For instance, I asked my students if it was acceptable for me to share parts of their own experiences in Kenya as teaching examples for other students. Most of them consented and the wishes of those who specifically asked me not to share any of their information with other students were respected as well. I had also shared with some of my students drafts of the paper I published on education and tourism (Ntarangwi 2000), so that they could offer feedback and also allow me an opportunity to gauge how accurate such feedback was useful for public consumption. Whenever I use an individual student's experience in my work I have sought his/her approval and asked if I could or could not disclose real names of such sources.

Conclusion

Tim Ingold's edited volume entitled *Key Debates in Anthropology* (1996) addresses, among other things, the issues of whether anthropology can be regarded as a science; whether it can say something general about social life; how culture shapes people's perceptions of their environment; and the place of language in forming a culture. These issues are critical not only in anthropology but also in many other disciplines where human activities and perceptions form a large part of the content. Some of these issues have been addressed in this chapter. I have, for instance, looked at my own subject position as a Kenyan anthropologist trained in America and at the experience of teaching anthropology to American students in Kenya. The connection between my own individual experiences as a member of a community and my role as a teacher teaching about that community becomes complex, especially when predicated upon some of the relations between anthropology, other disciplines and self-critique. As an individual, I was faced with the dilemma of possessing knowledge across cultures necessary to broker between my American students and the cultures of my own and other communities in East Africa. How could I avoid the problem of knowing and availing that knowledge to others when I was aware (through anthropological training) of how hard it is to reconcile the subjective, situated, socially constructed and ideologically mediated nature of the production and consumption of such knowledge? How could I avoid trying to present a good image of my community and my country to my students, especially given the context of negative images of Africa and Africans that American popular media often directs at these students? How much did I know about these cultures and how much should I have shared with my students? These and many other questions form the core of this chapter. I have argued that I was faced with a major challenge as a researcher and teacher, where the biggest issue was how to reconcile both these identities yet deal with the tendency among scholars to separate the two. Where does the Kenyan self, tied to seeing the good of my people and country, end, and where does the detached objective researcher start? Should these questions be posed in the first place?

Notes

1 http://web.stlawu.edu/ciis/html/off_campus/kenya/index.html, 3 November 2002.

2 Few people imbued with this kind of thinking ever stop to think of Africa as a continent with diverse geographical, economic, cultural and political realities.

3 I remember, at one Maasai Cultural Homestead (Boma) close to the Ngorongoro crater in Tanzania, listening to a male Maasai guide tell my students how Maasai warriors (morani) killed lions, drank blood for food every day, and spent most of their time dancing with their beautiful headdresses. These are the images many in the West have of Maasai warriors, and the guide was reproducing them for the students whom he saw as an important link in an information network that would bring future tourists to his boma.

4 This was usually reflected in various meetings I held with students upon their arrival in Kenya to establish the reasons they had for travelling for a semester abroad in Kenya.

5 I am aware of various works in anthropology that involve the shrinking of the distance that creates 'otherness', yet the majority of anthropological work continues to focus on some type of 'otherness'.

6 My doctoral research was mostly on the Swahili coast of Kenya where I took my students, and some of my later research has focused on tourism, one of the topics with which my students engage.

7 See Ntarangwi 2000 for an example of the kind of research I was conducting while teaching.

8 It is a result of this dilemma, and my understanding that some of my colleagues were reluctant to work with me towards ending what I saw as unjust treatment of local producers of knowledge, that I felt frustrated and subsequently left my position with the programme.

9 This has become apparent throughout my own encounters with different communities in Kenya and other parts of Africa: the failure of the development project and the fall of the nation-state, both vaunted as panaceas for change in Africa.

10 An understanding of the realities I have often observed in many Western people – who seem to be doing well materially, and yet socially, culturally and spiritually are still unfulfilled – has led me to question Westernisation as the answer to Africa's 'problems'.

References

Amselle, J., 2002, 'Globalisation and the Future of Anthropology', *African Affairs*, 101: 213–29.

Bell, D., P. Caplan and W.J. Karim (eds.), 1993, *Gendered Fields: Women, Men, and Ethnography*, London: Routledge.

Bruner, E. M., 1986, 'Experience and Its Expressions', in V. Turner and E. M. Bruner (eds.), *The Anthropology of Experience*, Urbana: University of Illinois Press, pp. 3–32.

Clifford, J. and G. Marcus (eds.), 1986, *Writing Culture: the Poetics and Politics of Ethnography*, Berkeley: University of California Press.

D'Amico-Samuels, D., 1991, 'Undoing Fieldwork: Personal, Political, Theoretical and Methodological Implications', in F. Harrison (ed.), *Decolonizing Anthropology: Moving Further Toward an Anthropology for Liberation*, Washington, DC: American Anthropological Association, pp. 68–87.

Freeman, D., 1983, *Margaret Mead and the Samoa: the Making and Unmaking of an Anthropological Myth*, Cambridge, Massachusetts: Harvard University Press.

Gibson, L. S., 1998, 'Teaching as an Encounter with the Self: Unravelling the Mix of Personal Beliefs, Education Ideologies, and Pedagogical Practices', *Anthropology and Education Quarterly*, 29, 3: 360–71.

Ginsburg, F. and A. L. Tsing, 1990, *Uncertain Terms: Negotiating Gender in American Culture*, Boston: Beacon Press.

Hammond, L. and G. Spindler, 2001, 'Not Talking Past Each Other: Cultural Roles in Educational Research', *Anthropology and Education Quarterly*, 32, 3: 373–8.

Hufford, D. J., 1995, 'The Scholarly Voice and the Personal Voice: Reflexivity in Belief Studies', *Western Folklore*, 54: 57–76.

Ingold, T. (ed.), 1996, *Key Debates in Anthropology*, London: Routledge.

Jackson, A. (ed.), 1987, *Anthropology at Home*, London: Tavistock.

Jacob, E., 2001, 'The Council on Anthropology and Education as a Crossroad Community: Reflections on Theory-Oriented and Practice-Oriented Research', *Anthropology and Education Quarterly*, 32, 3: 266–75.

Kaspin, D., 1997, 'On Ethnographic Authority and the Tourist Trade: Anthropology in the House of Mirrors', *Anthropological Quarterly*, 70: 53–7.

Kim, S., 1995, 'Fieldwork with a "Disguised" Worker in a South Korean Export Processing Zone', *Anthropology Today*, 11, 3: 6–9.

Kincheloe, J. L., 2003, *Teachers as Researchers: Qualitative Inquiry as a Path to Empowerment*, London: Routledge.

Limon, J., 1991, 'Representation, Ethnicity, and the Precursory Ethnography: Notes of a Native Anthropologist', in R. Fox (ed.), *Recapturing Anthropology*, Santa Fé: School of American Research Press, pp. 115–36.

McLancy, J. (ed.), 2002, *Exotic No More: Anthropology on the Front Lines*, Chicago, University of Chicago Press.

Malinowski, B., 1922, *Argonauts of the Western Pacific*, London: Routledge.

Mannheim, B. (ed.), 1979, *The Politics of Anthropology: from Colonialism and Sexism to the View from Below*, The Hague: Mouton.

Marcus, G. and M. Fischer, 1986, *Anthropology as Cultural Critique: an Experimental Moment in the Human Sciences*, Chicago: University of Chicago Press.

Mascarenhas-Keyes, S., 1987, 'The Native Anthropologist: Constraints and Strategies in Research', in A. Jackson (ed.), *Anthropology at Home*, London: Tavistock, pp. 83–98.

Mead, M., 1977, *Letters from the Field 1925–1975*, New York: Harper Books.

Moore, S. F., 1994, *Anthropology and Africa: Changing Perspectives on a Changing Scene*, Charlottesville: The University Press of Virginia.

Narayan, K., 1993, 'How Native is a "Native" Anthropologist?' *American Anthropologist*, 95, 3: 671–86.

Ntarangwi, M., 2000, 'Education, Tourism, or Just a Visit to the Wild?' *African Issues*, 28, 1 and 2: 54–60.

––––– 2003, *Gender Identity and Performance: Understanding Swahili Cultural Realities Through Song*, New Jersey: African World Press.

Ohnuki-Tierney, E., 1984, '"Native" Anthropologists', *American Ethnologist*, 11, 3: 584–6.

Rabinow, P., 1977, *Reflections on Fieldwork in Morocco*, Berkeley: University of California Press.

Ruby, J. (ed.), 1982, *A Crack in the Mirror: Reflexive Perspectives in Anthropology*, Philadelphia: University of Pennsylvania Press.

Sabania, N., 2002, 'But Where are the Cattle? Popular Images of Maasai and Zulu across the Twentieth Century', *Visual Anthropology*, 15: 313–46.

Strathern, M., 1995, 'The Nice Thing about Culture Is That Everyone Has It', in M. Strathern (ed.), *Shifting Contexts: Transformations in Anthropological Knowledge*, New York: Routledge, pp. 153–76.

Wallerstein, I., 1999, 'Social Sciences in the Twenty-First Century', *World Social Science Report*, UNESCO.

Watkins, J., 2001, 'Re-Searching Researchers and Teachers: Comment on "Not Talking Past Each Other"', *Anthropology and Education Quarterly*, 32, 3: 379–87.

12
Challenges and Prospects for Applied Anthropology in Kenya

Mary Amuyunzu-Nyamongo

I have had to answer many questions about applied anthropology since I studied the subject at the University of Nairobi in the mid-1980s. But the most common one has been: 'What is anthropology?' In retrospect, I realise that I asked the same question when faced with choosing between anthropology, philosophy and religion as an undergraduate. As a practising anthropologist, the question still dominates my professional and social interactions. This chapter examines my experiences as an anthropology student and practitioner in the population and health sector in Kenya. I also intend it as a guide for young people seeking careers in this field of social science.

Some of those who ask about anthropology are of the opinion that it is not a science. An epidemiologist I once worked with asked why it took so long to train a social scientist to do what is 'not so difficult'. He said that what a social scientist does 'can be done by any one because it is based on common sense'. The minority holding such views often lack an understanding of the work of anthropologists. Anthropologists, Seal et al. (2000) observe, need high levels of expertise to deal with the ethical, social and political dilemmas they encounter during fieldwork. The demand to fill key research positions with social scientists demonstrates the ongoing need for a better understanding of humanity. It is a role for which anthropologists are well equipped.

Anthropology as a degree course in Kenya

Kenya only started training anthropologists in the mid-1980s, despite the fact that Mzee Jomo Kenyatta, the country's first president, was a student of the eminent anthropologist Bronislaw Malinowski in the 1930s. In his book, Facing Mount Kenya, Kenyatta recognises the importance of anthropology in understanding human nature and in the fight for self-determination of his Kikuyu people. Although Kenyatta served as Chancellor of the University of Nairobi at its founding in 1971, anthropology was not among the courses offered, reflecting the then widely held perception that anthropology was a colonial tool. Many of the administrators who served in Kenya's colonial government happened to be anthropologists.

It was not until 1985 that Kenyatta's successor, Daniel arap Moi, directed that anthropology be taught at the University of Nairobi. The course was formally launched in 1986. As with all new projects, there were many teething problems. Almost everything – from lecturers to reference books – was in short supply. Lecturers had to be brought in from other departments such as sociology and history to fill in the gaps. This presented numerous challenges, as few of them were knowledgeable in the discipline, but this did not deter the discipline from taking root at the university. The range of courses offered included an introductory course as well as economic, ecological, medical and linguistic anthropology. Students taking a degree in anthropology were required to conduct fieldwork in one of the areas of study and write a dissertation in the third year.

My decision to study anthropology was taken rather abruptly. When I joined the university in 1986, new regulations had been put in place limiting the number of students per class. There was also a directive that one could not take government (political science) together with sociology, both of which were popular Bachelor of Arts courses. On the list of courses was a strange one named 'anthropology'. 'What is anthropology?' was therefore the main question asked by all prospective students. Speculation was that it was the study of bones and some, with arthropods in mind, jokingly called it the study of insects. From the very beginning the lecturers were required to demystify the discipline, a process that continues today. The parents and guardians of students are now more likely to understand the discipline and the competitiveness of its graduates in the job market.

Graduation and after

Being pioneer students in the discipline, employment prospects were central to most of us. Which employer would appreciate the role of anthropology? How would its legacy as a colonial tool affect our search for jobs? Upon graduation, a number of us pursued post-graduate studies, while others joined the job market. Remarkably, many were absorbed as 'cultural officers' in the Ministry of Culture and Social Services. Others joined research organisations such as the Kenya Medical Research Institute (KEMRI) and the African Medical and Research Foundation (AMREF). This diversity of engagement was useful in affirming the importance and flexibility of applied anthropology in employment. When our peers saw us employed in such a diversity of positions, they started to appreciate the importance of anthropology, even if such appreciation still has a long way to go.

Recently, while preparing for a meeting with the Czech ambassador to Kenya, who happened to be an anthropologist, the main question posed by colleagues was: can an anthropologist become an ambassador? The question is revealing. It assumes that an anthropological qualification does not necessarily fit one for certain professions. Indeed, during the twelfth Pan African Anthropological Association's meeting in Nairobi in 2002, a member of parliament with a doctorate in anthropology made a keynote address in which he articulated his application of the discipline's concepts in his political work. At the same meeting, a high-ranking anthropologist at the World Bank also addressed the conference participants, and brought her own anthro-pological training to bear on the way the bank deals with matters of money and lending to developing countries. This shows that anthropological skills can be applied across many fields. It is, there-fore, important for students to concentrate on understanding its concepts instead of worrying about the usefulness of their skills. This can best be enhanced through the full participation of their teachers who, ideally, will not only introduce them to the discipline but also articulate its ever-changing identity and application. Pels and Salemink (1999: 56) touch on the uneasy relationship between pure and applied anthropology when they observe that:

> The academic disavowal of practical application is, of course, an odd strategy of professionalisation when compared to other professions. In Anthropologyland, those who are not exclusively preoccupied with the construction of academic knowledge but are involved with its 'application' are often considered a lesser breed of scholars. The implicit and as Wright argues, unfounded assumption is that 'applied' work does not lead to a higher-rated achievement of formulating theory.... If one starts from

such an assumption, the history of anthropology can, indeed, be nothing but a history of ideas and methods.

Anthropology at the graduate level

As noted above, some of the graduates of anthropology from the University of Nairobi went on to postgraduate studies locally and abroad. I was among those who went to the United Kingdom. A postgraduate student of anthropology can expect different challenges to those awaiting graduates who seek a career in the applied field. I will use my personal experience to explain this. By the time I began studying anthropology at graduate level, I had been working in a multidisciplinary research institute in Kenya. As a member of the institute I was expected to come up with a research topic related to my work environment. Before I left for my graduate course, I drafted a research topic focusing on lymphatic filariasis, also known as elephantiasis, on the Kenyan coast. When I presented this to my university adviser in the UK, he felt it was too narrow and asked that I expand the area of focus and address some of the theoretical concerns within the field of anthropology. The result was that my research topic became 'The Management of Illness in a Plural Health Care Setting'. But when I returned to Kenya the scientific committee, which had to approve the proposal, said it was too broad. So in the end I had to write two research proposals, using appropriate formats for each of the two institutions. The multidisciplinary research institute required a research protocol with concise research questions, justifications, hypotheses and methodologies. My anthropological supervisor expected a more detailed proposal with a conceptual framework and an extensive literature review, in addition to my objectives and methodology. Consequently, during my fieldwork I was involved in two distinct yet connected studies to fulfil my dual obligations, one on lymphatic filariasis and the other on the management of illness (Amuyunzu 1994, 1996).

One of my most valuable experiences as a graduate student was the year of ethnographic fieldwork. Equally important for my employer's studies on lymphatic filariasis was my in-depth understanding of the community, which facilitated informed and timely contributions to the project teams. It is important to note, however, that during postgraduate studies the primary emphasis was on academic work, which can be a downside, especially for those preparing to join, or already working in applied fields.

Contributions to population and health research and interventions

Anthropological contributions to the health arena have become more widely recognised in the last two decades as a result of the failure of medical interventions implemented without understanding the cultures of the beneficiaries. Lambert and McKevitt (2002: 210) note that: 'Anthropology has biological, social and cultural branches but when applied to health issues it most commonly relates to the social and cultural dimensions of health, ill health and medicine.' The advent of HIV/AIDS, among other debilitating health conditions, and the recognition of their social nature, has underscored the importance of an anthropological perspective within research and intervention programmes. As an anthropologist in the population and health field, I have participated in a range of activities, some of which I discuss below.

Community mobilisation
This involves identifying key community persons, holding consultative meetings and preparing the community members for data collection and interventions. To be able to do this successfully, one needs to understand the community one is working in. An incident that occurred during my PhD fieldwork illustrates this point. During a campaign to control lymphatic filariasis among the Duruma people on Kenya's coast, a mass screening of community members was planned. Such activities took place at night, preferably after 10 pm when the microfilariae circulate in the peripheral blood. The project director suggested that we communicate this information to the community through primary school children. I observed that this would not yield the desired results since the Duruma are a patriarchal community where decision making is vested in male household heads. However, the decision was taken to use the school children anyway because they were readily available and would understand English. That night no one turned up for screening. The following day an urgent meeting of community leaders and heads of households was called. They subsequently mobilised the community to participate in the screening exercise, with a turn-out of more than 80 per cent.

Conducting formative research or diagnostic studies
Within the population and health field, the tendency to design data collection instruments without understanding community dynamics

is now a thing of the past. Through in-depth interviews, focus group discussions and observations, researchers are now able to design or adapt existing instruments to make them relevant to the prevailing circumstances of the specific community.

Methodologies that are becoming critical for anthropologists in the field include participatory data collection and other rapid appraisal tools. The popularity of 'rapid' tools is due to the need to identify problems and deal with them within a short period of time. For instance, participatory poverty assessments (PPAs) have been used in Kenya to facilitate the inclusion of 'voices of the poor' in the current poverty reduction strategy papers (PRSPs) (Government of Kenya 2001). Tools such as wealth ranking and gender analysis allow the communities to assess their own situations, and the strengths and weaknesses of their systems. In one community in Kenya, the community members recognised through gender analysis that the women were overworked, controlled none of the household resources and had little say in the decision making. Although this had always been the case, the men began to appreciate the women's role in the home much more than they had in the past. Participatory learning and action (PLA) tools generally empower the communities to identify their needs and homegrown solutions. Due to the fact that the success of using these tools depends heavily on appropriate community approaches, students of anthropology are usually sought to undertake such studies. Because of their training in qualitative methodology, anthropologists are often expected to be conversant with these applied methodologies, which is not always the case. I too have had to acquaint myself with these new tools, and with the growing academic critiques to which they are being subjected (for example, Cooke and Kothari 2001).

Conducting the qualitative aspects of a project

As members of multidisciplinary teams, anthropologists/social scientists often take responsibility for the qualitative aspects of a study. Mays and Pope (1995) state that social scientists 'reach the part other methods cannot', and that through the collection of qualitative data they have an ability to capture the views of 'ordinary' people in the real world. Miles and Huberman (1994) cite the locally grounded, richly holist and inherently flexible nature of the qualitative approach as its most important attributes.

Nevertheless, applied anthropologists have to familiarise themselves with quantitative tools so that they can engage meaningfully in the entire research process. Some have suggested that when anthropologies generate results through quantitative methodologies they fail to discuss their findings sufficiently. This failure may be due to their inability, or reluctance, to interpret the data statistically. Whatever the reason, this is a weakness that waters down such scientific presentations. Understanding quantitative tools also facilitates informed discussions in other fora, for example during conferences. As Lambert (1996) notes, 'fully multidisciplinary research needs to incorporate the conceptual frameworks and knowledge bases of participating disciplines'.

Designing and implementing community-based studies

These could be original ideas or part of ongoing activities. For example, while working on an adolescent intervention programme, we included a study on 'community perceptions regarding critical adolescent sexual and reproductive health needs'. This was informed by our understanding of the critical role parents, and the community at large, play in adolescents' lives, especially their sexual and reproductive health. Therefore it was necessary to bring them on board. This process highlighted the need to empower the parents with communication skills and led to the design of a training component for them as gatekeepers (Amuyunzu 1997b). In this way the role of the community vis-à-vis individual health was highlighted. Although behaviour change, for instance, focuses on the individual (in the use of condoms, for example), the community determines to a large extent the access to such products and the willingness of the individual to use them. Thus there are many more benefits in selling a product to the community rather than only to individual members.

Programme evaluation and consultancies

One important anthropological input in such activities is to focus on the social aspects of the project/programme being evaluated. This is critical at the planning phase, when the individual researcher has an opportunity to contribute to the inclusion of qualitative measures of achievement as part of the indicators in approaching problems that cannot be adequately assessed using quantitative measures alone. For instance, when designing a community-based health programme for the Turkana, most of the indicators derived were 'reduced from x per cent to y per cent'. The Turkana are a nomadic group of pastoralists inhabiting the northern part of Kenya. Their land is not agriculturally very productive and they experience long spells of drought that necessitate their movements in search of water and pasture for their animals. I proposed the inclusion of an indicator to capture community perceptions of improvement in their health. Although quantitative indicators may show improvement in specific aspects of the project, the community may not relate to these measures, especially in a community that is characterised by seasonal movement in and out of the villages. If their perceptions are not tapped, it is possible that any subsequent interventions may not be fully supported. In addition, this could invariably complicate follow-up activities and the sustainability of the gains made.

Participation in meetings, workshops and conferences

I have made presentations during conferences, some anthropological and some more multidisciplinary. The challenge is to ensure relevance and clarity of the information for different audiences. Such fora are vital avenues for learning and networking.

Anthropological conferences are an important part of my practice. I have attended the International Congress of Anthropological and Ethnological Sciences and I have been an active member of the Pan African and East African Anthropological Associations since their inception. During such meetings I interact with anthropologists in academia and in other applied fields. This is also the time to learn from a more conceptual and theoretical forum, in contrast to the more practical nature of my daily work. At such meetings I appreciate the importance of establishing linkages between the applied and theoretical/conceptual levels, especially for young and up-and-coming anthropologists.

Publishing

Publishing is critical in the applied field just as it is in academic circles, because it determines promotion and career development. Writing has been the most challenging aspect of my career. The key questions for anyone aspiring to be published include: 'Where do I publish? Do I have the necessary writing skills to have my papers published in competitive international journals?' To be a good writer, one has to read relevant publications and do so widely. But in Kenya getting access to relevant anthropological journals is a big problem. Compared with universities, non-governmental and research organisations sometimes offer enhanced access to the Internet and international subscription to internationally recognised journals. However, this access is often limited by what the organisations consider important journals, which may not always favour the anthropologist. Another handicap is what is considered a highly respected journal. None of the African-based population and health journals are highly ranked internationally and yet they are contextually relevant and subscription is cheaper. Publishing in these journals does not help the status of the scientists in the organisation. However, the highly ranked journals may not cater adequately for the needs of African-based social research. Decision makers in organisations may also not be conversant with anthropological journals, again disadvantaging the anthropologist as opposed to their peers in the 'hard' sciences.

The role of anthropologists in population and health issues

In the course of writing this chapter, I asked some of my colleagues to tell me what they thought about the role of anthropologists in population and health issues. Here are some of their comments:

> I see anthropologists as patient people who go to great lengths to understand social structures, unlike us epidemiologists who go to a community, administer a questionnaire and get out.

> Anthropologists are like journalists: they are non-judgmental and do not make recommendations. They are people who like to investigate but fail to give educated, scientific conclusions and recommendations. You cannot engage with people's lives and not help make decisions. I see anthropologists as 'go-betweens' among scientists.

> Someone who paves the way for real work to be done.

> Someone who writes a book on the basis of a single observation. Is this really a science?

> Anthropologists are good at explaining behaviour. Therefore they are expected to bring in ethnographic experiences that enhance the understanding of people's reproductive health behaviour.

Whatever one thinks of anthropologists, their crucial role in this field is not in dispute. As we have seen above, anthropological skills can be applied in a wide variety of activities. In population and health research, anthropologists tend to be the conscience of the study population. In a multidisciplinary set-up, scientists may be inclined to focus on numbers or on specific aspects of the community. It is imperative for the anthropologist to remind them of the individuals being studied and the necessity to develop a holistic understanding of their situation. The anthropologist has to put human faces on the statistics. For instance, in Kenya 700 people are reported to die daily of HIV-related infections (Amuyunzu-Nyamongo 2001). Anthropological contributions to the HIV/AIDS discourse provide more meaning to the experiences by putting them within specific contexts. Issues such as behavioural aspects of the condition, coping mechanisms, and socio-cultural and economic changes occurring as a result of the epidemic are important in underscoring its impact on the affected and infected. Information on the impact the disease is having on specific categories of people – women, children, youths, the elderly – humanises the disease experience. It shows that this is a condition that is afflicting real people. The elderly are becoming caretakers of orphans, a shift from their traditional role of playing with grandchildren while their children fend for them. The changes that are resulting from HIV and other socio-political and economic factors are a challenge to long-held anthropological views of African societies and should be documented. This not only contributes to understanding the situation but also leads to more focused and effective health interventions.

Lambert and McKevitt (2002) argue that an important contribution of anthropology is its empirical understanding of the context-specific nature of social processes. This focus, which anthropology emphasises through ethnographic studies, helps correct misleading generalisations that can potentially ignore the diversities of different settings. In some situations the anthropologist may be called upon to bridge the gap between the scientists and the community in what is popularly known as 'community mobilisation'. When conflict is anticipated or experienced in the community, the anthropologist is brought on board because she or he 'knows how to talk to people and understands the cultural issues at stake'. The main challenge for anthropologists is countering the 'magic key syndrome', which carries with it the assumption that they can 'fix it' or 'smooth the road' to the community. As practising anthropologists will attest, 'fixing it' is not as simple as is often assumed.

Cultural issues influence the adoption of interventions and it is imperative for programme implementers to understand the contact communities clearly. For instance, interest in basic sexuality research has often been accompanied by the use of qualitative research methods designed to understand human behaviour, its meanings and the impact of the socio-cultural context in which the behaviour occurs (Seal et al. 2000). The AIDS scourge helps to exemplify the role of the anthropologist. Short of effective, affordable vaccines or antiretroviral drugs, behaviour change remains the most reliable means of countering the spread of the epidemic (Macintyre et al. 2001). But behaviour change depends on factors that operate at the individual, community and cultural/structural levels. These factors include relative empowerment of the individuals, cultural norms and practices, and community mobilisation (UNAIDS 2002; Macintyre et al. 2001). An anthropologist is ideally placed to study and understand these aspects of the community.

Anthropologists, like other scientists, must compete in an increasingly congested and resource-constrained environment. Therefore, their work must provide answers to new questions or identify information or intervention gaps. Only in this way can they take advantage of the existing strengths and opportunities, both in academia and in applied fields, and justify the existence of their profession. The unpredictable nature of international research funding has a particularly negative effect on funds for prolonged ethnographic studies. The challenge for the anthropologist is not only to be competitive in seeking funds but to be able to do a good job in a relatively short time.

Conclusion

Anthropological contributions to population and health issues are currently enjoying unprecedented recognition. Young anthropologists need to be reassured of the applicability of their skills in different fields outside the academic environment. Interaction with other anthropologists is critical for continuous learning, while reference to current anthropological materials keeps the individual updated. Subscription to relevant and reputable journals is critical because it is important to acquaint oneself with the new thinking in the discipline. Aspiring to publish in such journals elevates the individual and institution and consequently enhances one's reputation as a credible scholar and practitioner. Although the applied field has challenges, it offers opportunities for individuals to translate the discipline's theories and concepts into real life situations. If anthropologists succeed in doing this, they will have made a tremendous contribution to the existence of humankind.

References

Amuyunzu, M., 1994, 'The Management of Illness in a Plural Health Care Setting: the Case of the Duruma of Coastal Kenya', unpublished PhD thesis, Cambridge University.

—— 1997a, 'Community Perceptions Regarding Chronic Filarial Swellings: a Case Study of the Duruma of Coastal Kenya', *East African Medical Journal*, 74, 7: 411–15.

—— 1997b, 'Community Perceptions Regarding Critical Adolescent Sexual and Reproductive Health', *International Journal of Health Promotion and Education*, 4, 4: 16–19.

—— 1998, 'Willing the Spirits to Reveal Themselves: Rural Kenyan Mothers' Responsibility in the Restoration of their Children's Health', *Medical Anthropology Quarterly*, 12, 4: 490–502

—— 1998, 'Socio-cultural Intricacies in the Nairobi, Kenya Bomb Blast', *Anthropology Newsletter*, November.

Amuyunzu-Nyamongo, M., 2001, 'HIV/AIDS in Kenya: Moving Beyond Policy and Rhetoric', *African Sociological Review*, 5, 2: 86–102.

Cooke, B. and U. Kothari, 2001, *Participation: The New Tyranny?*, London: Zed Books.

Government of Kenya, 2001, 'Poverty Reduction Strategy Paper', Vol. 1 and 2, Ministry of Planning and National Development.

Kenyatta, J., 1938, *Facing Mount Kenya*, London: Martin Secker and Warburg Ltd.

Lambert, H., 1996, *Encyclopaedia of Social and Cultural Anthropology. Medical Anthropology*, London: Routledge, pp. 358–61.

Lambert, H. and C. McKevitt, 2002, 'Anthropology in Health Research: from Qualitative Methods to Multidisciplinarity', *British Medical Journal*, 325: 210–13.

Macintyre, K., L. Brown and S. Sosler 2001, ' "It's Not What You Know but Who You Knew": Examining the Relationship between Behaviour Change and AIDS Mortality in Africa', *AIDS Education and Prevention*, 13, 2: 160–74.

Mays, N. and C. Pope (eds.), 1995, *Qualitative Research in Health Care*, London: British Medical Journal Publishing.

Miles, M. B. and A. M. Huberman, 1994, *Qualitative Data Analysis: an Expanded Source Book*, second edition, Thousand Oaks, California: Sage Publications.

Pels, P. and O. Salemink 1999, 'Introduction: Locating the Colonial Subjects of Anthropology', in P. Pels and O. Salemink (eds.), *Colonial Subjects: Essays on the Practical History of Anthropology*, Ann Arbor: University of Michigan Press.

Seal, D. W., F. R. Bloom and A. M. Somlai, 2000, 'Dilemmas in Conducting Qualitative Sex Research in Applied Field Settings', *Health Education and Behaviour*, 27, 1: 10–23.

Singer, M., 1992, 'The Application of Theory in Medical Anthropology: an Introduction', *Medical Anthropology Quarterly*, 14: 1–18.

UNAIDS, 2002, 'Report on the Global Epidemic', Joint United Nations Programme on HIV/AIDS.

13
Practising Anthropology at Home
Challenges and Ethical Dilemmas

W. Onyango-Ouma

The practice of anthropology in Kenya today is characterised by teaching, research and development work. Anthropologists trained locally and abroad teach in public and private universities. Those who teach also engage in research, but anthropologists are increasingly being employed specifically as social researchers. Examples include anthropologists working in agricultural and medical research institutions as well as archaeologists at the National Museums of Kenya. Applied anthropologists, both local and expatriate, work with development organisations where they apply anthropological knowledge to ensure that development programmes are appropriate to target populations.

This chapter examines the different perspectives of practising anthropology in one's own country, especially in the Third World. It highlights some of the challenges that one is likely to face while teaching anthropology or doing anthropological research. In teaching I explore students' perceptions of anthropology as a discipline and the ethics of student care. From a research angle, I explore the role of the anthropologist in collaborative research with researchers from other disciplines, reviewing the consultancy culture and the ethical dilemmas that arise from studying your own society.

The history of anthropology in Kenya

Anthropology as a discipline in public universities in Kenya has a unique relationship with the first two presidents of Kenya. Jomo Kenyatta trained under Bronislaw Malinowski at the prestigious London School of Economics, then went on to write an ethnography of his own people, the Kikuyu – *Facing Mount Kenya* (1938), with an introduction by Malinowski. Ironically, Kenyatta made no attempt to introduce anthropology as a discipline of study at university level in Kenya. It was Daniel arap Moi, the second president of Kenya, with no background in anthropology, who in 1986 asked the local university to develop a course that would take into consideration different cultures in Kenya. Moi felt that university graduates taking up employment in the public and private sectors should be able to understand and appreciate national cultures. The Institute of African Studies of the University of Nairobi, hitherto a cultural research institute, became the home of anthropology.

That Kenyatta was an anthropologist and yet made no effort to introduce anthropology as a discipline of study reveals his reservations about the discipline. Like many of his contemporaries, Kenyatta enjoyed the analytical benefits provided by anthropology but distrusted its politics. As Pels (1999) rightly observed, Kenyatta made no secret of what he thought anthropology stood for – the duplicity of Western 'pretenders to philanthropy' who claimed to 'monopolise the office of interpreting [the African's] mind and speaking for him' (Kenyatta 1965 [1938]: xviii). With this background, it was bound to take time before Kenyatta could be convinced that anthropology was of any use in post-independence Kenya. The situation in Kenya, however, was not any different from that of other post-independence states where scholars remained suspicious of anthropology's association with the colonialism from which they had just freed themselves. Sociology was given more prominence, while native anthropologists were sometimes banned by governments or rejected by other intellectuals in their countries (see Munthali 2001; Mafeje 2001).

During the colonial period some anthropologists saw their role as providing vital information to the colonial administration that could be used to assimilate the natives or rule them indirectly through their own established structures. Anthropologists of this period took it upon themselves, as did missionaries of that time, to provide first-hand descriptions of 'other' peoples. Evans-Pritchard, writing on the subject matter of social anthropology, argued that the social anthropologist 'studies primitive societies directly, living among them for months or years' (1951: 11). Asad was even more emphatic on the relationship between anthropology and colonialism in his argument that 'it is not a matter of dispute that social anthropology emerged as a discipline at the beginning of the colonial era' (1971: 15).

Anthropology's association with colonialism accounts for the way the discipline was received in independent states in the post-colonial period. Scholars who were championing nationalist interests denounced the colonial connections of anthropology and began to recover an indigenous history that challenged the functional anthropologist's dogma that only written records could provide a reliable basis for reconstructing history (see Asad 1973). In universities anthropology received a raw deal, probably because it was perceived to promote ethnicity through its single-site studies, which would threaten the unity of the multi-ethnic nascent states. That anthropology as an autonomous curriculum was introduced in Kenya only in 1986/7 although the first president of Kenya was an anthropologist and a former student of Malinowski is a good case in point. Even scholars like Okot p'Bitek, who had studied anthropology, shared the opinion that social anthropology had no place in an African university. According to p'Bitek, Africans had no interest in and could not indulge in perpetuating the myth of the 'primitive' (1970: 6), which was considered the preserve of anthropology in the colonial era. In this hostile environment Mafeje observes that anthropology, being a child of imperialism, had to adjust or die a natural death (2001: 24). This called for the few practising African anthropologists to lead the way in the deconstruction of colonial anthropology to make it relevant for the post-colonial period.

Anthropology is changing and is currently practised by 'natives' in the previously colonised states, although the West continues to dominate the terms of anthropological discourse. It is also interesting to note that in the West, where people were preoccupied with the study of 'others', anthropology has returned home, probably after discovery of their ignorance of their own societies. Munthali has referred to this trend as the 'homecoming of anthropology', occasioned by, among other factors, the end of colonialism, the reduction of funding for academic institutions, and the failure of other disciplines like sociology to explain Western societies adequately (2001: 115). The field is therefore increasingly becoming a flexible concept, as is what constitutes 'at homeness'.

Collaborative research projects and the role of the anthropologist

Researchers in other disciplines who recognise the importance of anthropology often seek the help of anthropologists to join them in collaborative projects in Kenya. From 1995 to 2000 I had an opportunity to be part of such a joint venture, in which research was conducted under a common framework in the fields of anthropology, parasitology, nutrition, health education and educational psychology. This collaboration was of a dual nature. It not only involved different disciplines but also brought together local and foreign researchers. On the one hand, there was the challenge of working on a common research problem with other disciplines that obviously had different research frameworks. On the other hand, within the anthropology component there was a need to reconcile the different knowledge traditions brought to the interface by local and foreign anthropologists.

Working with researchers from others disciplines presented the most interesting challenge. The research problem was biomedical in nature but the research approach adopted was multidisciplinary, with biomedical, psychological and anthropological aspects. Despite joint efforts, our biomedical colleagues felt that they dealt with 'real science', while anthropologists dealt with 'soft issues'. Anthropologists had to contend with the belief that they were only there to pave the way for 'real scientists' to come in with their complicated experiments. In line with this understanding, anthropologists carried out mobilisation activities to explain to the community the aim and purpose of the project. Anthropologists also conducted exploratory studies on community needs and priorities for purposes of designing detailed studies and interventions. According to our biomedical colleagues, anthropologists were mostly good at talking to people. Although in the project document the role of anthropologists was declared to be continuous in all aspects of project implementation with a direct impact on the community, it was later reduced to mobilisation and baseline studies. The funds allocated to anthropologists were redirected to 'real research activities' conducted by biomedical scientists.

Unaware of the need to involve anthropologists in all aspects of the project, our biomedical colleagues, who were in control, reduced us to the role of 'pacifiers'. They took most decisions related to biomedical interventions and sometimes consulted us only when problems developed. I was often called to sort out problems between our biomedical colleagues and the community. On one occasion some schoolchildren refused to take micronutrient supplements which were distributed free of charge in their schools. The action of the children interfered with planned follow-up activities and created gaps in the cohort data set. On another occasion women who delivered at home refused to comply with the requirement that their placentas be delivered to the health centre where blood samples were taken to test for malaria. This was after a rumour circulated that researchers intended to sell the placentas. Again this threatened the rigorous follow-up activities typical of experimental studies.

To solve the problem it became imperative to conduct home visits and talk to people in an informal way in order to understand why some members of the community refused to comply with requirements of the project to which they had previously consented. Surprisingly, we discovered that the schoolchildren's reason for non-compliance was that their parents had cautioned them against taking the tablets because they could be family planning pills. One reason for their suspicions was that the tablets were distributed at no cost.

The reason for non-compliance among the women was more intricate and culturally related. In the study community (the Luo in Western Kenya) the placenta (biero) is considered a very precious relic of a human being and as such should be buried in the family land. Burial of the biero binds the person to the land and invokes the notion of belongingness. In fact, one may claim the right of ownership to a piece of land where one's placenta is buried in the same way that one might if one's parents were buried there. Thus the project's requirement that the placenta be taken to the health centre and thereafter thrown in the centre's rubbish pit contradicted the community's desire to treat the placenta with dignity. The symbolic role of the biero among the Luo was brought out in the much-publicised S. M. Otieno burial dispute (Cohen and Odhiambo 1992). A strong case was made in court for the deceased to be buried in his ancestral land where his placenta had been buried at the time of his birth.

In the first case we were able to convince the parents that the tablets were not family planning pills by explaining why they were distributed at no cost. In the second case, having found out that the community valued the placenta, we reached a consensus that the women should be given back their placentas for appropriate burial at home after the taking of a specimen. In both cases there had been a misunderstanding due to different frames of understanding and conceptions of reality, which anthropologists had been able to bring to the surface. For instance, our biomedical scientists could not imagine that people might refuse to take the supplements simply because they were free. At the same time they could not understand the hue and cry about the placenta – a waste product, in their eyes.

Anthropology as a discipline of the past, and the ethics of student care

Although it is currently taught at the University of Nairobi as an autonomous curriculum leading to a Bachelor of Arts degree in Anthropology, the subject is yet to be granted its rightful place among the social sciences; students continue to perceive it as a subsidiary rather than an equal to its sister disciplines of sociology and political science. There is a misconception that anthropology only deals with past issues such as prehistory, archaeology and those traditional cultures that people want to forget. According to this view, anthropology is not capable of dealing with contemporary issues.

There is still limited public knowledge in Kenya of the subject matter of anthropology, which further perpetuates the myth that the discipline deals only with the past. In comparison to the high profile of archaeology, social/cultural anthropology is relatively invisible. The National Museums of Kenya and the British Institute in Eastern Africa have established a good infrastructure for conducting archaeological research over the years. By contrast, in the universities, the teaching of social anthropology overshadows research in the subject.

Students admitted to study anthropology are often not aware of what they are going to study. Once they have enrolled at the university they try as much as possible to shift from anthropology to other disciplines. In the 2001/2 academic year, of the 138 students admitted into the anthropology programme at the Institute of African Studies, 38 did not report, 55 sought transfers and only 45 remained in the programme. The same trend can be deduced from 2002/3 admissions. Of the 189 students admitted, 59 did not report, 62 sought transfers, and only 68 remained in the programme. The beneficiaries of the transfers are mainly economics and sociology departments in the same university. The department of sociology, for example, had a first-year student enrolment of about 600 in the 2002/3 academic year. Students who fail to report are probably those who were admitted but then did not make anthropology one of their final choices in high school, or those who failed to secure sponsorship for their education.

The desire to shift from anthropology to other disciplines continues even after the end of the first year. I once came across a student who wanted to shift from anthropology after one year of study despite the condition of going back to year one in his preferred course: he wanted to join the economics department because according to him economics offered good career prospects. Most of those who transfer to other disciplines see no good career prospects in studying anthropology. Such students are convinced that anthropology has very little to offer in a limited and competitive Kenyan job market. They lack information on career prospects that lie in studying anthropology and hence consider the discipline to be of very little relevance to current issues.

The misconception that anthropology as a discipline of study only deals with past issues could be attributed to lack of advocacy on the part of pioneer anthropologists in Kenya. This could partly be explained by Mafeje's argument that the nationalist governments in the post-colonial era banned anthropologists as 'peddlers of tribalism', forcing Africa's few anthropologists to go underground for many years (2001: 24). Consequently, the general public, including employers, are in dire need of what one might call 'public anthropology'. This would serve to inform the public on the subject matter of anthropology as a discipline and its relevance to current issues. Such efforts would incline more high school students to choose a career in anthropology, while employers would understand the knowledge and skills that anthropology graduates might offer. The current situation in Kenya is such that only international organisations and some local NGOs acknowledge the role of anthropologists. Such agencies specify in job adverts that they need an anthropologist. This move to recognise anthropology is not unique to Kenya but is common to many developing nations where economists and sociologists have dominated but often failed to deliver useful results.

Teaching in public universities in Kenya is not a well-paid job, especially when compared with what other organisations offer for the same level of expertise. This has adverse effects on the quality of service. As the saying goes – 'if you are reluctant to pay people well they will be reluctant to work for you'. The net result is that lecturers have to find alternative means to sustain themselves outside the university. The most common alternatives include research consultancies, and teaching in private universities. Those who fail to find these alternatives resort to income-generating activities completely different from their training. This group suffers from what Paul Nkwi, a Cameroonian anthropologist, has ably termed 'brain haemorrhage' – engagement in non-academic activities to supplement one's meagre income. Engagement in such diverse activities makes it difficult to concentrate fully on any one of them and lecturers end up 'moonlighting' here and there in order to meet deadlines. This has negative impacts on the quality of both teaching and research. Contributions to theory and methods through research and publications are rare.

The quality of teaching in delivering the curriculum is critical to an ethos of student care. Anthropological teachers have an obligation to teach/mentor their students according to established standards in the discipline. In other words, they have a duty to strive continually to improve their teaching/training techniques and conscientiously supervise, encourage and support students' studies, among other things (AAA 1998). Being gatekeepers of the discipline, lecturers should ensure that their students as future anthropologists are well grounded in theory and method, for example. Where these are compromised through engagement in other activities, lecturers stand accused of violating the ethics of student care.

Consultancy culture and ethics

Consultancies are usually offered by development aid agencies and NGOs funded by donors. Such agencies are often required to show positive progress in their work before further disbursement of funds, and this requires that independent consultants such as university lecturers evaluate their programmes. In consultancy work the consultant is often faced with the dilemma of what to focus on – do the work objectively and risk losing a future consultancy, or do the work as required by the agency and be in its good books for a future contract.

During my first year of teaching at the university a colleague proposed my name to a donor agency so that I could help them evaluate a school health project that they were funding. The project to be evaluated was being implemented by an organisation from the donor country. Initially it was the donor agency that approached me; after very candid discussions, the representative left convinced that I was the right person to do the evaluation since I had worked on similar issues in my doctoral studies. But he warned me that the advantage I had might not be liked by the organisation that was implementing the programme, since the evaluation was crucial for their continued funding.

In the follow-up meetings the implementing organisation was represented by the project coordinator. After discussions I was presented with clear-cut evaluation criteria, which elucidated how they wanted the evaluation to be done. Since I had worked on similar issues before, I raised questions concerning the methodology and made other suggestions but this did not go down well with the coordinator, who did not contact me thereafter. Later I was informed by the donor agency that the organisation had decided to invite a foreign consultant whose services were more expensive although he was less qualified than I was. It seemed that my determination to make a difference by being more responsive to disciplinary demands was my undoing in the world of consultancy. The colleague who had proposed my name later told me that I should have accepted everything without questioning, since the contract was lucrative.

The above example illustrates how difficult and tricky the world of consultancy can be. The question is – how does one decide what to prioritise when doing a consultancy? Is it just a question of economics, or ethics as well? For example, should one go ahead and participate in a consultancy when one is fully aware that the mandate contravenes certain scholarly and scientific principles? Anthropologists should be able to deal with such dilemmas, proceeding on the understanding that they have a responsibility for the integrity and reputation of their discipline. Anthropologists are subject to the general moral rules of scientific and scholarly conduct, and should not knowingly misrepresent facts to secure economic gains. As a matter of responsibility, anthropologists should be alert to the danger of compromising anthropological ethics as a condition of engaging in consultancy. Professional autonomy from the project sponsors should form the basis for engagement in consultancy.

Fieldwork at home: on being the 'other' at home

Between 1995 and 2002 I conducted different studies among informants with whom I share an ethnic identity. These studies were both anthropological and non-anthropological and were conducted among the Luo people in Bondo District in the western part of Kenya. This kind of fieldwork has been termed auto-ethnography – 'the anthropological study of a social cultural system by a member of the society concerned' (Seymour-Smith 1986: 19). Strathern refers to a somewhat similar venture as auto-anthropology – 'anthropology carried out in the social context which produced it' (1987: 17).

Perhaps I should start by questioning the ethnographer's sense of home – when is one at home? Am I at home among my professional peers, among those whose language I speak, in my country? If as human beings we have several identities, how do we define a home or even ourselves at any point in time? Or could home be a metaphor for the intimate relationships between that part of the world a person calls 'self' and the part of the world called 'other', as Jackson (1995) suggests?

Despite the difficulty in determining one's home at any given time, those who practise anthropology in their own countries/cultures have been branded as 'native anthropologists' rather than 'real anthropologists', who traditionally conduct their studies abroad. The paradigm that polarises 'native' and 'real' anthropologists (Narayan 1993) and by extension anthropology at home stems from the colonial setting. It was during this period that 'real anthropologists' went out to get the native's point of view through total immersion into other cultures by way of participant observation (see also Munthali 2001).

As I have stated elsewhere (Onyango-Ouma 2003) our main task as anthropologists should not be to decide who is an insider or an outsider. Instead we have to examine the ways in which each one of us is situated in relation to the people we study. In typical field situations we are often confronted with the reality that the grounds of familiarity and distance are shifting ones. Narayan (1993) suggested that a focus on the quality of relations with the people we study rather than a fixed distinction between insider and outsider would be valuable to our anthropological enterprise. Relationships are complex and shifting in different settings: an insider may as well be an outsider depending on where he/she is, as Nakhleh (1979) showed when navigating his local identity in his fieldwork. Even in one locale a person may have many strands of identification. During my fieldwork, for example, I realised that we can experience multiple identities depending on how we position ourselves and how the people we study position us. Munthali (2001) had a similar experience among his native Tumbuka of northern Malawi. He concluded that as we try to understand the behaviour of our 'objects' we should also know that they try just as hard to understand our behaviour (Munthali 2001: 120).

My fieldwork among the Luo in Bondo district was done in schools and communities with both adults and schoolchildren. I spoke the same language as my informants and shared many of their cultural attributes. But while in many respects I could be said to be doing 'anthropology at home', I realised I had many different identities, which simply stripped me of my local status and lumped me instead in the category 'other' at different times (Onyango-Ouma 2000). Some of these identities included:

1 *In-law identity.* I was from a different sub-group, one which is exogamous to the group where I was doing fieldwork, and that automatically gave me an in-law identity in various ways in which people dealt with me. During home visits my informants addressed me using the term *ora* (in-law), which was a status position with certain role expectations.

2 *Urban/élite identity.* Though I tried to go 'native', people still made the difference and associated me with the educated urban class. Throughout my fieldwork I used a bicycle, which was the common means of transport in the study area. But I was still considered an urbanite who was just trying to identify with the people.

3 *Educated identity.* Teachers could easily tell that I was more educated than them, even though I tried to play down our differences. In our daily conversations they asked questions that were basically meant to find out how much I knew about national and global issues.

4 *Adult identity.* In relation to schoolchildren whom I worked with and in understanding the field of childhood, I was positioned as an adult. Being an adult meant that I could only understand my informants from that particular position. Children also treated me as an adult in their responses to my questions.

Although I spoke the local language, my informants used the above identities to designate me as the 'other'. This made me reconsider my original idea that I was at 'home', or rather doing fieldwork at home (Onyango-Ouma 2003: 94). As a Western-trained post-colonial subject, my research was among the 'other', which would have been the choice of any Western anthropologist. I used the same anthropological tools as a Western anthropologist and hence the only advantage I might have had was the language and local nuances that eased my interpretations of social discourse and experiences.

The post-modern discourse on reflexivity, with its emphasis on the need to achieve distance between the anthropologist and those being studied, has further essentialised the dichotomy between the insider and outsider. Those studying at home have been considered insiders and hence incapable of maintaining distance or compromised in their attempts to do so. It is assumed that everything appears authentic to them as practitioners of the culture they are studying. One therefore needs to maintain distance by studying others because it is by juxtaposing other cultures alongside another that you can learn about them. Such arguments tend to give foreign (Western) anthropologists undue advantage over native anthropologists practising anthropology in Third World countries, especially because the tools of anthropological inquiry are very Western and thus standard.

It is my contention that at this historical moment the main concern for anthropologists should not be whether one is studying at home or abroad but how we relate to our informants during fieldwork and how we turn our material into monographs and articles. Anthropology is increasingly getting involved in current issues and social change at home and abroad, and it is futile to engage in polarising who is an insider and outsider. Rather, as Narayan points out:

> we might more profitably view each anthropologist in terms of shifting identifications amid a field of interpenetrating communities and power relations. The loci along which we are aligned or set apart from those we study are multiple and in flux (1993: 671).

The very nature of researching what for others is taken-for-granted reality creates an uneasy distance. Narayan (1993) has observed that even distance is a stance in itself and a cognitive-emotional orientation. We should therefore not assume that outsiders will automatically provide objective forms of representation of the societies they study. On the same note Pels further argues that 'the anthropological habit of presenting the facts of alternative cultural variations can be said to constitute a moral stance' (1999: 109).

Ethical dilemmas of doing anthropology at home

It occurred to me during my fieldwork that some ethical issues, while applying to all anthropologists (at home and abroad), are more demanding when working among 'your own people'. Mascarenhas-Keyes, a native anthropologist, has pointed out that anthropology at home requires a 'professionally induced schizophrenia between the "native self" and "professional self" (1987: 181). This is in reference to the contradictory nature of certain things or dilemmas that one is likely to encounter: one must adopt 'a multi-native strategy with a chameleon-like virtuosity' (Mascarenhas-Keyes 1987: 182). The dilemmas encountered actually translate into ethical questions and present yet another challenge to practising anthropology at home.

When you study your own society you are torn between obligations to the discipline and to the people you study (Onyango-Ouma 2003). Especially in Third World countries one is likely to have a different engagement with Western-based theories and books, which dominate the discipline. One is torn between mystification based on these theories and the desire for empiricism – to show the extraordinariness and uniqueness of the ordinary rather than the exoticism of the situation (Mascarenhas-Keyes 1987). Very often one is forced to speak to the discipline rather than to the people, who are 'merely viewed as fodder for professionally self-serving statements about a generalised Other' (Narayan 1993: 672). There is an ever-present demand to contribute to the discipline through technologies of written production in which disciplinary demands are prioritised over the voice of the people.

Our obligations to informants with regard to reciprocity of relations are more demanding when you are working at home. As opposed to foreign anthropologists who can easily engage in a 'quick-fix' anthropology, local anthropologists are bound to have a lifelong engagement with their field informants. For the outsider, the demand for the balanced reciprocity of relationships and information may be limited to the fieldwork period or continue only through sporadic correspondence with a few natives in the post-fieldwork period. By contrast, the local anthropologist is expected by informants to continue with those reciprocal relations long after fieldwork. The post-fieldwork period appears to be 'payback time' (Onyango-Ouma 2003: 94) for local anthropologists, who are often confronted with past informants' demands for gifts, favours and recognition in public places. Such demands are difficult to ignore when doing anthropology in your own community.

Claims of exploitation or one-sided personal gain (contradicting the ethical requirement that we should not exploit our informants) are commonly experienced when studying at home. When working among your own people informants find it difficult to understand why you are studying things that you are supposed to know in the first place. Munthali (2001) alludes to this when he confesses that he was branded a foolish person for asking silly questions to which he was expected to know the answers. Anthropologists working in 'other' societies can easily get away with an explanation that they are interested in learning the local culture. Faced with a local anthropologist, people take it that yours is a form of employment for which you are paid irrespective of the explanation given.

During my fieldwork I always had to grapple with the feeling that I was benefiting out of talking to my informants. According to them I had no reason not to contribute to funeral expenses, school development projects, and even individual undertakings, since I also benefited from them. This creates a dilemma regarding how far you can go in disclosing your source of funding and use of the research material (to gain academic qualifications, for example) when people are aware that you use their lives and experiences for your own personal gain. In this scenario as a local anthropologist one is accused of turning events or situations to one's own ends, through extracting raw materials for social and economic use. As Strathern has argued, 'the question is not one of extraction, but who has the power to convert a relation into a personal prestige [and economic gain]' (1987: 22).

The ethical dilemmas that arise from claims of informants' exploitation are not limited to 'anthropology at home' alone, but relate to research in general. Issues of exploitation and reciprocity remain contentious, for example, in biomedical research, where the study population has to part with blood or stool samples. In such studies the study population often see themselves as being exploited by researchers who use their samples for economic gain. Claims of exploitation are usually voiced even if the study population receives benefits such as free treatment from the research project.

Another kind of dilemma has to do with third party politics that are always masked in ethical claims between the researcher and the population being studied. Here I am referring to local authorities and institutions like schools to which our informants are subjects. While conducting research one is bound to such institutions and authorities ('powers that be') in one way or another, not only as a means of creating rapport but also to be seen to conform to local authorities as your informants do. In a school setting, daily visits to the headteacher's office and participation in the school activities (parades and assemblies, for example) serve as a way of conforming to the hierarchy of authority, with the headteacher at the apex.

However, even though the researcher may successfully conform to the local powers, a problem may arise when informants' participation in the research is seen as a threat by the local authority. The informants are then placed at risk of being victimised because of their involvement in research activities. An example at hand is when teachers in one of my study schools singled out research pupils for corporal punishment, claiming that they were rude. This action put me in a dilemma. On the one hand, I was aware that corporal punishment was not permitted in Kenyan schools and I felt tempted to intervene, but then I risked being kicked out of the school. On the other hand, the research was not supposed to cause harm in any way to the pupils. I kept on wondering whether or not I should intervene if children were at risk, because I risked losing access to and the trust of children if I did not intervene. This was further compounded by the fact that as a local anthropologist I knew that the teachers' action was illegal.

In the face of multiplex identities anthropology at home demands a kind of ethics that is based on 'moral negotiation', as suggested by Pels (1999). Negotiations over what it is right to do will involve relations with powers that be and informants. My experience involved 'emergent ethics' (ibid.) rather than following a code of ethics. In Pels's usage, emergent ethics refers to 'a set of moral agreements composed contingently, perhaps inconsistent, but at least appropriate for the situation at hand' (ibid.: 114). For instance, when I intervened in the teachers' decision to punish research pupils, I interfered with the running of the school – although I owed it a duty to behave well – but I found it right to do so.

To a large extent 'emergent ethics' apply equally when working abroad or in another society. Anthropologists working in other societies are also confronted with issues that they have to deal with on the basis of the situation rather than by following a code of ethics. However, the issues are more demanding and difficult to wish away while practising anthropology at home.

Conclusion

This chapter has discussed at length the challenges that I have faced in practising anthropology at home, and especially my experiences in teaching anthropology and conducting anthropological research in Kenya. The misconception that anthropology is a discipline of the past has led to the development of a negative attitude among students enrolling into the anthropology programme at the University of Nairobi. Within the field of collaborative multidisciplinary research there is the danger of anthropologists being relegated to deal with peripheral issues while 'real scientists' handle core issues. Poor salaries coupled with lack of funding for basic anthropological research drives anthropologists in the public universities into consultancies of various sorts. Such consultancies compromise the anthropologist's ability in order to meet the demands of the organisations awarding the contract and contribute little (if anything) to theory and methods in anthropology.

Yet even when one is pushed by circumstances to do anthropological research in local communities one has to live with the criticism that one is doing 'anthropology at home' and hence that one's objectivity is compromised. But as I have shown even an insider can only know about a society from particular locations (as an adult, child, female or male) within it, for cultures are not homogeneous and society is differentiated. Finally, studying one's society is not unproblematic: it raises ethical issues that confront the anthropologist as dilemmas. Such dilemmas are less likely to arise among those who study other cultures. The map of the terrain for practising anthropology at home in a Kenyan context is therefore riddled with challenges. These challenges can greatly inhibit the performance of anthropologists in both teaching and research. But there are important positive outcomes to strive for, not least connecting the local population to the research project.

References

American Anthropological Association (AAA), 1998, *Code of Ethics of the American Anthropological Association*, http://www.aaanet.org, 20 June 2004.
Asad, T., 1973, 'Introduction', in T. Asad (ed.), *Anthropology and the Colonial Encounter*, London: Ithaca Press, pp. 9–19.
Cohen, D. W. and E. S. Odhiambo, 1992, *Burying SM: The Politics of Knowledge and the Sociology of Power in Africa*, London: James Currey.
Evans-Pritchard, E. E., 1951, *Social Anthropology*, London: Cohen and West.
Jackson, M., 1995, *At Home in the World*, Durham: Duke University Press.
Kenyatta, J., 1965,1938, *Facing Mount Kenya: the Tribal Life of the Kikuyu*, New York: Vintage Books.

Mafeje, A., 2001, 'Anthropology in Post-Independence Africa: End of an Era and the Problem of Self-redefinition', *African Social Scientists Reflections, Part 1*, Nairobi: Heinrich Boll Foundation.

Mascarenhas-Keyes, S., 1987, 'The Native Anthropologist: Constraints and Strategies in Research', in A. Jackson (ed.), *Anthropology at Home*, London: Tavistock, pp. 180–95.

Munthali, A., 2001, 'Doing Fieldwork at Home: Some Personal Experiences among the Tumbuka of Northern Malawi', *The African Anthropologist*, 8, 2: 114–36.

Nakhleh, K., 1979, 'On Being a Native Anthropologist', in G. Huizer and B. Mannheim (eds.), *The Politics of Anthropology: from Colonialism and Sexism Toward a View from Below*, The Hague: Mouton Publishers, pp. 343–52.

Narayan, K., 1993, 'How Native is a "Native" Anthropologist?' *American Anthropologist*, 95: 671–86.

Onyango-Ouma, W., 2000, 'Children and Health Communication: Learning about Health in Everyday Relationships among the Luo of Western Kenya', Unpublished PhD Thesis, University of Copenhagen.

—— 2003, 'Anthropology at Home: Perspectives and Ethical dilemmas', *Mila*, 5: 90–7.

Okot p'Bitek, 1970, *African Religions in Western Scholarship*, Nairobi: Kenya Literature Bureau.

Pels, P., 1999, 'Professions of Duplexity: a Prehistory of Ethical Codes in Anthropology', *Current Anthropology*, 40, 2: 101–36.

Seymour-Smith, C., 1986, *Macmillan Dictionary of Anthropology*, London: Macmillan.

Strathern, M., 1987, 'The Limits of Auto-anthropology', in A. Jackson (ed.), *Anthropology at Home*, London: Tavistock, pp. 17–35.

Index